# LEVITICUS

*The Hodder Bible Commentary*

Edited by Lee Gatiss

# LEVITICUS

KATHERINE DAVIS

HODDER &
STOUGHTON

The Hodder Bible Commentary
Series Editor: Lee Gatiss
First published in Great Britain in 2025 by Hodder Faith
An imprint of John Murray Press
1



A CIP catalogue record for this title is available from the British Library

Hardback ISBN 978 1 473 69500 9
ebook ISBN 978 1 473 69518 4

Typeset in Bembo Std and Utopia by Palimpsest Book Production Ltd, Falkirk, Stirlingshire

Printed and bound in Great Britain by Clays Ltd, Elcograf S.p.A.

John Murray Press policy is to use papers that are natural, renewable and recyclable products and made from wood grown in sustainable forests. The logging and manufacturing processes are expected to conform to the environmental regulations of the country of origin.

Carmelite House
50 Victoria Embankment
London EC4Y 0DZ

www.hodderfaith.com
www.hodderbiblecommentary.com

John Murray Press, part of Hodder & Stoughton Limited
An Hachette UK company

The authorised representative in the EEA is Hachette Ireland,
8 Castlecourt Centre, Dublin 15, D15 XTP3, Ireland
info@hbgi.ie

# *Contents*

In memory of Stephanie Ruth and Moyra Dale
whose beautiful feet spoke the life-giving
message of the Son restoring us to a condition
of purity and to the presence of the Father.

# Series Preface

*The unfolding of your words gives light*
(Psalm 119:130)

The Hodder Bible Commentary aims to proclaim afresh in our generation the unchanging and unerring word of God, for the glory of God and the good of his people. This fifty-volume commentary on the whole Bible seeks to provide the contemporary church with fresh and readable expositions of Scripture which are doctrinally sensitive and globally aware, accessible for all adult readers but particularly useful to those who preach, teach and lead Bible studies in churches and small groups.

Building on the success of Hodder's NIV Proclamation Bible, we have assembled as contributors a remarkable team of men and women from around the world. Alongside a diverse panel of trusted Consultant Editors, they have a tremendous variety of denominational backgrounds and ministries. Each has great experience in unfolding the gospel of Jesus Christ and all are united in our aim of faithfully expounding the Bible in a way that takes account of the original text, biblical theology, the history of interpretation and the needs of the contemporary global church.

These volumes are serious expositions – not overly technical, scholarly works of reference but not simply sermons either. As well as carefully unpacking what the Bible says, they are sensitive to how it has been used in doctrinal discussions over the centuries and in our own day, though not dominated by such concerns at the expense of the text's own agenda. They also try to speak not only into a white, middle-class, Western context (for example), as some might, but to be aware of ways in which other cultures hear and need to hear what the Spirit is saying to the churches.

As you tuck into his word, with the help of this book, may the glorious Father 'give you the Spirit of wisdom and revelation, so that you may know him better' (Ephesians 1:17).

Lee Gatiss, Series Editor

## *Consultant Editors*

The Series Editor would like to thank the following Consultant Editors for their contributions to the Hodder Bible Commentary:

Shady Anis (*Egypt*)
Kirsten Birkett (*UK*)
Felipe Chamy (*Chile*)
Ben Cooper (*UK*)
Mervyn Eloff (*South Africa*)
Keri Folmar (*Dubai*)
Kerry Gatiss (*UK*)
Kara Hartley (*Australia*)
Julian Hardyman (*Madagascar*)
Stephen Fagbemi (*Nigeria*)
Rosanne Jones (*Japan*)
Henry Jansma (*USA*)
Samuel Lago (*USA*)
Andis Miezitis (*Latvia*)
Adrian Reynolds (*UK*)
Peter Ryan (*Australia*)
Sookgoo Shin (*South Korea*)
Myrto Theocharous (*Greece*)

# *Acknowledgements*

As I sat in an Old Testament survey class at theological college, listening to a fifty-minute overview of Leviticus, I asked myself why we do not teach Leviticus in our churches when we hold fast to the doctrine of Scripture built on 2 Timothy 3:15–16. This started a journey of learning to love Leviticus. I rediscovered an appreciation of praying 'hallowed be your name' as I realised that this one clause of the LORD's Prayer is praying Leviticus. I believe that one reason for the condition of the church in the western world today is that we have excised the whole book of Leviticus from our diet of Scripture, except for chapters and verses that are cherry-picked to justify our doctrine. My prayer is that the global church would discover the willingness to listen to God's instruction in Leviticus and ensure that the name of Jesus is sanctified and glorified in our church communities in the midst of a watching world.

This commentary is based on work from my doctoral study. I am so thankful for the kindness and patience of my doctoral supervisors, Professors Gordon Wenham and Gordon McConville. My doctorate was written at Tyndale House, Cambridge. I am thankful for this scholarly community and particularly for the encouragement of Dr Dirk Jongkind and Simon Sykes. My doctoral study would not have been possible without the kind and generous support of my parents, Jim and Wendy Smith. I am so blessed to be your daughter – thank you.

I wrote this commentary from our kitchen bench during

the first year of our daughter's life. This commentary would never have reached completion without the encouragement of my husband, Warren Davis. I am also thankful for the patience of our beautiful three – Austin, Theodore and Abigail – when life was not as smooth as it could have been because of my writing commitments. I also thank Sydney Missionary & Bible College for inviting me to write and teach amid a community that is centred on the whole counsel of Scripture and which is passionate about bringing the gospel of Jesus Christ to the ends of the earth. The gift of like-minded colleagues who are also friends has been a great blessing to me and my family.

Finally, thank you to the editor of this series, Lee Gatiss. I appreciate that this commentary took much longer to write than was desired. Thank you for your patience, for your desire to see authors engage with scholars from the Global South and for your helpful feedback.

# *Abbreviations*

| | |
|---|---|
| HALOT | L. Köhler, W. Baumgartner, M. E. J. Richardson, *Hebrew and Aramaic Lexicon of the Old Testament*, 2 vols, Leiden: Brill, 2001. |
| HUCA | *Hebrew Union College Annual* |
| JBL | *Journal for Biblical Literature* |
| JSOT | *Journal for the Study of the Old Testament* |
| LXX | The Septuagint, the Greek translation of the Old Testament |
| NIDOTTE | *New International Dictionary of Old Testament Theology and Exegesis* |
| TDOT | *Theological Dictionary of the Old Testament* |

## *Introduction*

# THE CONTEXT OF LEVITICUS

Before the LORD[1] redeemed Israel from slavery in Egypt, he promised in Exodus 6:7 that he would be their God and that he would take Israel as his people. He desired to redeem for relationship. Israel sealed their covenant relationship with the LORD at Sinai in Exodus 24 and the LORD provided instructions to Moses for the Tabernacle (Exodus 25–31). At the beginning of these instructions, the LORD expressed his motivation: 'let them make a sanctuary for me, and I will dwell among them' (Exodus 25:8). The LORD's motivation was to be in relationship, dwelling in the midst of his people. He was not obligated to live among Israel; he *wanted* to be present. Moreover, within the unfolding narrative of the Pentateuch, Exodus 25:8 was a watershed moment. By declaring his intention to live among his people, the LORD was announcing his intent to reverse humanity's expulsion from the Garden of Eden and overcome humanity's separation from his presence (Genesis 3:21–24). The first step to this goal was the building of the Tabernacle and the LORD's glory being present with and among his people.

However, before Moses could mediate the LORD's instructions

1 Please note that 'the LORD' is used in this commentary where the name YHWH occurs in the Hebrew text. This is significant as YHWH is the name by which he revealed himself to the Israelites as their covenant God (see Exodus 3:1–4:17; 6:1–8). When reading 'the LORD' in the NIV text and in this commentary, please keep in mind that this is referring to God's covenant name.

to the Israelites, God's people demonstrated their propensity to exchange the living God for a tame and hand-made image in Exodus 32:1–6. The irony could not be starker. As the LORD outlined his plan to be present among his people, the Israelites created a god that would be present with them and which they could approach on their own terms. The penalty that they deserved for their faithless idolatry was death as a nation (Exodus 32:9–10), but after Moses interceded on behalf of the Israelites, the LORD relented, and he promised that his presence would still go with Israel (Exodus 32:11–34:27). Two problems now existed as the Israelites created the LORD's Tabernacle in Exodus 35–40. How could the LORD be present in the midst of a people who had the propensity to be unfaithful? And how could he withhold his hand from acting against them when he also needed to be faithful to his own character?

Also, Moses was prevented from entering the newly created Tabernacle (Exodus 40:34–38).[2] If Israel's mediator was unable to approach the LORD, then how could the Israelites live with the LORD's holy presence in their midst? It was critical for this barrier to be overcome if Israel was to have life with the LORD dwelling among them as they travelled to the land of promise. This needs to be on the LORD's terms and not those of the Israelites due to the nature of God's holy presence as a consuming fire. The book of Leviticus was written and included between Exodus and Numbers to enable the LORD to dwell among his covenant people and for his people to have life with his presence in their midst as they travelled to the land and as they resided in the land.

How does the book of Leviticus achieve this purpose? By communicating the message that the LORD is to be sanctified and

2 L. Michael Morales, *Who Shall Ascend the Mountain of the LORD? A Biblical Theology of the Book of Leviticus* (Downers Grove: IVP Academic, 2015), 107, 114; Christophe Nihan, *From Priestly Torah to Pentateuch: A Study in the Composition of the Book of Leviticus* (Tübingen: Mohr Siebeck, 2007), 90, 105.

glorified in the midst of Israel (10:3; 22:32b). Leviticus communicates this message in a series of speeches (Leviticus 1–7; 11–15; 17; 18–20; 21–22; 23; 24:1–9; 25–26; 27) with three narratives placed at critical junctures in the book (Leviticus 8–10; 16; 24:10–23). The purpose of these speeches is to instruct the priesthood and Israelites about how they can ensure that the LORD is sanctified in their midst, while the narratives illustrate how the LORD is to be glorified in Israel. After we explore each speech and narrative in Leviticus, this commentary places each passage within the context of biblical theology as we look forward into the New Testament and read Leviticus as Christian Scripture. As we read Leviticus in light of the mystery revealed in Jesus Christ, we realise that at the crux of Leviticus are precious truths of the Christian faith. God is with us, and we have an imperishable hope in the new creation where God will permanently restore his presence among his covenant people.

# 1

# Approaching the Holy God in Israel's Midst

## LEVITICUS 1–7

Leviticus 1–7 is the LORD's provision for Israel to approach him so that covenant fellowship can be maintained with his holy presence in their midst.[1] This provision is a series of gifts through which the Israelites can enter the LORD's presence. The first three gifts in Leviticus 1–3 instruct God's people about approaching the LORD in good relationship. The final two gifts in Leviticus 4:1–6:7 then instruct the Israelites about how they are to restore their relationship with God and with their neighbour when those relationships are fractured by offence and guilt. Below is a brief overview of each of the five gifts explained in 1:3–6:7.

<table>
<tr><th></th><th>Gift</th><th>Text</th><th>Purpose</th></tr>
<tr><td rowspan="3">Gifts for approaching the LORD in good relationship</td><td>1. Burnt offering</td><td>1:3–16</td><td>To enter the LORD's presence.</td></tr>
<tr><td>2. Grain offering</td><td>2:1–16</td><td>To remember the covenant relationship between Israel and the LORD.</td></tr>
<tr><td>3. Fellowship offering</td><td>3:1–17</td><td>To celebrate peace in relationship between an Israelite household and the LORD.</td></tr>
</table>

1 Felix Chingota, 'Leviticus' in *Africa Bible Commentary*, edited by Tokunboh Adeyemo (Grand Rapids: Zondervan, 2006), 134, highlights, 'In Mesopotamia or Egypt an ordinary person was not allowed either to participate in any acts of divine service or to view the text of the ritual, but in Israel the priest's manual was an open book, a textbook for all Israel.'

| | | | |
|---|---|---|---|
| *Gifts for restoring relationship* | 4. Sin offering | 4:1–5:13 | To restore relationship with the LORD. |
| | 5. Guilt offering | 5:14–6:7 | To repair the relationship with the LORD and with a neighbour by dealing with the guilt of an offence. |

After outlining these five gifts in 1:3–6:7, the LORD then instructs the priesthood (6:8–7:21) and the Israelites (7:22–36) about their responsibilities when gifts are offered to him.

Some readers might have a visceral reaction to the killing and cutting up of livestock in Leviticus 1–7. In contexts such as rural Italy or Alexandria in Egypt, there is an everyday connection between field and plate in a tangible way. Children grow up knowing that a life has been taken so that they can eat. In contexts like these, what is described below is not as removed from everyday life as it is for readers who buy their meat from a supermarket. Many westerners live in a sanitised culture where the killing and preparation of meat is far removed from our daily context and where we buy meat that is wrapped so that no liquid escapes into our shopping. I would encourage readers to confront the raw reality of animal slaughter as a means of acknowledging that the sacrifice of our Saviour was not a sanitised affair. It was bloody and brutal. Being able to enter the rawness of these sacrifices teaches us to appreciate the cost of a life being sacrificed so that we can have confidence approaching the living and holy God.

## 1. *When God's people approach the* LORD • *Leviticus 1:1–2*

Leviticus 1:1 resumes the narrative from Exodus 40:34–35. While Moses is outside the Tabernacle, the LORD calls to Moses and speaks to him with a message that is to be mediated to the

Israelites.[2] This message begins in 1:2c and concludes with a summary statement in 7:37–38, which are 'bookends' to the LORD's message in 1:2–7:36. These 'bookends' remind the reader of the topic of this first section in Leviticus, which is the bringing of gifts to the LORD.

*The burnt offering*

**1** The LORD called to Moses and spoke to him from the tent of meeting. He said, **2** 'Speak to the Israelites and say to them: "When anyone among you brings an offering to the LORD, bring as your offering an animal from either the herd or the flock.

The LORD's message begins in 1:2c with an everyday situation for the Israelites, which is, 'When anyone among you brings an offering to the LORD . . .' The Hebrew word that the NIV translates as 'anyone' is *ʾādām*, which may be familiar from Genesis 1:26–27. In Genesis 1:26–27, *ʾādām* refers to humanity, male and female, whom God made 'in his image'. Leviticus 1:2c is another example where *ʾādām* retains its meaning of 'people' more generally.[3] By using *ʾādām,* and not a more gender-specific word, 1:2c conveys the *accessibility* of bringing an offering to God.

When an Israelite wishes to bring a gift for the LORD, then 1:2d provides clarity about what he or she is to do. They are to bring an animal as a gift, which is to be from a herd of cattle or from a flock (i.e., sheep or goats). While this is the general principle, there are two exceptions. The first exception is when the gift-giver cannot afford an animal. In this instance, they are to bring either a dove or a pigeon (e.g., 1:14–16). The second exception is the grain offering described in 2:1–16, which does

2 See John. E. Hartley, *Leviticus* (Dallas: Thomas Nelson, 1992), 9, for the view that the Tent of Meeting is the same as the Tabernacle in Leviticus. For this reason, we will use these two terms interchangeably.

3 Hartley, *Leviticus*, 9.

not require an animal. This general situation in 1:2c–d reminds us that while we might be motivated to bring a gift to the LORD, we are to approach God on his terms, not on our own, and this requires the willingness to listen to his instructions.

## *2. The burnt offering: entering the presence of a holy God • Leviticus 1:3–16*

The LORD gives more specific instructions in 1:3–6:7 about five types of gifts of which the first is the burnt offering (1:3–16). The burnt offering instructions unfold in three stages: a gift from the herd (1:3–9), from the flock (1:10–13) and of a bird (1:14–17). The first section, focusing on an offering from the herd, is much more detailed. The following two sections about gifts from the flock or of a bird are shorter and summarised since 1:3–9 has already provided the complete picture from the perspective of the gift-giver.[4]

**3**' "If the offering is a burnt offering
from the herd, you are to offer a male
without defect. You must present it at
the entrance to the tent of meeting
so that it will be acceptable to the
LORD. **4** You are to lay your hand on
the head of the burnt offering, and
it will be accepted on your behalf to
make atonement for you. **5** You are
to slaughter the young bull before
the LORD, and then Aaron's sons
the priests shall bring the blood
and splash it against the sides of the
altar at the entrance to the tent of
meeting. **6** You are to skin the burnt
offering and cut it into pieces. **7** The
sons of Aaron the priest are to put fire
on the altar and arrange wood on the
fire. **8** Then Aaron's sons the priests
shall arrange the pieces, including
the head and the fat, on the wood
that is burning on the altar. **9** You are
to wash the internal organs and the
legs with water, and the priest is to
burn all of it on the altar. It is a burnt
offering, a food offering, an aroma

4 Gordon J. Wenham, *The Book of Leviticus* (Grand Rapids: Eerdmans, 1979), 49.

pleasing to the LORD.
**10** '"If the offering is a burnt offering
from the flock, from either the
sheep or the goats, you are to offer
a male without defect. **11** You are to
slaughter it at the north side of the
altar before the LORD, and Aaron's
sons the priests shall splash its blood
against the sides of the altar. **12** You
are to cut it into pieces, and the
priest shall arrange them, including
the head and the fat, on the wood
that is burning on the altar. **13** You
are to wash the internal organs and
the legs with water, and the priest is
to bring all of them and burn them
on the altar. It is a burnt offering, a
food offering, an aroma pleasing to
the LORD.
**14** '"If the offering to the LORD is
a burnt offering of birds, you are
to offer a dove or a young pigeon.
**15** The priest shall bring it to the altar,
wring off the head and burn it on
the altar; its blood shall be drained
out on the side of the altar. **16** He is
to remove the crop and the feath-
ers[a] and throw them down east of
the altar where the ashes are. **17** He
shall tear it open by the wings, not
dividing it completely, and then the
priest shall burn it on the wood that
is burning on the altar. It is a burnt
offering, a food offering, an aroma
pleasing to the LORD.

---

a 16 Or *crop with its contents*; the meaning of the Hebrew for this word is uncertain.
a 2 Or *representative*; also in verses 9 and 16

Verse 3 focuses on the burnt offering to be offered from a herd of cattle, which must fulfil certain characteristics. First, it must be male (that is, a bull), and the second characteristic is that it must be 'without defect' (1:3b). While the NIV describes what the bull should not have (i.e., a defect), the Hebrew is much more positive. The Hebrew word is *tāmim*, which means 'whole, entire, have integrity'.[5] That is, the bull must be complete as opposed to being broken, marked or having a blemish.[6] The gift-giver

---

5 Ludwig Köhler and Walter Baumgartner, 'תָּם', in *HALOT*, Volume IV (Leiden: Brill, 2001), 1742; J. P. J. Olivier, 'תמם', in *NIDOTTE*, Volume 4, edited by Willem A. VanGemeren (Grand Rapids: Zondervan, 1997), 306–7.

6 Also Ming Him Ko, *Leviticus* (UK: Langham Global Library, 2018), 16–7.

must actively choose a gift that embodies these characteristics, a bull that is whole.

Having chosen an unblemished bull, the Israelites must approach the entrance of the Tent of Meeting with the living bull that they wish to offer (1:3c). The next phrase, 'so that it will be acceptable to the LORD', has a double meaning. First, if the offering is going to be accepted by the LORD, then it must be brought to the Tent of Meeting and not to another location (see 17:1–9). Second, by presenting the living bull at the entrance, the priests can check that the gift fulfils the requirements of being a bull that is whole.[7] The living animal must be accepted as a suitable gift before the rest of the process can go ahead.

Once the gift has been accepted, the gift-giver presses his or her hand on top of the living bull's head (1:4). The purpose of the hand-pressing is for the gift-giver to identify with the living animal, and for the animal to be identified with the gift-giver.[8] This hand pressing continues as the gift-giver reaches to the neck of the bull with a knife and slaughters it (1:5). As the unblemished bull is surrendered from life to death, the gift-giver's identification with the bull is so that the animal can be accepted on the gift-giver's behalf.[9] The act of hand-pressing expresses, 'Let this unblemished bull be accepted in my stead.'[10] As the gift-giver asks for the bull to be accepted on his or her behalf, and as the living bull is given over to death, 'atonement' is made for the gift-giver. It is then the sole responsibility of the priest to bring the blood of the slaughtered gift to the altar (1:5b–c), located at the entrance of the Tent of Meeting. The priest then splatters

---

7 Leigh M. Trevaskis, *Holiness, Ethics and Ritual in Leviticus* (Sheffield: Sheffield Phoenix, 2011), 182.

8 Roy Gane, *Cult and Character: Purification Offerings, Day of Atonement, and Theodicy* (Winona Lake: Eisenbrauns, 2005), 53; Rolf P. Knierim, *Text and Concept in Leviticus 1:1–9* (Tübingen: Mohr Siebeck, 1992), 37; Trevaskis, *Holiness*, 183.

9 Knierim, *Text and Concept*, 36–7.

10 Trevaskis, *Holiness*, 182–4.

the blood on every side of that altar for two purposes. The first is to make atonement (see below) and the second is to give the blood to the LORD to whom it belongs (Leviticus 3:16; 17:10–16).[11]

Once the blood has been splattered on the altar, the burnt offering is wholly offered to the LORD (1:6–9). The priest places *all* the pieces of the gift onto the wood, which includes the head and the fat (1:8). The entrails and legs must be washed before being placed on the fire too (1:9).

With the process of the burnt offering explained, it is worth asking what the purpose of the gift is and why atonement is necessary. At the beginning of the sequence, the gift-giver was outside the Tabernacle, selecting the gift that exemplifies the characteristics of being a bull without blemish (1:3). The gift-giver moves from outside the Tent of Meeting to being inside, at the entrance, through the agency of the whole process. We can infer from the movement of the burnt offering process that its purpose is for the gift-giver to be able to approach the LORD.[12]

Also, a bull without blemish needs to be accepted on the gift-giver's behalf for atonement to be made. This suggests that the unblemished bull represents what the gift-giver is not – without blemish.[13] To enter the presence of a holy God requires wholeness and integrity. While the gift-giver may not be motivated by the need to repair a broken relationship, no one is faultless. Our created condition is marred by our rebellion against God, which is why entering God's presence requires atonement. Atonement turns away God's anger when entering and pays the price (the unblemished blood of another) for the penalty of our broken condition in the presence of a holy God.

---

11 Martin Noth, *Leviticus* (Kent: SCM, 1977), 22; James. W. Watts, *Leviticus 1–10* (Leuven: Peeters, 2013), 200.

12 Knierim, *Text and Concept*, 78. Contrary to Ko, *Leviticus*, 21, who views the purpose of the burnt offering as 'to attract the divine presence'.

13 Trevaskis, *Holiness*, 202, 206.

## Moving forward into the New Testament

The burnt offering accentuates that a life without blemish being surrendered to death on our behalf is the *only* means by which we can approach the living and holy God. This helps us grasp what Jesus's sacrifice achieved. We can now approach God because Jesus's condition *is* what we *are not*. He exemplifies our original created condition of wholeness and being without blemish (1 Peter 1:19). He was given to death in our place so that he can be accepted on our behalf. Because Jesus's blood was shed for us, we can enter God's presence without fear of consequence (Hebrews 10:19–20).

Also, the provision of another two types of burnt offerings in 1:10–17 highlights a key point. Not every Israelite will have access to a bull that is without blemish, nor a sheep or a goat. Every Israelite would have access to a dove or pigeon, irrespective of its condition, although it still might be costly. The three provisions for a bull, sheep/goat or a dove ensure that every Israelite can enter the presence of their holy covenant God; there is no exclusion based on socio-economic background.

## *3. The grain offering: remembrance of the covenant • Leviticus 2*

The second gift is the grain offering, which is the only offering in Leviticus 1–7 where blood is not required to be shed. Verses 1–3 outline the basic requirements. The essential ingredient is 'finest flour' or, otherwise translated, 'semolina flour' (2:1). Then the gift-giver is to add olive oil and incense. The purpose of the incense is to give a 'pleasing aroma' when the gift is burnt as a food offering (2:2). Once all the ingredients are brought together, the gift-giver takes the mixture to a priest at the Tent of Meeting.

*The grain offering*

**2** ' "When anyone brings a grain offering to the LORD, their offering is to be of the finest flour. They are to pour olive oil on it, put incense on it **2** and take it to Aaron's sons the priests. The priest shall take a handful of the flour and oil, together with all the incense, and burn this as a memorial[a] portion on the altar, a food offering, an aroma pleasing to the LORD. **3** The rest of the grain offering belongs to Aaron and his sons; it is a most holy part of the food offerings presented to the LORD.

**4** ' "If you bring a grain offering baked in an oven, it is to consist of the finest flour: either thick loaves made without yeast and with olive oil mixed in or thin loaves made without yeast and brushed with olive oil. **5** If your grain offering is prepared on a griddle, it is to be made of the finest flour mixed with oil, and without yeast. **6** Crumble it and pour oil on it; it is a grain offering. **7** If your grain offering is cooked in a pan, it is to be made of the finest flour and some olive oil. **8** Bring the grain offering made of these things to the LORD; present it to the priest, who shall take it to the altar. **9** He shall take out the memorial portion from the grain offering and burn it on the altar as a food offering, an aroma pleasing to the LORD. **10** The rest of the grain offering belongs to Aaron and his sons; it is a most holy part of the food offerings presented to the LORD.

**11** ' "Every grain offering you bring to the LORD must be made without yeast, for you are not to burn any yeast or honey in a food offering presented to the LORD. **12** You may bring them to the LORD as an offering of the firstfruits, but they are not to be offered on the altar as a pleasing aroma. **13** Season all your grain offerings with salt. Do not leave the salt of the covenant of your God out of your grain offerings; add salt to all your offerings.

**14** ' "If you bring a grain offering of firstfruits to the LORD, offer crushed heads of new grain roasted in the fire. **15** Put oil and incense on it; it is a grain offering. **16** The priest shall burn the memorial portion of the crushed grain and the oil, together with all the incense, as a food offering presented to the LORD.

The grain offering has two parts. First, a handful of the flour and oil, with all the incense, is burned entirely on the altar. Like the burnt offering, this is described as a 'food offering, an aroma pleasing to the LORD' (2:2). The second part is given to Aaron and his sons as part of their food provision. The LORD describes this second part as 'a most holy part of the food offerings presented to the LORD'. The portion given to the priests has the status of being 'most holy' to convey that the priestly share is important to the LORD.

Verses 8–10 repeat the crux of the grain offering process from 2:2–3 and this repetition highlights three points. First, obedience to the LORD's instruction about the ingredients and preparation is critical for the gift to have a pleasing aroma to the LORD. Second, the gift is given to the LORD as a 'memorial'. Third, the LORD provides for his vocational servants from the gifts that are given to him.

Before progressing further, explaining the second point about the grain offering being a 'memorial' is important so that we can grasp the purpose of this gift. The Hebrew term translated 'memorial portion' (see 2:2, 9) is *ʾazkārāṯâ*, which is based on the root term *zākar*, meaning 'to remember'.[14] When the Israelite gives a grain offering to the LORD, it is offered as a remembrance. A reasonable question is, 'What are the Israelites remembering when bringing a grain offering?' To answer this question, we need to explore 2:11–13.

Verses 11–13 identify what is to be excluded from the gift and what is to be included. Verse 11 focuses on *exclusion* and the verse has two parts. The first prohibits the grain offering from being made with leaven, that is, an agent added to the flour mixture that causes the bread to rise. This is an already familiar prohibition from 2:4, 5. The second part of 2:11 is the reason for the prohibition, which is that the Israelites are instructed not to burn leaven or honey as a food offering. While leaven has already been prohibited in the Passover and Feast of Unleavened Bread in Exodus 12:1–20, the exclusion of honey is a surprise.

14 See also Ko, *Leviticus*, 23.

The most likely explanation is that raw honey is acidic and reacts with yeast to cause bread to rise.[15]

Verse 13 states what is to be *included* in *every* grain offering, which is salt. The Israelites are to ensure that the 'salt of the covenant with your God' is never missing from the grain offering. Since the grain offering is to be a remembrance, and salt must be included to have this remembrance function, then the remembrance is most likely of their covenant relationship with God.[16] As an Israelite brings their grain offering to the LORD, they are actively remembering their covenant allegiance. It is a tribute of faithful loyalty to their covenant God.[17]

## *4. The fellowship offering: celebrating peace in relationship • Leviticus 3*

The third kind of offering is the fellowship offering. The Hebrew term for 'fellowship offering' is *šəlāmim*, where the root *šālôm* means peace in relationship.[18] The fellowship offering is voluntary and motivated by the desire of the gift-giver to celebrate peace in relationship with the LORD and then within the family household.[19] As such, this is the only gift where most of the sacrificed animal is returned to the gift-giver so that it can be shared as part of a family feast (see 7:11–21; Deuteronomy 12:6–7, 18).

15 Also, Chingota, 'Leviticus', 136; Jay Sklar, *Leviticus* (Downers Grove: IVP Academic, 2014), 99.

16 Chingota, 'Leviticus', 136; Ko, *Leviticus*, 23; Wenham, *Leviticus*, 71.

17 Wenham, *Leviticus*, 69.

18 Richard. E. Averbeck, 'שָׁלֹם', in *NIDOTTE*, Volume 4, edited by Willem A. VanGemeren (Grand Rapids: Zondervan, 1997), 137.

19 Contrary to Chingota, 'Leviticus', 136, who views the fellowship offering to be 'achieving harmonious living with God and with other human beings'.

### *The fellowship offering*

**3** ' "If your offering is a fellow-
ship offering, and you offer
an animal from the herd, whether
male or female, you are to present
before the LORD an animal without
defect. **2** You are to lay your hand
on the head of your offering and
slaughter it at the entrance to the
tent of meeting. Then Aaron's sons
the priests shall splash the blood
against the sides of the altar. **3** From
the fellowship offering you are to
bring a food offering to the LORD: the
internal organs and all the fat that is
connected to them, **4** both kidneys
with the fat on them near the loins,
and the long lobe of the liver, which
you will remove with the kidneys.
**5** Then Aaron's sons are to burn it on
the altar on top of the burnt offering
that is lying on the burning wood; it
is a food offering, an aroma pleasing
to the LORD.

**6** ' "If you offer an animal from
the flock as a fellowship offering to
the LORD, you are to offer a male
or female without defect. **7** If you
offer a lamb, you are to present it
before the LORD, **8** lay your hand on
its head and slaughter it in front of
the tent of meeting. Then Aaron's
sons shall splash its blood against
the sides of the altar. **9** From the
fellowship offering you are to bring
a food offering to the LORD: its fat,
the entire fat tail cut off close to the
backbone, the internal organs and
all the fat that is connected to them,
**10** both kidneys with the fat on them
near the loins, and the long lobe of
the liver, which you will remove with
the kidneys. **11** The priest shall burn
them on the altar as a food offering
presented to the LORD.

**12** ' "If your offering is a goat, you
are to present it before the LORD,
**13** lay your hand on its head and
slaughter it in front of the tent of
meeting. Then Aaron's sons shall
splash its blood against the sides of
the altar. **14** From what you offer you
are to present this food offering to
the LORD: the internal organs and
all the fat that is connected to them,
**15** both kidneys with the fat on them
near the loins, and the long lobe of
the liver, which you will remove with
the kidneys. **16** The priest shall burn
them on the altar as a food offering,
a pleasing aroma. All the fat is the
LORD's.

**17** ' "This is a lasting ordinance for
the generations to come, wherever
you live: you must not eat any fat or
any blood." '

Verse 1 describes the peace offering from the stance of the gift-giver. The gift-giver has the choice of choosing a bull or a cow, but either way the animal must be presented before the LORD 'without blemish' (ESV). That is, the gift must be whole and complete so that it can be accepted as a pleasing aroma to the LORD. Once brought to the Tent of Meeting, the gift-giver performs the familiar act of pressing his or her hand on the gift's head and then slaughtering the animal (see also 1:4–5). While the sacrifice does not have an atoning function, the hand-pressing retains its purpose of identification between the gift-giver and the gift as the animal is transferred from life to death. The priest is then responsible for giving to the LORD all the parts of the gift that belong to him, which is the blood, the internal organs and fat (3:3–5, 16–17). This includes splashing the blood against the sides of the altar, arranging the organs and fat on top of the burnt offering and burning the pieces as a food offering that has a pleasing aroma to the LORD (3:5). The provisions for the fellowship offering of a lamb (3:6–11) and of a goat (3:12–16) follow the same sequence of actions.

While the fellowship offering is about celebrating peace in relationship with the LORD and within family community, the shape of the text highlights how we are to relate to God in a way that reflects peace in relationship. The gift-giver honours the LORD by ensuring that the gift represents wholeness and completeness, which is necessary for the gift to have a pleasing aroma (3:1–5, 6, 9–11, 14–16). Also, by giving to the LORD all that belongs to him (i.e., the blood and the fat), the gift-giver honours the LORD and all that belongs to him (3:16–17).

## Moving forward into the New Testament

Under the new covenant, we celebrate the relationship of peace that we have with God and, through him, with one another by the LORD's Supper. The key difference between the fellowship offering and the LORD's Supper is that the latter remembers that the peace we enjoy with God is solely through the blood of Jesus shed for us (Ephesians 2:14–18; Colossians 1:20). Through his blood, we have peace with God, and we extend that peace to one another (Colossians 3:15). It is good practice, therefore, to ensure that we are in relationships of peace with fellow believers before we share in the LORD's Supper together.

However, Leviticus 3 moves beyond the celebration of peace in relationships to what this means for our relationship with God in everyday life. The shape of the passage reminds us that we are to give to God what belongs to him. We no longer offer the blood or fat of sacrifices as a food offering to God because Jesus's gift of himself on our behalf is a once-for-all sacrifice (1 Peter 3:18; Hebrews 9:12). Yet it is because Jesus gave up his life for us that the teaching of Leviticus 3 is even more applicable now. Jesus bought our lives with his blood; our lives belong wholly to him (Romans 7:4).

## 5. *The sin offering: reconciliation with the LORD • Leviticus 4:1–5:13*

The sin (4:1–5:13) and guilt (5:14–6:7) offerings focus on restoring broken relationship when offence threatens the wholeness of covenant relationship with the LORD. While Leviticus 1:3–16 addressed the consequence of the brokenness of our humanity before God through the burnt offering, the sin offering is for a specific situation outlined in 4:2.[20]

20 The NIV translates the name of this offering as 'sin offering'. While 4:1–5:13 focuses on situations where the impurity being removed by the gift is caused by offence and guilt, this diminishes how this offering functions to purify more broadly in other situations (e.g., Leviticus 12). These instances, however, are not the focus of 4:1–5:13.

*The sin offering*

**4** The LORD said to Moses, **2** 'Say to the Israelites: "When anyone sins unintentionally and does what is forbidden in any of the LORD's commands –

**3** ' "If the anointed priest sins, bringing guilt on the people, he must bring to the LORD a young bull without defect as a sin offering[a] for the sin he has committed. **4** He is to present the bull at the entrance to the tent of meeting before the LORD. He is to lay his hand on its head and slaughter it there before the LORD. **5** Then the anointed priest shall take some of the bull's blood and carry it into the tent of meeting. **6** He is to dip his finger into the blood and sprinkle some of it seven times before the LORD, in front of the curtain of the sanctuary. **7** The priest shall then put some of the blood on the horns of the altar of fragrant incense that is before the LORD in the tent of meeting. The rest of the bull's blood he shall pour out at the base of the altar of burnt offering at the entrance to the tent of meeting. **8** He shall remove all the fat from the bull of the sin offering – all the fat that is connected to the internal organs, **9** both kidneys with the fat on them near the loins, and the long lobe of the liver, which he will remove with the kidneys – **10** just as the fat is removed from the ox[b] sacrificed as a fellowship offering. Then the priest shall burn them on the altar of burnt offering. **11** But the hide of the bull and all its flesh, as well as the head and legs, the internal organs and the intestines – **12** that is, all the rest of the bull – he must take outside the camp to a place ceremonially clean, where the ashes are thrown, and burn it there in a wood fire on the ash heap.

**13** ' "If the whole Israelite community sins unintentionally and does what is forbidden in any of the LORD's commands, even though the community is unaware of the matter, when they realise their guilt **14** and the sin they committed becomes known, the assembly must bring a young bull as a sin offering and present it before the tent of meeting. **15** The elders of the community are to lay their hands on the bull's head before the LORD, and the bull shall be slaughtered before the LORD. **16** Then the anointed priest is to take some of the bull's blood into the tent of meeting. **17** He shall dip his finger into the blood and sprinkle it before the LORD seven times in front of the

curtain. 18 He is to put some of the
blood on the horns of the altar that is
before the LORD in the tent of meet-
ing. The rest of the blood he shall
pour out at the base of the altar of
burnt offering at the entrance to the
tent of meeting. 19 He shall remove
all the fat from it and burn it on the
altar, 20 and do with this bull just
as he did with the bull for the sin
offering. In this way the priest will
make atonement for the community,
and they will be forgiven. 21 Then he
shall take the bull outside the camp
and burn it as he burned the first
bull. This is the sin offering for the
community.

22 ' "When a leader sins uninten-
tionally and does what is forbidden in
any of the commands of the LORD his
God, when he realises his guilt 23 and
the sin he has committed becomes
known, he must bring as his offering
a male goat without defect. 24 He is
to lay his hand on the goat's head
and slaughter it at the place where
the burnt offering is slaughtered
before the LORD. It is a sin offering.
25 Then the priest shall take some
of the blood of the sin offering with
his finger and put it on the horns of
the altar of burnt offering and pour
out the rest of the blood at the base
of the altar. 26 He shall burn all the
fat on the altar as he burned the fat of
the fellowship offering. In this way
the priest will make atonement
for the leader's sin, and he will be
forgiven.

27 ' "If any member of the commu-
nity sins unintentionally and does
what is forbidden in any of the
LORD's commands, when they real-
ise their guilt 28 and the sin they
have committed becomes known,
they must bring as their offering for
the sin they committed a female goat
without defect. 29 They are to lay their
hand on the head of the sin offering
and slaughter it at the place of the
burnt offering. 30 Then the priest is
to take some of the blood with his
finger and put it on the horns of the
altar of burnt offering and pour out
the rest of the blood at the base of
the altar. 31 They shall remove all the
fat, just as the fat is removed from the
fellowship offering, and the priest
shall burn it on the altar as an aroma
pleasing to the LORD. In this way the
priest will make atonement for them,
and they will be forgiven.

32 ' "If someone brings a lamb as
their sin offering, they are to bring
a female without defect. 33 They
are to lay their hand on its head

and slaughter it for a sin offering at
the place where the burnt offering
is slaughtered. 34 Then the priest
shall take some of the blood of the
sin offering with his finger and put
it on the horns of the altar of burnt
offering and pour out the rest of the
blood at the base of the altar. 35 They
shall remove all the fat, just as the
fat is removed from the lamb of the
fellowship offering, and the priest
shall burn it on the altar on top of
the food offerings presented to the
LORD. In this way the priest will make
atonement for them for the sin they
have committed, and they will be
forgiven.

5 '"If anyone sins because they
do not speak up when they hear
a public charge to testify regarding
something they have seen or learned
about, they will be held responsible.
2 '"If anyone becomes aware that
they are guilty – if they unwittingly
touch anything ceremonially unclean
(whether the carcass of an unclean
animal, wild or domestic, or of any
unclean creature that moves along
the ground) and they are unaware
that they have become unclean, but
then they come to realise their guilt;
3 or if they touch human unclean-
ness (anything that would make
them unclean) even though they are
unaware of it, but then they learn
of it and realise their guilt; 4 or if
anyone thoughtlessly takes an oath
to do anything, whether good or evil
(in any matter one might carelessly
swear about) even though they are
unaware of it, but then they learn
of it and realise their guilt – 5 when
anyone becomes aware that they
are guilty in any of these matters,
they must confess in what way they
have sinned. 6 As a penalty for the
sin they have committed, they must
bring to the LORD a female lamb or
goat from the flock as a sin offering[a];
and the priest shall make atonement
for them for their sin.

7 '"Anyone who cannot afford a
lamb is to bring two doves or two
young pigeons to the LORD as a
penalty for their sin – one for a sin
offering and the other for a burnt
offering. 8 They are to bring them
to the priest, who shall first offer
the one for the sin offering. He is
to wring its head from its neck, not
dividing it completely, 9 and is to
splash some of the blood of the sin
offering against the side of the altar;
the rest of the blood must be drained
out at the base of the altar. It is a
sin offering. 10 The priest shall then
offer the other as a burnt offering

in the prescribed way and make atonement for them for the sin they have committed, and they will be forgiven.

11 ' "If, however, they cannot afford two doves or two young pigeons, they are to bring as an offering for their sin a tenth of an ephah[b] of the finest flour for a sin offering. They must not put olive oil or incense on it, because it is a sin offering.
12 They are to bring it to the priest, who shall take a handful of it as a memorial[c] portion and burn it on the altar on top of the food offerings presented to the LORD. It is a sin offering.
13 In this way the priest will make atonement for them for any of these sins they have committed, and they will be forgiven. The rest of the offering will belong to the priest, as in the case of the grain offering." '

a 3 Or *purification offering*; here and throughout this chapter
b 10 The Hebrew word can refer to either male or female.
a 6 Or *purification offering*; here and throughout this chapter
b 11 That is, probably about 1.6 kilograms
c 12 Or *representative*

The sin offering is for the situation where someone realises that he or she has broken the LORD's commands (4:2). Verse 2 describes this action as sinning 'unintentionally'. The Hebrew verb translated as 'sins' is *ḥāṭā*, which is one word that contains two ideas. First, the action of *ḥāṭā* is to miss the path or the way. This also includes wandering from the path. When someone 'sins unintentionally', the path that is missed is that set out by God's commands. God provides instructions for his people not to give unnecessary restrictions just because he can; rather, he commands his people to clearly point out how to maintain a peaceful relationship with him. When a person breaks God's commands by doing what is not to be done, or by not doing what God has asked to be done, they have missed the path that God has set before them and have wandered from their way.

Second, while the verb is an action word, it conveys the idea that the action has incurred guilt, and this guilt has a penalty. This guilt is not about feeling guilty. Rather, guilt refers to an objective legal condition that is a consequence of doing what is prohibited or not doing what God has commanded. This guilt remains unless the penalty is paid. Both the action and the resulting guilt fracture our relationship with God. The sin offering deals with the offence of the action before God, while the guilt offering deals with the penalty incurred. Both are needed for the relationship between the offending Israelite and the LORD to be restored.

However, the person's sin in 4:2 is 'unintentional', which suggests that the breaking of God's command is unwitting. This encompasses several situations. It could be where a person does not know a command and, once it is known, realises they have done wrong. Or they might know the command, but they do what is prohibited without knowing.[21] The idea is that the act of sinning was not deliberate, contrived or premeditated. The sin offering is God's gracious provision for his people to acknowledge their guilt before him after sinning unintentionally and to restore their relationship with the LORD.

After 4:2 describes the situation in which a person should bring a sin offering to the LORD, 4:3–31 describes how different groups of people in the Israelite community should bring their sin offering: a priest (4:3–12), the whole community of Israel (4:13–21), a leader (4:22–26) and an individual (4:27–31). This list demonstrates that every person, irrespective of status or position, has the responsibility of bringing a sin offering. There are no exclusions; every person is accountable to God for their guilt when they have unintentionally broken God's commands. Moreover, a community can wander from the path of obedience and of covenant faithfulness too. The act of sinning is not just an individual act; we can sin as a community and so are culpable together before God.

As noted above, the first set of instructions for the sin offering is for when a priest sins. The sin offering instructions describe

21 Sklar, *Leviticus*, 110.

the process for the priest first because of his status as a servant of the LORD who serves in his holy presence. As such, the guilt a priest incurs has consequence for the whole Israelite community. For this reason, 4:3 describes the situation: 'If the anointed priest sins, bringing guilt on the people . . .' Because his actions have consequences for the people, as well as himself, he is to bring a sin offering before the LORD 'for the sin he has committed'. This offering is to be a 'young bull' with the characteristic of being without blemish. That is, the bull is to exemplify the characteristic of wholeness and completeness as a sin offering. If the bull's sacrifice is to be for the sin committed, then the bull must represent what the gift-giver is not: one without blemish for the one with blemish.

The culpable priest, like any other person, is to bring the unblemished bull to the entrance of the Tent of Meeting (4:3–4). Although the priest's status enables him to enter God's presence, he cannot presume to do so because of his guilt. The priest presses his hand on the bull's head as an act of identification after which he sacrifices the bull before the LORD (4:4). The priest is permitted to collect the bull's blood himself and approach the curtain that separates the LORD's Most Holy Place from the Holy Place where only the priests are allowed to serve (Exodus 26:31–35). With the blood of his sin offering, the priest is to stand before the separating curtain, dipping his finger into the blood and then sprinkling the blood seven times before the curtain (Leviticus 4:6). This is the first instance in Leviticus where we are introduced to the primary function of sacrificial blood. The blood of an unblemished sacrifice can purify. The reason for this is that blood represents the life of another (see 17:10–16) and when this life is without blemish, it can remove impurity from God's presence. In this instance, the guilt caused by an act of sin is a kind of impurity. This impurity needs to be removed from God's presence by a process of purification so that God's holy presence can continue dwelling among his people.[22] The act of sprinkling the blood seven times before the curtain represents the complete purification of the place where God's presence dwells in the midst of his covenant nation.[23]

The priest then places blood on the sides of the altar that 4:7 describes is 'before the LORD'. The rest of the blood is poured at the base of altar as the means by which blood is given to God. Just as the blood needs to be given to the LORD, so too does the fat. For this reason, 4:8–10 instructs the priest to take all the fat from the slaughtered bull and to burn the fat on the altar of the burnt offering. This way, all that belongs to the LORD is given to the LORD in the context of the sin offering.

While the blood and fat are given to the LORD, the bull has been sacrificed for the culpable priest's sin and so, in its death, the bull now represents the culpability of the priest. The rest of the bull – all its flesh, head, legs, skin, internal organs – is not to be burnt before the LORD. Instead, it needs to be taken outside the camp and destroyed by burning (4:12).[24] This is a significant step in the process. Since sin is a kind of impurity, it cannot remain in God's presence nor among the Israelites (i.e., in the camp). The sacrificial bull needs to be removed from the place where God's people live to represent the removal of sin from the covenant community.

Verses 13–21 then address a situation where the whole Israelite community sins unintentionally. That is, together they wander from God's path by breaking God's commands. Again, this situation is where the community is unaware or ignorant of what they have done, but at some point realise both their sin and their guilt before God (4:13). The process for their sin offering is very similar to that for the priest explained above. However,

22 Also, Wenham, *Leviticus*, 89.

23 Hartley, *Leviticus*, 60; Sklar, *Leviticus*, 111–2.

24 Wenham, *Leviticus*, 91.

since the whole Israelite community is culpable and shares guilt, the elders as representatives press their hands on the bull's head and the bull is then slaughtered. Once more, the hand-pressing identifies the bull with the culpability and guilt of the Israelite community.

In 4:16–18, a priest has the responsibility for purifying the place where God's presence dwells by sprinkling the blood seven times against the separating curtain (4:17) and then purifying the altar (4:18). The sacrifice achieves its goal through the death of the bull for the sin of the Israelite community. This goal is the purifying of the place where God's presence dwells by the sacrificial blood, and by giving to God all parts of the sacrifice that belong to him. Verse 20 says, 'In this way the priest will make atonement for the community and they will be forgiven.'

The root of the verb translated as 'forgiven' in 4:20 is *salaḥ*, which means to restore relationship. Moreover, this restoration is the consequence of atonement being made.[25] Atonement was achieved through the bull becoming sin for the culpable community and through the purification of the place where God dwells by the blood of an unblemished sacrifice. By atonement being made, the fracture in Israel's relationship is overcome and the relationship restored. Felix Chingota observes that the 'use of the passive voice, *they will be forgiven*, makes it clear that though the anointed priest is the one who performs the ritual, the actual forgiveness comes from the LORD'.[26]

In the remainder of the section on the sin offering, the text describes the sin offering for a leader (4:22–26), for any individual in the community (4:27–31), when a lamb is offered instead of a bull (4:32–35) and where someone fails to give testimony in a

---

25 Jacob Milgrom, *Leviticus 1–16* (New York: Doubleday, 1991), 245; Watts, *Leviticus 1–10*, 346–7.

26 Chingota, 'Leviticus', 137.

justice process (5:1–13). Each sin offering process, irrespective of the situation, repeats the same steps as explained above for the priest and for the Israelite community. The repetition teaches us that when individuals or the community have broken God's commands and so are guilty, they are to seek restoration of their relationship with God by the sacrifice of an unblemished bull for their sin.

## Moving forward into the New Testament

Regardless of who we are, we have all sinned (Romans 3:9–23; 5:12–19). That is, we have all thought, desired and acted in ways where we have wandered away from right relationship with God. We are all guilty. The consequence, as seen with the slaughter of each sacrifice, is death because anyone who is impure cannot be in a peaceful relationship with a holy God nor live in his presence. Since a holy God dwelled in Israel's midst, they had to bring bull after bull to seek forgiveness. But this came to a chilling climax when the impurity of Israel's sin and guilt reached such a point that their sin offerings failed, and God removed his people into exile (Isaiah 1:2–25; Micah 6:6–16). There was a need for a permanent solution if God's presence were to be restored permanently among his covenant people and there be life, not death or exile.

This is one reason Jesus came to live among us and shared our humanity. By becoming human, he became like us so that he can represent us and be identified with us (Hebrews 2:14–18). His character was without blemish, and he died physically whole (Hebrews 2:17–18; 1 Peter 1:19). Because he identified with us in our humanity, he could become sin for us in his unblemished sacrifice (2 Corinthians 5:21). He also suffered the consequence of our sin on the cross where he endured the separation from God that our sin and guilt deserved (Matthew 27:45–46). Where there was no provision for atonement and reconciliation, whether it be in Leviticus

4:1–5:13 or later in 20:1–17, Jesus's sacrifice is effective to cover *all* our sin and guilt – past, present and future. Such is the abundance of grace to be found in Jesus (Romans 5:20–21). We are freed from carrying the burden of our guilt because our guilt has been effectively dealt with. But, as the apostle Paul states clearly and strongly in Romans 6:1–14, knowing that we have received this grace, we do not persist in sin. To do so would be to presume on the grace we have received in Christ. Instead, knowing that Jesus has dealt with the impurity and guilt of our sin for us, we actively turn away from that sin and seek to live with integrity as we follow Jesus.

Moreover, the blood of Jesus's unblemished sacrifice is a powerful purifier for us. His blood has purified God's heavenly dwelling place in his once-for-all sacrifice (Hebrews 9:11–28). His blood restores us to a pure condition so that God's presence can dwell among us without fear of consequence. In 'the already and the not yet', between Jesus's ascension and when he returns again, Jesus has sent his Spirit to live in us, and this is only possible because we have been purified by his blood (Acts 2:14–39).[27] The Holy Spirit dwelling in us now is a guarantee of our future beyond physical death when God's presence will be restored permanently in the midst of his covenant people in the new heavens and the new earth (Ephesians 1:13–14; Revelation 21–22). As we await this glorious future now, we belong to God and serve him because we have been purified by the blood of Christ (Hebrews 9:14).

27 This commentary adopts the phrase 'the already and the not yet' from D. A. Carson, *How Long O Lord? Reflections on Suffering and Evil* (Second edition; Grand Rapids: Baker Academic, 2006), 110, 123.

## *6. The guilt offering: dealing with the penalty of our guilt • Leviticus 5:14–6:7*

The purpose of the guilt offering is to make reparation when an Israelite has offended the LORD (5:14–16, 17–19) or a neighbour by damaging their property (6:1–7).

*The guilt offering*

14 The LORD said to Moses: 15 'When anyone is unfaithful to the LORD by sinning unintentionally in regard to any of the LORD's holy things, they are to bring to the LORD as a penalty a ram from the flock, one without defect and of the proper value in silver, according to the sanctuary shekel.[d] It is a guilt offering. 16 They must make restitution for what they have failed to do in regard to the holy things, pay an additional penalty of a fifth of its value and give it all to the priest. The priest will make atonement for them with the ram as a guilt offering, and they will be forgiven.

17 'If anyone sins and does what is forbidden in any of the LORD's commands, even though they do not know it, they are guilty and will be held responsible. 18 They are to bring to the priest as a guilt offering a ram from the flock, one without defect and of the proper value. In this way the priest will make atonement for them for the wrong they have committed unintentionally, and they will be forgiven. 19 It is a guilt offering; they have been guilty of[e] wrongdoing against the LORD.'

6 [a]The LORD said to Moses: 2 'If anyone sins and is unfaithful to the LORD by deceiving a neighbour about something entrusted to them or left in their care or about something stolen, or if they cheat their neighbour, 3 or if they find lost property and lie about it, or if they swear falsely about any such sin that people may commit – 4 when they sin in any of these ways and realise their guilt, they must return what they have stolen or taken by extortion, or what was entrusted to them, or the lost property they found, 5 or whatever it was they swore falsely about. They must make restitution in full, add a fifth of the value to it and give it all to the owner on the day they present their guilt offering. 6 And as a penalty they must bring

to the priest, that is, to the LORD,
their guilt offering, a ram from the
flock, one without defect and of the
proper value. 7 In this way the priest
will make atonement for them before
the LORD, and they will be forgiven
for any of the things they did that
made them guilty.'

d 15 That is, about 12 grams
e 19 Or *offering; atonement has been made for their*
a In Hebrew texts 6:1-7 is numbered 5:20-26, and 6:8-30 is numbered 6:1-23.

The first situation in 5:14–16 is where an Israelite has been unfaithful to the LORD by sinning against the LORD's 'holy things' (5:15). 'Holy things' refers to anything that has been dedicated to the LORD, which includes property such as the Tent of Meeting, gifts given to the LORD and food to be given to priests. Once again, 5:15 reminds the reader that the offence was not intentional. In this situation, the guilt offering has two stages. The first stage in 5:16 is the Israelite bringing to the Tent of Meeting an unblemished ram for a guilt offering. This ram is called a 'penalty', that is, the price of the guilt incurred by the wrongdoing against the LORD's property. For this reason, the ram is also to be given a monetary value (i.e., silver shekels).

The second stage of the guilt offering is financial compensation where the Israelite must add an additional one-fifth of the ram's monetary value (5:16). This payment of an additional one-fifth has the purpose of making reparation for the wrongdoing and seeks in good faith to restore the relationship with the LORD. Once the penalty of the ram and the financial compensation are given to the priest, it is the responsibility of the priest to make atonement with the ram as the 'penalty'. The goal of the whole process is for the Israelite who committed the wrong to be restored in relationship with the LORD and so be forgiven. The second situation in 5:17–19 echoes 4:2, which is when anyone wanders from the LORD's path by doing what the LORD has prohibited (5:17).

The third situation in 6:1–7 is when an Israelite has wronged his or her neighbour by committing an offence against their property (6:2–3). Significantly, 6:2 begins the situation with, 'If anyone sins and is unfaithful to the LORD . . .' Offence against a neighbour is first an act of unfaithfulness against God. For this reason, there are two parts to the guilt offering process once the Israelite realises that he or she is guilty of the offence. The first part is the restoration of the property to the neighbour, plus an additional payment of one-fifth of the property's value (6:4–5). This restitution is to be completed by the Israelite on the day that he or she brings a guilt offering to the LORD, which is the second part of the process. This guilt offering of an unblemished ram is the penalty for the offence against the LORD (6:6). The priest then makes atonement with the ram to remove the person's guilt, and the Israelite is forgiven their offence.

## Moving forward into the New Testament

While the sin offering is concerned with the removal of sin and guilt from the Israelite community, the guilt offering is about paying the penalty of guilt when an Israelite has sinned against the LORD.[28] The penalty is dealt with by the sacrifice of the ram, which provides atonement through its death. The fact that the penalty can only be satisfied with the death of an offering in the gift-giver's place suggests that the only acceptable penalty is that of a life. Such is the seriousness of our unfaithfulness against God. Like the sin offering, a permanent solution is needed because we stubbornly continue to be unfaithful, whether we come to the knowledge of our sin or not. Irrespective, we remain culpable for our guilt, and we have a debt owing to God. This debt is impossible to satisfy by ourselves. This makes Jesus's death on our behalf remarkable. He not only became sin for us in his unblemished sacrifice, but he also atoned for the penalty of our guilt with his own life (Colossians 2:14).

---

28 Contrary to Chingota, 'Leviticus', 139–40, this guilt is not emotive but rather a legal status before the LORD due to an offence committed.

Having said the above, there are two other parts of the guilt offering that are good for us to put into practice. The first is the recognition of our offence and guilt against God and acknowledging this before him. Under the new covenant, we do not acknowledge this with a ram, but by confessing our sin to God. We humble ourselves in dependence on him and the sacrifice that Jesus made on our behalf (1 John 1:7–9). Cultivating this habit daily will keep us humble and will protect us from taking Jesus's sacrifice for granted. The second is reparation when we have wronged our neighbour when property is involved. The principle of reparation from the guilt offering is that we are to make good for how we have wronged our neighbour and seek to restore relationship with him or her.

## *7. Instructions for the priesthood • Leviticus 6:8–7:21*

Leviticus 6:8–7:21 is addressed to the priesthood, but these instructions would have been read in the hearing of every Israelite too. Just as these instructions would have been of benefit to the Israelites, so too they are of benefit to us. Moreover, 6:8–7:21 cycles through the different types of gifts introduced previously in 1:2–6:7. The same order is maintained except for the fellowship offering, which is placed last in 7:11–21 since it naturally introduces the topic of eating in 7:22–36. Rather than exploring each offering systematically, we will explore the whole section through the lens of three issues.

*The burnt offering*

**8**The LORD said to Moses: **9**'Give
Aaron and his sons this command:
"These are the regulations for the
burnt offering: the burnt offering
is to remain on the altar hearth
throughout the night, till morning,
and the fire must be kept burning
on the altar. **10**The priest shall then
put on his linen clothes, with linen
undergarments next to his body, and
shall remove the ashes of the burnt

offering that the fire has consumed
on the altar and place them beside
the altar. 11 Then he is to take off
these clothes and put on others, and
carry the ashes outside the camp to
a place that is ceremonially clean.
12 The fire on the altar must be kept
burning; it must not go out. Every
morning the priest is to add firewood
and arrange the burnt offering on the
fire and burn the fat of the fellowship
offerings on it. 13 The fire must be
kept burning on the altar continu-
ously; it must not go out.

*The grain offering*

14 ' "These are the regulations for
the grain offering: Aaron's sons are
to bring it before the LORD, in front
of the altar. 15 The priest is to take
a handful of the finest flour and
some olive oil, together with all the
incense on the grain offering, and
burn the memorial[b] portion on the
altar as an aroma pleasing to the
LORD. 16 Aaron and his sons shall
eat the rest of it, but it is to be eaten
without yeast in the sanctuary area;
they are to eat it in the courtyard of
the tent of meeting. 17 It must not
be baked with yeast; I have given
it as their share of the food offer-
ings presented to me. Like the sin
offering[c] and the guilt offering, it is
most holy. 18 Any male descendant
of Aaron may eat it. For all gener-
ations to come it is his perpetual
share of the food offerings presented
to the LORD. Whatever touches it will
become holy." '[d]

19 The LORD also said to Moses,
20 'This is the offering Aaron and his
sons are to bring to the LORD on the
day he[e] is anointed: a tenth of an
ephah[f] of the finest flour as a regular
grain offering, half of it in the morn-
ing and half in the evening. 21 It must
be prepared with oil on a griddle;
bring it well-mixed and present the
grain offering broken[g] in pieces
as an aroma pleasing to the LORD.
22 The son who is to succeed him as
anointed priest shall prepare it. It is
the LORD's perpetual share and is to
be burned completely. 23 Every grain
offering of a priest shall be burned
completely; it must not be eaten.'

*The sin offering*

24 The LORD said to Moses, 25 'Say
to Aaron and his sons: "These are
the regulations for the sin offering:
the sin offering is to be slaughtered
before the LORD in the place where
the burnt offering is slaughtered; it
is most holy. 26 The priest who offers
it shall eat it; it is to be eaten in the
sanctuary area, in the courtyard of

the tent of meeting. **27** Whatever touches any of the flesh will become holy, and if any of the blood is spattered on a garment, you must wash it in the sanctuary area. **28** The clay pot that the meat is cooked in must be broken; but if it is cooked in a bronze pot, the pot is to be scoured and rinsed with water. **29** Any male in a priest's family may eat it; it is most holy. **30** But any sin offering whose blood is brought into the tent of meeting to make atonement in the Holy Place must not be eaten; it must be burned.

*The guilt offering*

**7** ' "These are the regulations for the guilt offering, which is most holy: **2** the guilt offering is to be slaughtered in the place where the burnt offering is slaughtered, and its blood is to be splashed against the sides of the altar. **3** All its fat shall be offered: the fat tail and the fat that covers the internal organs, **4** both kidneys with the fat on them near the loins, and the long lobe of the liver, which is to be removed with the kidneys. **5** The priest shall burn them on the altar as a food offering presented to the LORD. It is a guilt offering. **6** Any male in a priest's family may eat it, but it must be eaten in the sanctuary area; it is most holy.

**7** ' "The same law applies to both the sin offering[a] and the guilt offering: they belong to the priest who makes atonement with them. **8** The priest who offers a burnt offering for anyone may keep its hide for himself. **9** Every grain offering baked in an oven or cooked in a pan or on a griddle belongs to the priest who offers it, **10** and every grain offering, whether mixed with olive oil or dry, belongs equally to all the sons of Aaron.

*The fellowship offering*

**11** ' "These are the regulations for the fellowship offering anyone may present to the LORD:

**12** ' "If they offer it as an expression of thankfulness, then along with this thank-offering they are to offer thick loaves made without yeast and with olive oil mixed in, thin loaves made without yeast and brushed with oil, and thick loaves of the finest flour well-kneaded and with oil mixed in. **13** Along with their fellowship offering of thanksgiving they are to present an offering with thick loaves of bread made with yeast. **14** They are to bring one of each kind as an offering, a contribution to the LORD; it belongs to the priest who splashes the blood of the fellowship offering against the altar. **15** The meat of their fellowship offering of thanksgiving must be eaten on the day it is offered; they must leave none of it till morning.

**16** ' "If, however, their offering is the result of a vow or is a freewill offering, the sacrifice shall be eaten on the day they offer it, but anything left over may be eaten on the next day. **17** Any meat of the sacrifice left over till the third day must be burned. **18** If any meat of the fellowship offering is eaten on the third day, the one who offered it will not be accepted. It will not be reckoned to their credit, for it has become impure; the person who eats any of it will be held responsible.

**19** ' "Meat that touches anything ceremonially unclean must not be eaten; it must be burned. As for other meat, anyone ceremonially clean may eat it. **20** But if anyone who is unclean eats any meat of the fellowship offering belonging to the LORD, they must be cut off from their people. **21** Anyone who touches something unclean – whether human uncleanness or an unclean animal or any unclean creature that moves along the ground[b] – and then eats any of the meat of the fellowship offering belonging to the LORD must be cut off from their people." '

---

**b** 15 Or *representative*

**c** 17 Or *purification offering*; also in verses 25 and 30

**d** 18 Or *Whoever touches them must be holy*; similarly in verse 27

**e** 20 Or *each*

**f** 20 That is, probably about 1.6 kilograms

**g** 21 The meaning of the Hebrew for this word is uncertain.

**a** 7 Or *purification offering*; also in verse 37

**b** 21 A few Hebrew manuscripts, Samaritan Pentateuch, Syriac and Targum (see 5:2); most Hebrew manuscripts *any unclean, detestable thing*

## Food portions for the priesthood

A major emphasis in 6:8–7:21 is who can eat from the gifts given to the LORD and where they must be eaten. In the grain offering instructions, after the priest has offered the food offering to the LORD as a remembrance of the covenant (6:15), the rest is given to the priests for food (6:16–17). The parts given to the priests are given by the LORD from the gifts given to him (6:17). The

LORD is generously providing for his servants. For this reason, the parts given to the priesthood are considered 'holy'. Anything set apart to and for God has the status of being holy. For this reason, the food needs to stay in a place that is holy and can only be eaten by those who are holy (6:16). These instructions are the same for the sin (6:24–30) and guilt offerings (7:1–10). There is provision for the priests to eat some sin and guilt offerings (6:26, 29; 7:3–6), depending on the extent of atonement that the sacrifice provided.

This emphasis on the LORD giving food to the priests from the gifts he has received is God giving permission for the priests to gain their livelihood from their service to the LORD. This is not to be taken for granted by the priesthood, nor abused (e.g., 1 Samuel 2:12–17), but neither are the Israelites to deprive the priesthood of their food. The apostle Paul draws on these instructions in 1 Corinthians 9:1–18 as he highlights that those who are involved in gospel work have an appropriate expectation that they will gain their livelihood from their work for the gospel. While Paul argues that he did not make use of this expectation (1 Corinthians 9:15–18), his reference to Leviticus 6:18–7:21 affirms that the provision of a living for those set apart for God's service is still just as applicable under the new covenant as it is under the old.

## The nature of holiness

By exploring who can eat from the gifts given to the LORD and where they can be eaten, we learn that the holy must be kept to the holy. This is an emphasis that continues throughout 6:8–7:21. For instance, in the sin offering instructions, 6:27 says, 'Whatever touches any of the flesh will become holy.' This suggests that the state of being holy is contagious. Also, any clay pot involved in the cooking of the meat must be smashed (6:28). Clay kitchen implements are renowned for being porous and so they absorb natural juices.[29] In contrast, any meat leftovers in a bronze cooking pot can easily be scrubbed out. The holy must be kept to the holy because holiness is contagious.

In the fellowship offering instructions, we learn the consequences of when the holy is not kept to the holy and comes into contact with impurity. In 7:19, God states that any meat from the fellowship offering is to be burned if it touches anything 'unclean' (i.e., 'impure'). The meat has the status of being 'holy' as it is part of an offering given to God, and so we learn from 7:19 that what is holy cannot come into contact with what is considered impure. Anything impure cannot be set apart for God (i.e., have the status of being 'holy').

Similarly, in 7:20–21, if a person is in a condition of impurity and eats the meat of the fellowship offering, then the penalty is that they must be 'cut off from their people'. Being 'cut off' is a penalty of permanent exclusion from the Israelite community.[30] While this might sound like a harsh penalty, it shows the serious consequence of impurity encountering what is holy (see 10:10).

## Eating the fellowship offering in a worthy condition

Leviticus 7:11–21 outlines situations where an Israelite might bring a fellowship offering motivated by thankfulness (7:12–15), by a vow or as a freewill gift (7:16–18). In each instance, the instructions are about how the Israelite is to bring their fellowship offering and how it is to be eaten by the gift-giver's household. For instance, in 7:15, the meat of the thanksgiving offering must be eaten on the day it is sacrificed and none should be left until morning. This is different from the vow or freewill offering where leftovers may be eaten the next day, but any remaining

29 Baruch A. Levine, *Leviticus* (Philadelphia: JPS, 2003), 40; Sklar, *Leviticus*, 131.

30 Contrary to Ko, *Leviticus*, 68–9, who follows Milgrom, *Leviticus 1–16*, 457–8.

on the third day must be burned completely (7:16–17) since it is considered to be in a condition of impurity (7:18). If anyone eats the impure meat, the sacrifice becomes unacceptable in retrospect and the person who eats from it is to be held to account. This highlights that there are acceptable and unacceptable times for eating the fellowship offering.

This topic of impurity continues into 7:19–21. Verses 20–21 explain that a person in a condition of impurity, for whatever reason (see explanation of Leviticus 11–15), cannot eat of the fellowship offering belonging to the LORD. The household must be in a condition that is worthy of participation, that is, not in an impure condition. Stated positively, they must be in a pure condition (see 10:10). The condition in which God's people participate in the fellowship offering feast is vital for its acceptance with the LORD.

The LORD's Supper is a fellowship feast of thanksgiving. While we do not bring a sacrifice to God as an expression of thankfulness, we celebrate the crucified Lamb who was sacrificed for us by sharing bread and wine that symbolise his body and blood (1 Corinthians 11:23–26). The reason we participate in this feast together is that we have participated in Jesus's death and resurrection. We enact our participation in Jesus's death when we eat the bread and drink the wine and so remember the basis by which we have peace with God and peace with one another. Furthermore, because of what Jesus achieved on the cross for us, we have been purified by his blood. We are now in a condition of purity because of his work for us. While our worthiness to participate is entirely dependent on Jesus's completed work for us, it is still good for us to cultivate the practice of examining ourselves before participating in the LORD's Supper (1 Corinthians 11:27–32). We can prepare ourselves by reflecting on how we have sinned against God, confessing our sin to him, turning away from that sin and reminding ourselves of the forgiveness we have in Christ. In this way, we are ready to participate in the LORD's Supper in a condition that honours Jesus.

## *8. Instructions for the Israelites • Leviticus 7:22–36*

Leviticus 7:22–36 addresses two further matters that affect how the Israelites bring their gifts to the LORD.

*Eating fat and blood forbidden*

**22** The LORD said to Moses, **23** 'Say to the Israelites: "Do not eat any of the fat of cattle, sheep or goats. **24** The fat of an animal found dead or torn by wild animals may be used for any other purpose, but you must not eat it. **25** Anyone who eats the fat of an animal from which a food offering may be[c] presented to the LORD must be cut off from their people. **26** And wherever you live, you must not eat the blood of any bird or animal. **27** Anyone who eats blood must be cut off from their people." '

*The priests' share*

**28** The LORD said to Moses, **29** 'Say to the Israelites: "Anyone who brings a fellowship offering to the LORD is to bring part of it as their sacrifice to the LORD. **30** With their own hands they are to present the food offering to the LORD; they are to bring the fat, together with the breast, and wave the breast before the LORD as a wave offering. **31** The priest shall burn the fat on the altar, but the breast belongs to Aaron and his sons. **32** You are to give the right thigh of your fellowship offerings to the priest as a contribution. **33** The son of Aaron who offers the blood and the fat of the fellowship offering shall have the right thigh as his share. **34** From the fellowship offerings of the Israelites, I have taken the breast that is waved and the thigh that is presented and have given them to Aaron the priest and his sons as their perpetual share from the Israelites." '

**35** This is the portion of the food offerings presented to the LORD that were allotted to Aaron and his sons on the day they were presented to serve the LORD as priests. **36** On the day they were anointed, the LORD commanded that the Israelites give this to them as their perpetual share for the generations to come.

---

c 25 Or *offering is*

The first matter, in 7:22–27, ensures that the Israelites do not eat the fat or blood of livestock, or of any animal. The reason for these instructions is already familiar to the hearer of Leviticus 1–7. Both the fat and blood belong to the LORD (3:17). By refraining from eating the fat and blood, the Israelites are honouring what belongs to God.

The second matter, in 7:28–36, is how the fellowship offering is to be offered to the LORD and the giving of food to the priests from gifts presented to God. Verses 35–36 remind the hearer of two important points. The first is that the priestly share is the LORD's provision for his servants from the day they were set apart for their role (7:35). The second point is that God has commanded the Israelites to give the priests their share (7:36). The LORD is instructing his people to be generous as he is generous.

## *9. Summary conclusion • Leviticus 7:37–38*

Leviticus 1–7 concludes in 7:37–38 with a summary statement. This summary begins by naming all the gifts that have been addressed in Leviticus 1–7. Curiously, the ordination offering is mentioned. This is the gift that each priest is to give to the LORD when being set apart for his service and it is explained as part of the grain offering instructions in 7:19–23.

**37** These, then, are the regulations for the burnt offering, the grain offering, the sin offering, the guilt offering, the ordination offering and the fellowship offering, **38** which the LORD gave Moses at Mount Sinai in the Desert of Sinai on the day he commanded the Israelites to bring their offerings to the LORD.

Verse 38 emphasises who gave these instructions, the context in which these instructions were given and their purpose. These instructions are from the LORD that he gave to his mediator

Moses when the Israelites resided at Sinai. In this context, the Israelites have just been redeemed from Egypt (Exodus 12–18) and have sealed their covenant relationship with the LORD (Exodus 19–24). They are a newly formed covenant community who need to learn how to approach the holy God living in their midst. The LORD does not leave them to flounder or guess, but clearly provides these instructions so that his covenant people can bring their gifts to him. However, while these instructions are provided in Leviticus 1–7, Aaron and his sons still need to be set apart as priests so that they can mediate Israel's gifts to the LORD, which is the focus of the next section in Leviticus 8–10.

## 2

# The Opening Ceremony of the Tabernacle

## LEVITICUS 8–10

Leviticus 8 focuses on Aaron and his sons being set apart as priests to serve the LORD, so that the Israelites can bring their gifts to God in a fiery opening ceremony in Leviticus 9. As Aaron offers Israel's inaugural gifts based on Leviticus 1–7, Leviticus 9 emphasises that this opening ceremony unfolds just as the LORD commanded. However, Leviticus 10 depicts what happens when the priests break the LORD's commands. It is the difference between life and death. This warning introduces two fundamental ideas that are foundational for the whole of Leviticus: the LORD is to be set apart by those who approach him, and he is to be glorified in the sight of all the people (10:3).

### *1. The priesthood established • Leviticus 8*

To this point in the Pentateuch's narrative, we have heard God's plans for the Tabernacle (Exodus 25–31), seen God's people create the Tabernacle according to God's commands (Exodus 35–40), and we have also heard God's plan for the Israelites to bring gifts to express devotion in relationship and to restore the relationship when broken (Leviticus 1–7). The LORD provides the priesthood to serve him in his Tabernacle (Exodus 28–29) and to offer Israel's gifts to him (Leviticus 1–7). However, the priests have yet to be commissioned, and this needs to happen before Israel's gifts can be offered to the LORD. Leviticus 8 depicts Moses doing exactly as the LORD commanded as he consecrates Aaron and his sons as Israel's first priests to serve God in his holy presence.

*The ordination of Aaron and his sons*

8 The LORD said to Moses, 2 'Bring Aaron and his sons, their garments, the anointing oil, the bull for the sin offering,[a] the two rams and the basket containing bread made without yeast, 3 and gather the entire assembly at the entrance to the tent of meeting.' 4 Moses did as the LORD commanded him, and the assembly gathered at the entrance to the tent of meeting.

5 Moses said to the assembly, 'This is what the LORD has commanded to be done.' 6 Then Moses brought Aaron and his sons forward and washed them with water. 7 He put the tunic on Aaron, tied the sash round him, clothed him with the robe and put the ephod on him. He also fastened the ephod with a decorative waistband, which he tied round him. 8 He placed the breastpiece on him and put the Urim and Thummim in the breastpiece. 9 Then he placed the turban on Aaron's head and set the gold plate, the sacred emblem, on the front of it, as the LORD commanded Moses.

10 Then Moses took the anointing oil and anointed the tabernacle and everything in it, and so consecrated them. 11 He sprinkled some of the oil on the altar seven times, anointing the altar and all its utensils and the basin with its stand, to consecrate them. 12 He poured some of the anointing oil on Aaron's head and anointed him to consecrate him. 13 Then he brought Aaron's sons forward, put tunics on them, tied sashes round them and fastened caps on them, as the LORD commanded Moses.

14 He then presented the bull for the sin offering, and Aaron and his sons laid their hands on its head. 15 Moses slaughtered the bull and took some of the blood, and with his finger he put it on all the horns of the altar to purify the altar. He poured out the rest of the blood at the base of the altar. So he consecrated it to make atonement for it. 16 Moses also took all the fat around the internal organs, the long lobe of the liver, and both kidneys and their fat, and burned it on the altar. 17 But the bull with its hide and its flesh and its intestines he burned outside

the camp, as the LORD commanded
Moses.

18 He then presented the ram for
the burnt offering, and Aaron and
his sons laid their hands on its head.
19 Then Moses slaughtered the ram
and splashed the blood against the
sides of the altar. 20 He cut the ram
into pieces and burned the head,
the pieces and the fat. 21 He washed
the internal organs and the legs with
water and burned the whole ram on
the altar. It was a burnt offering, a
pleasing aroma, a food offering
presented to the LORD, as the LORD
commanded Moses.

22 He then presented the other
ram, the ram for the ordination, and
Aaron and his sons laid their hands
on its head. 23 Moses slaughtered the
ram and took some of its blood and
put it on the lobe of Aaron's right
ear, on the thumb of his right hand
and on the big toe of his right foot.
24 Moses also brought Aaron's sons
forward and put some of the blood
on the lobes of their right ears, on the
thumbs of their right hands and on
the big toes of their right feet. Then
he splashed blood against the sides
of the altar. 25 After that, he took the
fat, the fat tail, all the fat around
the internal organs, the long lobe
of the liver, both kidneys and their
fat and the right thigh. 26 And from
the basket of bread made without
yeast, which was before the LORD,
he took one thick loaf, one thick loaf
with olive oil mixed in, and one thin
loaf, and he put these on the fat por-
tions and on the right thigh. 27 He
put all these in the hands of Aaron
and his sons and they waved them
before the LORD as a wave offering.
28 Then Moses took them from their
hands and burned them on the
altar on top of the burnt offering as
an ordination offering, a pleasing
aroma, a food offering presented
to the LORD. 29 Moses also took the
breast, which was his share of the
ordination ram, and waved it before
the LORD as a wave offering, as the
LORD commanded Moses.

30 Then Moses took some of the
anointing oil and some of the blood
from the altar and sprinkled them
on Aaron and his garments and on
his sons and their garments. So he
consecrated Aaron and his garments
and his sons and their garments.

31 Moses then said to Aaron and his
sons, 'Cook the meat at the entrance
to the tent of meeting and eat it there
with the bread from the basket of
ordination offerings, as I was com-
manded: "Aaron and his sons are to
eat it." 32 Then burn the rest of the

meat and the bread. **33** Do not leave
the entrance to the tent of meet-
ing for seven days, until the days of
your ordination are completed, for
your ordination will last seven days.
**34** What has been done today was
commanded by the LORD to make
atonement for you. **35** You must stay
at the entrance to the tent of meeting
day and night for seven days and do
what the LORD requires, so that you
will not die; for that is what I have
been commanded.'

**36** So Aaron and his sons did every-
thing the LORD commanded through
Moses.

**a** 2 Or *purification offering*; also in verse 14

Leviticus 8:1–3 begins with the LORD speaking to Moses with instructions that assume we are familiar with Exodus 28–29. Exodus 28–29 is made up of three sections (28:1–43; 29:1–37; 29:38–46), which shape the narrative in Leviticus 8.[1] Since Exodus 28–29 shapes Leviticus 8, it is worth exploring the three parts of Exodus 28–29 briefly before explaining Leviticus 8.

The first part of Exodus 28–29 is 28:1–43, which identifies who the priests are to be (28:1) and what they are to wear as they serve the LORD in the Tabernacle (28:2–43). In 28:1, the LORD gives permission for Aaron and his sons (Nadab, Abihu, Eleazar and Ithamar) to be brought to Moses 'from among the Israelites' so that 'they may serve me as priests'. Since they are 'from among the Israelites', Aaron and his sons can identify with Israel as they represent the Israelites before the LORD. After 28:1 identifies who the priests are, 28:2–43 describes the clothing to

1 See also Chingota, 'Leviticus', 142; Watts, *Leviticus 1–10*, 439. There is general recognition that Leviticus 8 is an outworking of Exodus 29. For example, see Bryan D. Bibb, *Ritual Words and Narrative Worlds in the Book of Leviticus* (New York: T&T Clark, 2009), 109–11; Frank H. Gorman Jr., *The Ideology of Ritual: Space, Time and Status in the Priestly Theology* (Sheffield: JSOT, 1990), 104; Richard S. Hess, 'Leviticus 10:1: Strange Fire and an Odd Name', *Bulletin for Biblical Research* 12, no. 2 (2002): 646; Philip P. Jenson, *Graded Holiness: A Key to the Priestly Conception of the World* (Sheffield: JSOT, 1992), 119; Ko, *Leviticus*, 75–6.

be created for them. Although the priests represent the Israelites, their clothing makes them distinct from the other Israelites and marks them out as having a particular purpose within Israel, which is to serve the LORD in his dwelling place (i.e., the Tabernacle). These clothes were created in Exodus 39:1–31 and as the narrator recounts how they were made, the refrain, 'as the LORD had commanded Moses' in verses 1, 5, 7, 21, 26, 29 and 31 emphasises that the priestly clothes were completed exactly as the LORD instructed.

The second part, in Exodus 29:1–37, explains how Moses is to 'consecrate' Aaron and his sons as priests. The act of consecrating is the act of setting apart to a particular status of belonging solely to the LORD (i.e., to be holy). In this instance, Aaron and his sons are being consecrated to serve the LORD in his presence and so they need to reflect the state of the one whom they serve, which is holy. This idea of consecration is the transferring of Aaron and his sons from being in a common state to being in a holy state.[2]

The reason the priests need to be holy is evinced in 29:38–46, which is the third part of Exodus 28–29. The LORD reveals in 29:38–46 that, with the priesthood consecrated and with burnt offerings given, he will meet and speak with his people, and that 'the place will be consecrated by my glory' (29:42–43). If Aaron and his sons are to serve in a place (i.e., the Tabernacle) set apart by the LORD's glory, then they need to have the status of being holy. No one can be in the presence of God's glory without being both pure and holy (see later discussion of Leviticus 10:10). As noted above, these three parts of Exodus 28–29 shape the events of Leviticus 8.

As Moses gathers the Israelite community in Leviticus 8:3 at the entrance of the Tent of Meeting, they gather so that they can witness the enactment of the priesthood's consecration from

2 See also Chingota, 'Leviticus', 142–3.

Exodus 29. There are seven points from the detail of Leviticus 8 that are helpful to explore.

First, before Moses clothes Aaron and his sons, 8:6 notes that Moses washes their bodies with water. The priesthood are being set apart to serve the LORD in a place that is to be maintained in a condition of purity (see 10:10). The act of washing is a symbol that they are being transferred from one condition and status (impure and common) to a different condition and status (pure and holy).[3] While the idea of purity here does not contain the idea of cleanliness, the act of washing is a reminder that the priests are set apart to serve the LORD in a place that is both pure *and* holy (see 10:10). Aaron and his sons will repeat this washing every time they put on their priestly clothes as a constant reminder that they are to remain in a condition of purity and in a state of being holy since where they serve is to remain in a pure condition and a holy status because of the God whom they serve.

Second, the order in which Moses dresses Aaron is significant. Moses clothes Aaron from the undergarments to the top garments. He begins by clothing Aaron with the linen tunic, which is an undergarment designed to preserve Aaron's dignity underneath the ephod (see Exodus 28:39–41). An embroidered sash is then tied around Aaron's waist, after which the robe and ephod are placed on him. The design of the robe is described in Exodus 29:31–35 as being made of blue cloth with a woven collar and then with embroidered pomegranates of blue, purple and scarlet around the bottom hem. The pomegranates are symbolic of blessing that the LORD provides Israel, especially in the land of promise (e.g., Numbers 13:23). Then bells are interspersed

---

3 Compare Ko, *Leviticus*, 76. While Ko, building on Gorman's work, recognises that the act of washing 'designates the person's move from one status to another', Ko does not differentiate between purity as a condition and being holy as a state. He seems to conflate the two distinct ideas.

between the pomegranates so that they ring with Aaron's movement. These bells are designed as a safety feature so that the ringing is heard when he enters the Most Holy Place (Exodus 28:34–35). Entering the earthly dwelling place of a holy God is dangerous. The holy presence that had to restrain himself from acting against those feasting on Mount Sinai in Exodus 24:11 and who was a consuming fire on top on Mount Sinai in Exodus 24:17 is the same presence that fills the Most Holy Place inside the Tabernacle. Aaron will need to approach that same holy presence to fulfil his role. For this reason, the sound of the bells is a reminder to the LORD that Aaron is entering his presence as he serves the LORD and maintains the Tabernacle in a condition of purity.

Third, Aaron's clothing is a reminder that he represents the Israelites before the LORD *and* he is holy to the LORD. The golden breastpiece, which Moses places over the ephod in 8:8, symbolises Aaron's identification with the Israelites and his representative function before the LORD for Israel. Exodus 28:29–30 explains the purpose of the breastpiece. Each tribe was named after one of Jacob's sons, which is the reference to the 'sons of Israel' in Exodus 29:29. The high priest's golden breastpiece bears the names of the twelve sons to represent the names of the twelve tribes before the LORD. As Aaron moves about the Tabernacle, his identification and representation with the twelves tribes is a reminder to the LORD of the covenant relationship and the people among whom he dwells. Yet, as Moses places the turban on Aaron's head and sets a golden plate into it, the engraving reminds both Aaron and Israel that the priesthood are 'holy to the LORD' (Exodus 28:36). This emblem is a daily reminder that the priesthood are set apart to a particular status, which is to serve the LORD. What the LORD desires of the priesthood is a microcosm of Israel's life in the land. Just as the priesthood are holy to the LORD in the Tabernacle so that they can mediate between Israel and the LORD, so too Israel is to be holy to the LORD in the land as they are to be set apart from the nations to represent the LORD to them.[4]

Fourth, blood needs to be shed and placed on Aaron and his sons for them to be transferred from the status of being common to being holy (see later explanation of Leviticus 10:10). With the ram of the ordination offering transferred from life to death in the stead of Aaron and his sons in 8:23, Moses places blood on Aaron's right earlobe, his thumb and his big toe, to symbolise that the whole of Aaron is being set apart to serve the LORD.[5] Moses repeats the same symbolic action with Aaron's sons in 8:24. Similarly, in 8:30, Moses splatters a mixture of oil and blood on the priestly clothes that Aaron and his sons will wear as they serve the LORD. Again, the purpose of this action is to symbolise that the clothes they wear are to be set apart in a pure condition to the LORD. *Everything* in the LORD's presence must be in a condition of purity and have the status of being holy (see 10:10).

Fifth, after blood is placed on Aaron (8:23) and his sons (8:24), Moses takes all the fat of the ordination offering (8:25), three different loaves of bread and the right thigh of the sacrificed ram (8:26). He then places them in the hands of Aaron and his sons to wave before the LORD (8:27). This might sound rather gruesome, but it is how Aaron and his sons acknowledge that what they are waving before the LORD belongs to the LORD. In 8:28, Moses takes the fat, the loaves and the thigh and places them on the altar to be burnt entirely as a pleasing aroma to the LORD. Similarly, Moses takes the breast of the sacrificed ram in 8:29 and waves it before the LORD. Again, he is acknowledging that the part of the sacrifice he is waving belongs to the LORD.

4 See Carmen Joy Imes, *Bearing God's Name: Why Sinai Still Matters* (Downers Grove: IVP, 2019).

5 Wenham, *Leviticus*, 143.

In this instance, the LORD has given the breast to Moses as his food portion.

Sixth, Moses instructs Aaron and his sons to remain at the entrance to the Tent of Meeting for seven nights in 8:33 so that the consecration process can reach completion. Two questions might arise for hearers of 8:33. First, why do Aaron and his sons need to remain at the entrance for seven whole days? Ko helpfully observes that, from an anthropological perspective, remaining in the doorway is a transitional location.[6] They are neither inside nor outside. That is, 'Aaron and his sons are living in a "non-state," a state that does not belong to the initial condition, or to the final or transferred condition.'[7] Until the seven days are finished, their transfer to the state of being holy is not yet complete. This leads to the second question, which is whether the number seven has significance, and it does. The number seven represents completeness, and so the instruction for Aaron and his sons to remain at the entrance for seven nights symbolises that they are completely set apart to serve the LORD.[8]

Finally, throughout the whole process, Moses does 'as the LORD commanded' (8:9, 13, 17, 21, 29). Verses 34–36 repeat three times that the process is completed 'just as the LORD commanded Moses', with the final refrain in 8:36 forming a frame (an *inclusio*) with 8:4.[9] This emphasis suggests that Leviticus's narrator wishes the hearer to know that the priesthood have been set apart by Moses in accordance with the LORD's purposes. Now the priesthood are ready to mediate the Israelites to the LORD as they serve in the LORD's presence as servants who belong solely to him.

---

6 See Ko, *Leviticus*, 82–4.

7 Ko, *Leviticus*, 82. However, please note that Ko here conflates the idea of state and condition, which are two distinct, albeit related, terms for Leviticus. See the explanation of Leviticus 10:10.

8 Also, Chingota, 'Leviticus', 144; Sklar, *Leviticus*, 148.

9 Robert Alter, 'Leviticus', in *The Five Books of Moses: A Translation with Commentary* (New York: Norton, 2008), 572.

## Moving forward into the New Testament

There are glimpses of both the priests and Israel fulfilling their mediatory purpose in the rest of the Old Testament. But over time, both the priesthood and Israel neglect their purpose (e.g., 1 Samuel 3–4; Micah 3:9–12) and embody patterns of behaviour contrary to their holy status of belonging solely to the LORD (e.g., Micah 6). The impurity caused by Israel's persistent rebellion could no longer be dealt with by offerings and sacrifices (Isaiah 1:10–31). Idols were placed in the LORD's Temple (Ezekiel 8). Although the LORD warned Israel patiently and repeatedly that they had failed to embody their purpose among the nations as a people holy to the LORD, they failed to heed the warning that God would purify his people through his justice. In the midst of failure, both by the priesthood and by Israel, the LORD envisioned raising up a priest-king who, in the form of a servant, would fulfil the purposes of both the priesthood and Israel (Isaiah 49:1–6; 52:13–53:12). He would mediate Israel to the LORD, while also bearing the penalty of Israel's rebellion in his own body, and he would mediate the nations to the LORD and the LORD to the nations.

As we step forward into the New Testament, we witness Jesus embodying the priest-king figure of the servant and being faithful where both the priesthood and Israel failed (Matthew 4:1–17). By his body becoming a sacrifice for the rebellion of Israel and the nations, he secured peace with God for all who are willing to participate in his death and resurrection (Ephesians 2:1–3:6). Through his death, resurrection and ascension, Jesus enabled a way for the nations to be restored to relationship with God and so mediates not only Israel to God, but the nations to God too. He did not achieve this by offering his own sacrifices first. There was no need because he embodied wholeness and holiness to the LORD and, for this reason, his offering of his own body was an acceptable once-for-all sacrifice on our behalf (Hebrews 8–9).

Although Jesus's work in his death, resurrection and ascension fulfils the role of both priesthood and Israel in the world, Jesus invites new covenant believers from every tribe and nation to join in the task of being a holy and royal priesthood. As inheritors of the blessings that we have in Jesus (1 Peter 1:3–12), we inherit the task of mediating Jesus to the nations as a people holy to the LORD, and we are called to embody our status (1 Peter 1:13–2:25). We do not do this by sacrifice and offerings because this work is complete. Instead, we participate in our task of mediating Jesus to the world by embodying our holy status of belonging to God in Jesus Christ and by bearing Jesus's name among the nations. As the apostle Peter writes:

> But you are a chosen people, a royal priesthood, a holy nation, God's special possession, that you may declare the praises of him who called you out of darkness into his wonderful light. Once you were not a people, but now you are the people of God; once you had not received mercy, but now you have received mercy. (1 Peter 2:9–10)

Having received this mercy and knowing the imperishable hope we have in Jesus, we are motivated to share what we have received in Christ with those who do not know him. Moreover, we do this because of an even greater vision of every tribe and nation gathered around the throne of God, proclaiming:

> Salvation belongs to our God,
> who sits on the throne,
> and the Lamb . . .
> Praise and glory
> and wisdom and thanks and honour
> be to our God for ever and ever.
> (Revelation 7:10, 12)

## *2. A fiery opening ceremony: obedience to command • Leviticus 9*

The opening ceremony of the Tabernacle begins in Leviticus 9 after the consecration of the priesthood has reached completion in Leviticus 8.[10] The goal of the opening ceremony, where Aaron will offer the inaugural gifts for Israel, is conveyed at the end of 9:4: 'For today the LORD will appear to you.'

### *The priests begin their ministry*

**9** On the eighth day Moses
summoned Aaron and his
sons and the elders of Israel. **2** He
said to Aaron, 'Take a bull calf for
your sin offering[a] and a ram for your
burnt offering, both without defect,
and present them before the LORD.
**3** Then say to the Israelites: "Take a
male goat for a sin offering, a calf and
a lamb – both a year old and without
defect – for a burnt offering, **4** and
an ox[b] and a ram for a fellowship
offering to sacrifice before the LORD,
together with a grain offering mixed
with olive oil. For today the LORD will
appear to you." '
**5** They took the things Moses com-
manded to the front of the tent of
meeting, and the entire assembly
came near and stood before the
LORD. **6** Then Moses said, 'This is
what the LORD has commanded you
to do, so that the glory of the LORD
may appear to you.'
**7** Moses said to Aaron, 'Come to the
altar and sacrifice your sin offering
and your burnt offering and make
atonement for yourself and the
people; sacrifice the offering that
is for the people and make atone-
ment for them, as the LORD has
commanded.'
**8** So Aaron came to the altar and
slaughtered the calf as a sin offering
for himself. **9** His sons brought the
blood to him, and he dipped his
finger into the blood and put it on
the horns of the altar; the rest of the
blood he poured out at the base of

10 The temporal phrase beginning 9:1, 'On the eighth day', contextualises the events of 9:1–10:7 immediately after the completion of the consecration process. As per Milgrom, *Leviticus 1–16*, 571; Nihan, *From Priestly Torah*, 90.

the altar. **10** On the altar he burned
the fat, the kidneys and the long lobe
of the liver from the sin offering, as
the LORD commanded Moses; **11** the
flesh and the hide he burned outside
the camp.

**12** Then he slaughtered the burnt
offering. His sons handed him the
blood, and he splashed it against the
sides of the altar. **13** They handed him
the burnt offering piece by piece,
including the head, and he burned
them on the altar. **14** He washed the
internal organs and the legs and
burned them on top of the burnt
offering on the altar.

**15** Aaron then brought the offering
that was for the people. He took the
goat for the people's sin offering and
slaughtered it and offered it for a sin
offering as he did with the first one.

**16** He brought the burnt offering
and offered it in the prescribed way.
**17** He also brought the grain offering,
took a handful of it and burned it on
the altar in addition to the morning's
burnt offering.

**18** He slaughtered the ox and the
ram as the fellowship offering for
the people. His sons handed him the
blood, and he splashed it against the
sides of the altar. **19** But the fat por-
tions of the ox and the ram – the fat
tail, the layer of fat, the kidneys and
the long lobe of the liver – **20** these
they laid on the breasts, and then
Aaron burned the fat on the altar.
**21** Aaron waved the breasts and the
right thigh before the LORD as a wave
offering, as Moses commanded.

**22** Then Aaron lifted his hands
towards the people and blessed
them. And having sacrificed the
sin offering, the burnt offering and
the fellowship offering, he stepped
down.

**23** Moses and Aaron then went
into the tent of meeting. When they
came out, they blessed the people;
and the glory of the LORD appeared
to all the people. **24** Fire came out
from the presence of the LORD and
consumed the burnt offering and the
fat portions on the altar. And when
all the people saw it, they shouted
for joy and fell face down.

**a** 2 Or purification offering; here and throughout this chapter
**b** 4 The Hebrew word can include both male and female; also in verses 18 and 19.

It is easy to read the end of 9:4 and glance over the significance of this moment. The LORD has already appeared to the Israelites in theophany as fire descended on Mount Sinai in Exodus 19:16–19 and which remained during the giving of the covenant codes (Exodus 20–23), the covenant-sealing ceremony (Exodus 24) and while Moses ascended the mountain into the cloud to receive instructions for the Tabernacle (Exodus 25–31). Furthermore, this consuming fire at the top of Sinai was present and visible while the Israelites exchanged the worship of the LORD for the worship of a handmade image in 32:1–6, so breaking at least the first two commands of the Decalogue (Exodus 20:2–6). Their pledge to be faithful in covenant relationship with the LORD in Exodus 24:3–8 all too soon turned to faithlessness in Exodus 32:1–6. The exchange was for the approachable and tame instead of the LORD's holy presence (see Exodus 19:21–2; 24:11).[11] While the LORD's reaction was a desire to destroy the people for their unfaithfulness (Exodus 32:7–10), he relented in response to Moses's intercession (Exodus 32:11–14) and, furthermore, he agreed to forgive their rebellion and not to remove his presence from Israel (Exodus 33–34).

With the Tabernacle created for the LORD's presence to dwell in Israel's midst, a critical question emerged: how can a holy God be present among a rebellious people? The only means by which the LORD can appear before the Israelites, and the Israelites' lives be preserved, is if gifts such as the sin and burnt offerings are given to the LORD through sacrifice.

In this context, we can understand the significance of the Israelites bringing all they need to offer these gifts in Leviticus 9:5. These animals will be sacrificed on their behalf so that their lives can be preserved when the glory of the LORD appears before them. With everyone gathered before the Tabernacle, and therefore before the LORD, Moses announces in 9:6 that the following instructions in 9:7 are what the LORD has commanded so that 'the glory of the LORD may appear to you'. These instructions are directed to Aaron since he is commanded to offer the gifts

11 See G. Geoffrey Harper, 'Endangered or Dangerous? YHWH's Presence and Impurity in Leviticus Perspective', *JSOT* 46 no. 4 (2022): 480–94.

described in 9:3–4, first for himself and then for the Israelites. As Milgrom notes, 'This sequence is essential. The priests cannot atone for others until they have atoned first for themselves.'[12] In 9:8–21, Aaron is depicted as offering his gifts and the gifts for the Israelites just as the LORD commanded (see Leviticus 1–7). Noticeably, the burnt offerings for Israel have not yet been consumed by fire as pleasing aromas for the LORD. The burnt offerings are laid on the altar, ready for the fire to be set.

Once all the gifts are offered, Aaron lifts his hands towards the people in blessing then steps down from the altar (9:22). Afterwards, Moses and Aaron enter the Tabernacle. The problem at the end of Exodus is resolved. Where once Moses could not enter when the LORD's glory had filled the Tabernacle, both Moses *and* Aaron are now entering because the gifts offered to the LORD have made atonement for their impurity. After Moses and Aaron bless the people for a second time, the glory of the LORD appears to all and fire immediately comes out from the LORD's presence in 9:24, consuming the burnt offering and the fat. The people's lives are preserved because of the sacrifices; the fire consumes the burnt offerings rather than the people. God's glory cannot be seen unhindered by an impure people unless atonement has been made with the life of another being taken and the people being purified by its blood.[13] The offerings have been given and consumed in their stead. Such is the nature of the LORD's glory and our impurity! The two cannot coexist without those who are impure being put to death. With the gifts offered on behalf of the Israelites, they can see the LORD's glory and live. No wonder the reaction of the Israelites is to shout for joy and fall face down when they see what happens! Their gifts are accepted by the LORD because the sacrifices have been offered as the LORD commanded.

---

12 Milgrom, *Leviticus 1–16*, 578.

13 See also Ko, *Leviticus*, 90.

## Moving forward into the New Testament

This reading of Leviticus 9 in context evinces three points for theological reflection and application. First, this opening ceremony exemplifies that the Lord's provision of gifts enables his presence and glory to be among his people and for the life of Israel to be preserved. The Lord is a consuming fire because of the utter purity of his holiness. God's people are tainted by rebellion; they cannot see God's glory and live. Holiness and impurity cannot come into contact. The only way is for God's people to be purified through the shedding of another's blood on their behalf. For God's presence to be permanently restored to his covenant people, there needed to be a permanent solution to this problem of a holy God dwelling among an impure people. As we move forward into the New Testament, this permanent solution is revealed in Jesus's atoning sacrifice whose blood is powerful to purify our whole beings (Hebrews 9:11–14). Because we are purified by his blood, God has given his spirit to dwell in and among us (Ephesians 1:11–14) while we await our imperishable future in a new heaven and a new earth where God's presence will be permanently restored to his covenant people (Revelation 21:1–4). This will not be an appearing of his glory for a moment with a flash of consuming fire; this future will be of God's people dwelling in the light of God's glory with the fullness of life (Revelation 21:22–6). This is only possible because the crucified and risen Lamb is present, whose sacrifice purified a people from every tribe and nation. Knowing the power of Jesus's sacrifice for us, how much more is our joy in Christ and our thankfulness and praise of the Lamb who was slain!

Second, sacrifices were able to be consumed instead of the Israelites when God's glory appeared because there was a priesthood who could mediate Israel to the Lord. However, these priests needed to offer gifts for themselves before they could offer gifts on behalf of Israel. Furthermore, this opening ceremony was the first of countless days where access to the LORD was through sacrifice and where the blood of sacrifices was brought into the Tabernacle to ensure that the place where the LORD dwelled remained in a pure condition. While the Israelites and priesthood did as the LORD commanded, a holy God could be present with his people. But as we move forward into the Old Testament, we witness sacrifices failing because both the people and the priesthood failed to do as the LORD commanded. The impurity of Israel's rebellion and unfaithfulness grew to such a point that God sent his people into exile (Ezekiel 10, 18). Just as Israel needed a permanent solution to their impurity, so too they needed a high priest who could permanently be their mediator before the LORD. For this reason, Jesus also became our great high priest who not only purified us by his own blood in a once-for-all sacrifice but is also present before the Father's throne of grace as he intercedes on our behalf (Hebrews 4:14–16; 9:23–8).

Third, Leviticus 8–9 highlights a significant pattern. This pattern is of command, obedience to command and then acceptance, which is the pattern of the law. While Israel is redeemed and set apart as God's people, order is maintained within this relationship by the LORD giving commands, which are to be obeyed by God's people, and which in turn leads to the people's acceptance with the LORD's presence residing among them. This is evident in Leviticus 9 as commands are given to Aaron and the Israelites (9:2–4) with the expectation that these commands will be fulfilled (9:6), which is affirmed by the recurring phrase, 'as the LORD [Moses] commanded' (9:7, 10, 21). The outcome of Aaron's and Israel's obedience is that the gifts are accepted on their behalf and the people's lives preserved (9:24). However, this pattern fails because of the nature of God's people who can confess their intent to follow the LORD's commands and yet, in the next moment, wander away from him. Part of being honest before God is acknowledging that we cannot fulfil God's commands perfectly because our disposition is stained by our sinfulness. We cannot gain God's acceptance by our obedience. There is only one who can because of his perfect obedience to the Father: Jesus. He perfectly fulfils the pattern of command, obedience and acceptance. By his obedience, we are accepted by God and we are freed from this pattern to pursue faithfulness to God in Jesus. We pursue faithfulness to Jesus's command not to be accepted by him, but solely for his glory and praise as we bear his holy name.

### *3. A second fiery display: the LORD must be glorified in Israel's midst • Leviticus 10:1–3*

Following the fiery opening ceremony in 9:1–24, the scene changes in 10:1 to focus on Aaron's sons, Nadab and Abihu, in the Tabernacle.

*The death of Nadab and Abihu*

**10** Aaron's sons Nadab and
Abihu took their censers,
put fire in them and added incense;
and they offered unauthorised fire
before the LORD, contrary to his
command. 2 So fire came out from
the presence of the LORD and con-
sumed them, and they died before
the LORD. 3 Moses then said to
Aaron, 'This is what the LORD spoke
of when he said:

'"Among those who approach
me
I will be proved holy;
in the sight of all the people
I will be honoured."'

Aaron remained silent.

Three simple actions are the difference between life and death. Nadab and Abihu take a censer each, put fire in it and place incense on top. We are told immediately by the narrator that these actions are contrary to the LORD's instructions (see Exodus

30:7–10).[14] Tension is heightened further when we remember that their rebellious actions are in the Tabernacle – the place where the LORD dwells. The consequence is immediate (10:2). Fire comes out from the LORD's presence and consumes Nadab and Abihu. The contrast with the previous scene could not be starker. In 9:24, the same wording is used: 'Fire came out from the presence of the LORD and consumed . . .' In this instance, the burnt offering and pieces of fat were consumed, not the people.[15] The sacrifices were accepted by the LORD and the people lived in the presence of the LORD's glory. In 10:1–2, however, there are no sacrifices present. Nadab and Abihu are consumed. The consequence of their rebelliousness is death.

Nadab and Abihu's fiery end in 10:2 could seem overly dramatic. All they do is offer incense in the LORD's presence; is that worth being consumed by fire? This question diminishes the seriousness of rebellion and the danger of the LORD's holiness. As Chingota highlights, 'Each time the divine presence is juxtaposed with sin, there is a reaction from the LORD.'[16] Nadab and Abihu were privileged to serve the LORD in his presence and this privilege requires following the LORD's instructions so that life and relationship can be maintained as the LORD dwells in Israel's midst. With Nadab and Abihu's fiery end, we are confronted with the penalty of rebellion: death. Knowing the extent of

---

14 Ko, *Leviticus*, 94–6, suggests that the phrase 'contrary to his command' in 10:1 leaves ambiguity as Nadab and Abihu suffer the penalty for doing something that the LORD did not command them to do, that is, there is neither permission nor prohibition. Please note that, at this point, Ko follows Bibb, *Ritual Words*, 121–2. However, contrary to both Ko and Bibb, there is clarity in Exodus 30 about who offers incense and the timing of when this incense should be offered. When it comes to worship in the Tabernacle, there is no grey area where the priests can choose to do as they wish.

15 Walter Houston, 'Tragedy in the Courts of the LORD: A Socio-Literary Reading of the Death of Nadab and Abihu', *JSOT* 90 (2000): 32–3.

16 Chingota, 'Leviticus', 145.

our own rebellion, we are also confronted with the realisation that we can never be in the presence of the LORD and live; we too would die. This points us to the need for sacrifice, where another is offered in our stead so that the penalty we deserve can be borne for us and we can live in the presence of God.

Nadab and Abihu's rebellion and ensuing death in 10:1–2 raises a fundamental question about the responsibility of the priesthood. Moses turns to Aaron in 10:3, who is now a grieving father, and refers to the fiery event of 10:2 as an example of what the LORD meant when he said:

> Among those who approach me
> I will be proved holy;
> in the sight of all the people
> I will be honoured.[17]

As the priests serve the LORD in his presence, they model what it means to set the LORD apart as holy. While the actions of the priesthood cannot make the LORD holy, since he is holy in and of himself, either their actions can treat him as holy by choosing obedience as they approach him, or their actions can trivialise his holiness by their rebelliousness. When the LORD is approached with the respect that his holiness deserves, then the lives of the priesthood are preserved as they serve in the LORD's presence, but when they despise the LORD's holiness by breaking his commands, the consequence is death.[18] If the priesthood do not approach the LORD with respect, then how will the Israelites? The priesthood have the responsibility of honouring the LORD in the sight of all Israel.

---

17 Please note that the verbs translated as 'I will be proved holy' and 'I will be honoured' can also be understood reflexively i.e., 'I will sanctify myself' and 'I will glorify myself'. Also, Milgrom, *Leviticus 1–16*, 603; Morales, *Who Shall Ascend*, 145, 146; Wenham, *Leviticus*, 155.

18 Ko, *Leviticus*, 93.

## Moving forward into the New Testament

The priesthood serving the LORD in the Tabernacle is a reminder to Israel about their role as a kingdom of priests as they serve the LORD among the world's nations. Israel's obedience to the LORD's commands respects the holiness of their covenant God in the midst of a watching world. Conversely, their rebelliousness despises the holiness of their covenant God, which is the reason, after many warnings, the LORD's glory left the Temple in Jerusalem (Ezekiel 10) and God's covenant people were removed from the land and into exile (e.g., Ezekiel 12). As we move forward into the New Testament, we who believe in Jesus and participate in his death and resurrection have been made a kingdom of priests to serve the LORD in the world while we await the coming again of our LORD Jesus Christ (1 Peter 2:4–10; Revelation 1:6; 5:10). While our lives have been purchased by the blood of Christ and we have full acceptance before God by what Jesus has done for us, either our conduct before a watching world can bring glory to God and lead others to do the same, or our conduct can dishonour Christ among the nations, which can bring the gospel into disrepute. Our responsibility as believers whose lives have been purchased by the blood of Jesus is to live in full obedience to our LORD, to bring honour to his name among the nations in the hope that those nations will too be present around the throne of Jesus declaring honour, praise and glory to him (1 Peter 2:11–25).

## *4. The purpose of the priesthood • Leviticus 10:4–20*

Leviticus 10:4–20 is a sequence of two scenes unfolding in the aftermath of the two fiery events in Leviticus 9 and 10:1–3. The priests must finish the gift offering process from the opening ceremony (chapter 9). The deaths of Nadab and Abihu represent a significant complication for the completion of the Tabernacle's opening ceremony. The two scenes in 10:4–7 and 10:12–20 address these issues and make a point that Aaron and his two remaining sons act with integrity and do not replicate the disobedience of Nadab and Abihu.

**4** Moses summoned Mishael and
Elzaphan, sons of Aaron's uncle
Uzziel, and said to them, 'Come here;
carry your cousins outside the camp,
away from the front of the sanctuary.'
**5** So they came and carried them, still
in their tunics, outside the camp, as
Moses ordered.

**6** Then Moses said to Aaron and his
sons Eleazar and Ithamar, 'Do not
let your hair become unkempt[a] and
do not tear your clothes or you will
die and the LORD will be angry with
the whole community. But your rela-
tives, all the Israelites, may mourn
for those the LORD has destroyed by
fire. **7** Do not leave the entrance to
the tent of meeting or you will die,
because the LORD's anointing oil is
on you.' So they did as Moses said.

**8** Then the LORD said to Aaron,
**9** 'You and your sons are not to
drink wine or other fermented drink
whenever you go into the tent of
meeting, or you will die. This is a last-
ing ordinance for the generations to
come, **10** so that you can distinguish
between the holy and the common,
between the unclean and the clean,
**11** and so you can teach the Israelites
all the decrees the LORD has given
them through Moses.'

**12** Moses said to Aaron and his
remaining sons, Eleazar and Itha-
mar, 'Take the grain offering left over
from the food offerings prepared
without yeast and presented to the
LORD and eat it beside the altar, for it
is most holy. **13** Eat it in the sanctuary
area, because it is your share and
your sons' share of the food offer-
ings presented to the LORD; for so I
have been commanded. **14** But you
and your sons and your daughters
may eat the breast that was waved
and the thigh that was presented.
Eat them in a ceremonially clean
place; they have been given to you
and your children as your share of
the Israelites' fellowship offerings.
**15** The thigh that was presented and
the breast that was waved must be
brought with the fat portions of the
food offerings, to be waved before
the LORD as a wave offering. This
will be the perpetual share for you

and your children, as the LORD has
commanded.'
**16** When Moses enquired about
the goat of the sin offering[b] and
found that it had been burned, he
was angry with Eleazar and Itha-
mar, Aaron's remaining sons, and
asked, **17** 'Why didn't you eat the sin
offering in the sanctuary area? It is
most holy; it was given to you to take
away the guilt of the community by
making atonement for them before
the LORD. **18** Since its blood was not
taken into the Holy Place, you should
have eaten the goat in the sanctuary
area, as I commanded.'
**19** Aaron replied to Moses, 'Today
they sacrificed their sin offering
and their burnt offering before the
LORD, but such things as this have
happened to me. Would the LORD
have been pleased if I had eaten the
sin offering today?' **20** When Moses
heard this, he was satisfied.

a 6 Or *Do not uncover your heads*
b 16 Or *purification offering*; also in verses 17 and 19

Between the two scenes in 10:4–7 and 10:12–20, verses 8–11 highlight the responsibilities of the priesthood. Since the explanation of 10:8–11 is crucial for understanding Leviticus and will help us understand what is at stake in the two scenes enfolding these instructions, the commentary below focuses first on 10:8–11.

The LORD's instructions in 10:8–11 begin with the general principle that neither Aaron nor his sons are to undertake their responsibilities in the Tabernacle when under the influence of alcohol. Some scholars surmise from this that Nadab and Abihu were drunk, which led to their disobedience and so their deaths.[19] However, there is no evidence of this connection in 10:1–3. This instruction is more precautionary. Being under the influence of alcohol would diminish their capacity to ensure that the LORD is set apart as holy and glorified among the people. More specifically, being under the influence of alcohol would diminish their capacity to make two critical distinctions that the LORD identifies in 10:10.

19 For example, Hartley, *Leviticus*, 135; Hess, 'Leviticus 10:1', 197.

The first distinction in 10:10 is between the holy and the common. The holy and the common are opposites, which can be seen in Figure 1. Someone or something is either holy or common; there is no middle ground.

Figure 1

For the common to become holy, it needs to be consecrated, which means to be set apart as holy. We have already seen this process in action when the priesthood and furniture for the Tabernacle were consecrated to be holy in the service of the LORD. Because the LORD is holy, all that encounters his presence must share the status of being holy. Moreover, the status of being common is not at all negative; it is a neutral term. All in the created world is common, but what is common has not been set apart as holy. Put positively, the 'common' describes the normal state from which a person, people, animal or object can be set apart as 'holy' for a particular purpose.[20]

This introduces us to a crucial idea about the distinction between the holy and the common. Each is a 'status'.[21] A person's

20 See also Watts, *Leviticus 1–10*, 540; Wenham, *Leviticus*, 19.

21 For the idea that the holy and common are two states, while the impure and pure are two conditions, see Richard E. Averbeck, 'Clean and Unclean',

status, for instance, is either common or holy. Similarly, an object's status is either common or holy. The common can become holy when consecrated, but when the holy is treated as common, the holy is profaned. A problem emerges when the holy is profaned. For instance, when the LORD is treated as though he is no different from the rest of creation, especially when we disregard his instructions, we are treating him as though he is common when he is holy, and so we profane his holiness. The consequence, though, is not that his holiness is impacted, but that we who profane his holiness are deserving of consequence. Figure 2 illustrates these relationships.

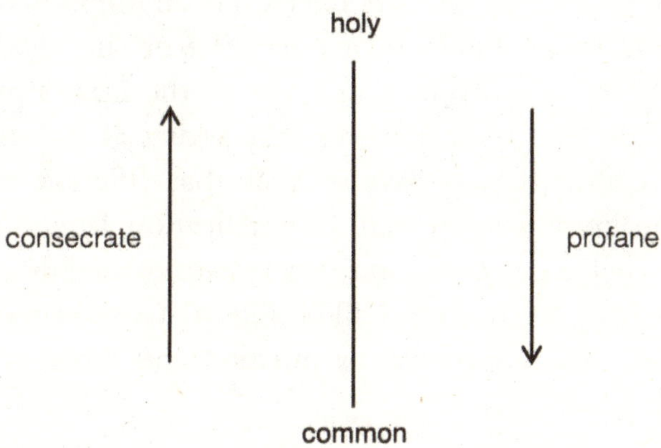


Figure 2

The second distinction in 10:10 is between the impure and the pure. The NIV uses the language of 'the unclean and the clean', but this language suggests hygiene and cleanliness, which is not what this distinction is about. To avoid this association, this commentary uses the language of impurity and purity. Again, impurity and purity are opposites and are conditions.[22]

---

in *NIDOTTE*, Volume 4, edited by Willem A. VanGemeren (Grand Rapids: Zondervan, 1997), 481; Morales, *Who Shall Ascend*, 155; Trevaskis, *Holiness*, 68–70.
22 Averbeck, 'Clean and Unclean', 481; Morales, *Who Shall Ascend*, 155; Trevaskis,

That is, when a person is considered impure, they are in a condition of impurity; similarly, when a person is considered pure, they are in a condition of purity. The purpose of the LORD's instructions in Leviticus 11–15 is to teach the Israelites about the distinction between purity and impurity, and about the consequence when someone or something is in a condition of impurity.

As we explore Leviticus 11, it will soon become evident that a person cannot be in a condition of impurity and approach the LORD, because impurity is the antithesis to the LORD's utter purity. The impure cannot be in contact with holiness without dire consequence. Therefore, for a person in an impure condition to be restored to a condition of purity, he or she needs to be purified. We have already seen in 4:1–5:13 the LORD's provision for the sin (purification) offering that addresses this need. As we explore Leviticus 11–15, we will see that different causes of impurity require different means of purification. In contrast, the process by which a person's condition is transformed from purity to impurity is by becoming defiled. Figure 3 shows the difference between when someone is purified and when someone is defiled.

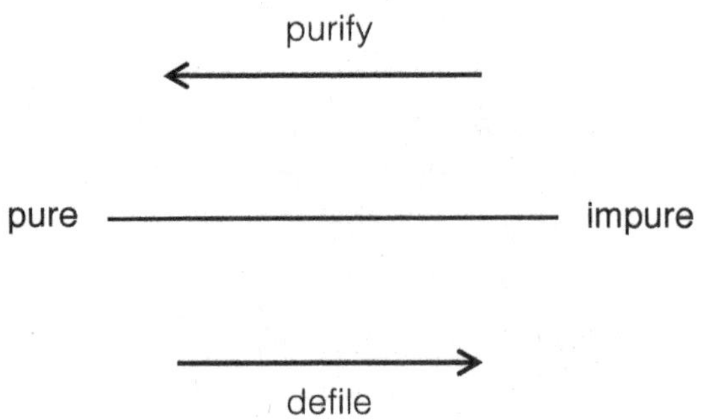


Figure 3

*Holiness*, 68–70.

Putting these pieces together, there are certain states and conditions that can coexist, and there is one combination that has a lethal consequence. In the following diagram, we can see that the holy and the pure happily coexist, and this is the combination where there is life and flourishing in the LORD's presence.[23] Similarly, an Israelite can be in a common state and in a pure condition and still approach the LORD. The critical factor is that the Israelite is in a pure condition. This is the reason the quadrants on the left-hand side of Figure 4 are the same shade of light grey. However, as we move into the right-hand quadrants,

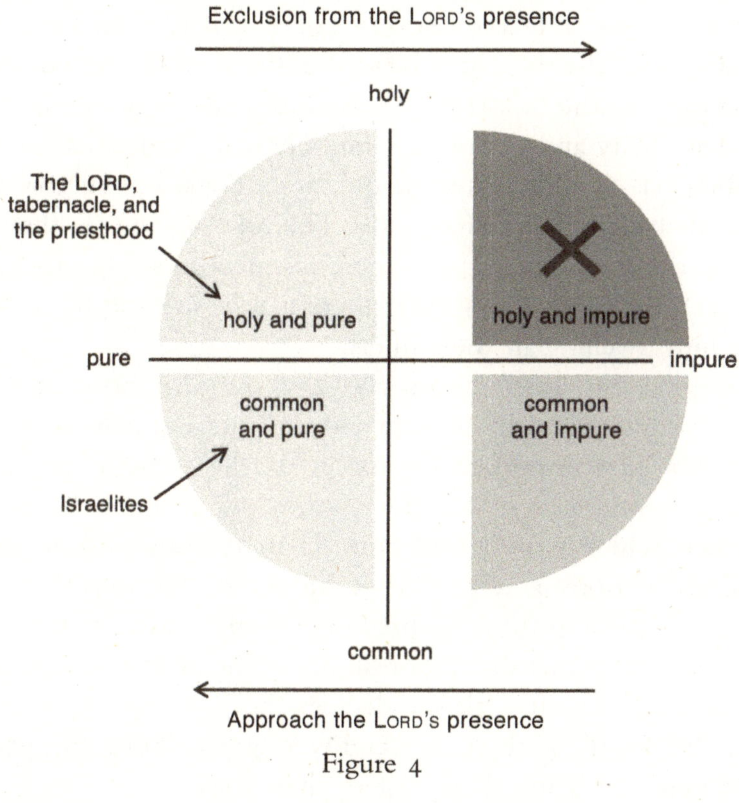


Figure 4

23 The diagram is an adaptation of Matthew Thiessen's illustration in *Jesus and the Forces of Death: The Gospels' Portrayal of Ritual Impurity within First-Century Judaism* (Grand Rapids: Baker Academic, 2020), 10.

the common factor is that each represents an impure condition. If an Israelite is in a common state but in an impure condition, they are not to have contact with the divine in the Tabernacle. To be restored to God's presence, they need to be restored to a condition of purity by a process of purification (see explanation in Leviticus 11–15). However, the final quadrant represents the holy meeting the condition of impurity, which must not happen within the Israelite community. The consequence is severe and lethal. For this reason, every care is taken to ensure that the holy and the impure remain separate.

This may raise a few questions. For instance, a reader might wonder why the Israelites have the status of being common when they are the LORD's holy people, or another question could be what purity and impurity mean. These are crucial issues, and Leviticus 11–15 addresses these questions. For now, the goal is to know that these distinctions exist. The role of the priesthood is to help the Israelites navigate these distinctions so that they can approach the LORD and so that there can be life and flourishing with him dwelling in their midst.

Grasping the distinctions above about the holy and the common and about the impure and the pure can help us understand why it is important for Aaron and his sons to keep away from the influence of alcohol as they serve the LORD in his presence, which is holy and pure. Their responsibility to make these distinctions is a matter of life in relationship with the LORD or exclusion from his presence. Furthermore, in 10:11, the LORD highlights that the responsibility of the priesthood includes teaching the Israelites 'all the decrees the LORD has given them through Moses'. With such weighty responsibilities, the priesthood needs to bring their best to their roles.

Before exploring the two scenes that encompass these instructions in 10:8–11, there are two issues that are helpful to address. First, these distinctions between the holy and the common and between the pure and impure still matter under the new covenant. In Leviticus 11–15 we see how these distinctions play out in the tangible aspects of everyday life – in the kitchen, in childbirth, in regard to sex, with a woman's monthly period and dealing with mould and illness. The purpose of these distinctions in everyday life is so the Israelites would learn about the nature of these distinctions as they relate to the LORD and as they relate to one another (see Leviticus 18–20). Under the new covenant, we no longer make these distinctions in the tangible aspects of everyday life, but these distinctions remain in our relationships as we relate to the LORD and as we relate to one another (e.g., see Colossians 3:5–14).

Second, it may have occurred to some readers that if priests were required to avoid alcohol, should those with pastoral responsibilities today follow the same pattern? While pastoral leaders have a radically different role from the priesthood since we have our great high priest and we are no longer in need of a priest other than him, we still bear great responsibility as we teach, rebuke, correct and train God's people in righteousness so that they might be 'thoroughly equipped for every good work' (2 Timothy 3:17). In my Australian Anglican context, every person with pastoral responsibility and oversight needs to adhere to a code of conduct called *Faithfulness in Service.*[24] It is not a coincidence that number 6.8 of these guidelines states, 'You are not to undertake any pastoral ministry when you are impaired by alcohol or any other mind-altering or addictive substances.'[25]

As noted above, the LORD's instructions in 10:8–10 are encompassed by two scenes in 10:4–7 and 10:12–20. The first scene begins in 10:4–5 with Moses giving instructions for Nadab

24 *Faithfulness in Service: A national code for personal behaviour and the practice of pastoral ministry by clergy and church workers* (Seventh Edition, Sydney: Anglican Church of Australia Trust Corporation, 2017).

25 *Faithfulness in Service*, 27.

and Abihu's bodies to be moved outside the camp so that the Israelite community can begin their grieving process. However, Moses gives specific instructions in 10:6–7 to Aaron and his two remaining sons, Eleazar and Ithamar, about their participation in the funeral rites. In ancient Near Eastern culture, mourning occurred in community, and the mourning process involved outward signs of grief. These signs included tearing clothes, putting on sackcloth, covering yourself with ashes and letting hair and beards grow long. In 10:6, Moses refers to these mourning rituals and prohibits Aaron, Eleazar and Ithamar from participating because they are still serving the LORD in the Tent of Meeting and the Tabernacle. Significantly, Moses warns Aaron and his two remaining sons that they too will die if they ignore these prohibitions; moreover, God will be angry with the whole Israelite community.

Surely, though, Aaron has a right to grieve the deaths of his two sons, and Eleazar and Ithamar their brothers? Yet by accepting the privilege of serving as priests in the LORD's presence, they have certain responsibilities that they cannot suddenly neglect for any reason.[26] One such responsibility is respecting what is holy; their clothing is holy and should not be ripped. Moreover, they have been set apart as holy and, until the opening ceremony is complete, they cannot abandon the place where they serve the LORD.[27] Also, in the Israelite worldview, the culpability of one affects the whole, especially with the priesthood since they represent the Israelites within God's presence. For this reason, the intentional disobedience of Aaron and his sons would affect the standing of the whole community before the LORD. The narrator

26 Ko, *Leviticus*, 98.

27 As Ko, *Leviticus*, 98, states, 'Their relatives can mourn on behalf of them, but they have to conduct themselves faithfully according to the dictates of the ritual laws. In this way, the officiating priests exist in an intermediate state, witnessing the boundary of life and death, absorbing both happiness and sorrow, behaving as a mediator between God and humans.'

deliberately observes in 10:7 that Aaron, Eleazar and Ithamar do as Moses has commanded.

The second scene in 10:12–20 depicts Aaron and his sons completing the offerings from the opening ceremony (chapter 9). This scene begins in 10:12–15 with Moses instructing Aaron, Eleazar and Ithamar about the responsibility to eat their portions of the grain offering and fellowship offerings. In this context, Moses checks that the meat of the sin offering has been eaten by Aaron and his sons (10:16–18). He finds that Eleazar and Ithamar have burnt the entirety of the sin offering outside the camp instead!

To understand this scene, we need to recall the instructions for the sin offering from 6:24–30. When atonement is made for an individual Israelite and blood is *not* brought before the curtain of the Most Holy Place, 6:24–30 instructs the priesthood to eat the flesh of these sin offerings. In contrast, when the sin offerings make atonement for the priesthood or for the Israelite community, the priesthood are to take the gift outside the camp and burn it completely (4:11–12, 18–21).

With this context in mind, the detail of 10:16–18 starts to fall into place. Moses points out in 10:18 that the sin offering is in the category of atonement for the individual Israelites and is to be eaten by the priests.[28] However, Eleazar and Ithamar treated the sin offering as though it made atonement before the curtain of the Most Holy Place and burnt the entirety of the sin offering outside the camp (10:16). When we realise that there is a dissonance between Moses' instructions and what the priests have done, tension emerges. The last time priests did not adhere to the LORD's instructions, they died! Now Eleazar and Ithamar have done what they ought not to have done. But

28 Please note, contrary to Ko, *Leviticus*, 102, that this is a case of confused categories of the sin offering, rather than Moses's misinterpreting and misapplying the LORD's instructions for the sin offering.

Aaron's response in 10:19 demonstrates that their actions were not motivated by rebellion but by a sincere desire to do right by the LORD. Because the guilt of Nadab and Abihu affected their father (i.e., Aaron), Eleazar and Ithamar treated the sin offering as though it was a sin offering for making atonement for the sin of a priest (see 4:1–12).[29] Since Aaron's reasoning demonstrates a desire to do what is right, Moses is at peace with the decision and there is no consequence (10:20).

Why, though, did Aaron and his sons need to eat the sin offering, and why would Aaron's unworthiness because of Nadab and Abihu's rebellion affect his ability to participate? Moses gives the reason in 10:17. By consuming the flesh, they are bearing the guilt of the Israelite community as a means of making atonement for the Israelites before the LORD.[30] This is a new idea in Leviticus. When the elders press their hands on the living goat's head, the goat is identified with the guilt of the people caused by their sin and then the goat is killed as the penalty that the guilt deserves. The action of eating is the act of internalising this guilt and so bearing the guilt of the people. The priesthood eat as representatives of the Israelites. It would not have been appropriate for Aaron to bear the guilt of the people on the day that Nadab and Abihu died because of their rebellion.

---

29 Similarly, Houston, 'Tragedy in the Courts', 34, suggests that the reason for Aaron's silence in 10:3 is that he shares the 'dishonour' of his two, now dead, sons. This dishonour could be a cause for not eating as much as it is a cause for silence.

30 See Gane, *Cult and Character*, 91–6, for an overview of this question. He concludes, 'Thus far we cannot escape the conclusion . . . that priestly consumption of sacrificial flesh is an integral part of the purification-offering ritual and makes some kind of contribution to expiation. It is not merely priestly enjoyment of compensation for service already rendered, including applying blood to the altar. Levine is right that the priestly meal of purification-offering meat accomplishes both things at once.'

## Moving forward into the New Testament

These two scenes remind us that the Lord's holiness is not to be trifled with. We see an anxiety about ensuring the holy is respected so that life can be preserved and consequence avoided. But as new covenant believers, we do not have this anxiety. What has changed? There is certainly one aspect that has not: God is still just as holy and he is still a 'consuming fire' (Hebrews 12:28–29). The holy is still to be respected with reverential awe. However, Jesus as both priest and sacrifice entered the heavenly Most Holy Place in complete obedience. Because of his complete obedience, there is no need to worry about how Jesus respects the holy. He is utterly holy and respects the holy. Furthermore, his sacrifice was once for all and so he has done away with the need for a priesthood to negotiate the holy daily to offer sacrifices for the purification of God's people (Hebrews 9:11–10:9). However, although we now have access to God's throne with confidence, through the blood of Jesus and through his high priesthood (see Hebrews 4:14–16), we must not forget that we need to approach him in a manner that respects his holiness, which is the reason we begin the Lord's Prayer, 'Our Father in heaven, hallowed be your name.'

# 3

# The Distinction Between Purity and Impurity

## LEVITICUS 11–15

A vital role for the priesthood is to make distinctions between what is holy and common, and what is impure and pure (10:10). It is not a coincidence that the next five chapters instruct the Israelites about how to make the distinction between what is pure and impure and about the consequences of being in an impure condition. Leviticus 11–15 teaches these two points by using tangible aspects of everyday life such as table fellowship (Leviticus 11); childbirth (Leviticus 12); the appearance of our bodies, clothes and homes (Leviticus 13–14); and bodily fluids (Leviticus 15). The goal is for the Israelites to apply this distinction between purity and impurity in their attitudes and behaviour in their covenant relationship with the LORD (11:44–45).

### *1. The distinction between purity and impurity by food • Leviticus 11*

Food is a central part of our lives irrespective of our culture and people group, and irrespective of whether we have much or little. We gather around food, and the act of eating maintains social cohesion. Our relationship with food says much about the health of our culture. However, while we can all relate to food as that which brings us together in community, we all have different cultural values about what is acceptable and unacceptable to eat. In my Australian context, personal preference often shapes the foods we eat and the food sources that we avoid. However, we do have some boundaries. For instance, we generally avoid eating animals that we associate with our cuddly household pets. We do, however, eat our national animal – the wallaby. Kangaroo meat, when slow-cooked with red wine, makes a lovely Bolognese. In Chinese culture, there are no food sources that are taboo.[1] So when we approach Leviticus 11, we need to be aware that making distinctions between food sources, with some being acceptable and others being unacceptable, may be unfamiliar for Chinese believers.[2] Yet the concept of food taboos may be familiar for others. For example, the African believer may come from a tribe that believes impurity is transmitted through food.[3] Similarly, a Muslim-background believer would also be practised at making distinctions between food sources. When exploring Leviticus 11, it is worth reflecting on how our culture of origin shapes how we relate to food sources.

The purpose of Leviticus 11 is to teach the Israelites about the distinction between purity and impurity using food. Each day an Israelite makes decisions about what to eat and what he or she chooses to avoid, and while these decisions would become a habit, the Israelite would be living the choice to be associated with purity and to avoid what is impure. It is worth stating that there is nothing innate within the animals, sea creatures, birds, insects or reptiles that makes them inherently pure or impure. Instead, in his freedom to do so, the LORD chose to designate certain characteristics that would represent the condition of purity and other characteristics that would represent the condition of impurity as a means of teaching the Israelites how to make the distinction between purity and impurity within the whole of life (see 11:44–45; 18:1–20:27).

1 Ko, *Leviticus*, 105.

2 Ko, *Leviticus*, 105.

3 Chingota, 'Leviticus', 149.

### *Clean and unclean food*

**11** The LORD said to Moses and
Aaron, **2** 'Say to the Israel-
ites: "Of all the animals that live on
land, these are the ones you may eat:
**3** you may eat any animal that has a
divided hoof and that chews the cud.
**4** ' "There are some that only chew
the cud or only have a divided hoof,
but you must not eat them. The
camel, though it chews the cud, does
not have a divided hoof; it is ceremo-
nially unclean for you. **5** The hyrax,
though it chews the cud, does not
have a divided hoof; it is unclean for
you. **6** The rabbit, though it chews the
cud, does not have a divided hoof; it is
unclean for you. **7** And the pig, though
it has a divided hoof, does not chew
the cud; it is unclean for you. **8** You
must not eat their meat or touch their
carcasses; they are unclean for you.
**9** ' "Of all the creatures living in the
water of the seas and the streams
you may eat any that have fins and
scales. **10** But all creatures in the
seas or streams that do not have
fins and scales – whether among
all the swarming things or among
all the other living creatures in the
water – you are to regard as unclean.
**11** And since you are to regard
them as unclean, you must not eat
their meat; you must regard their
carcasses as unclean. **12** Anything
living in the water that does not have
fins and scales is to be regarded as
unclean by you.
**13** ' "These are the birds you are
to regard as unclean and not eat
because they are unclean: the eagle,[a]
the vulture, the black vulture, **14** the
red kite, any kind of black kite, **15** any
kind of raven, **16** the horned owl, the
screech owl, the gull, any kind of
hawk, **17** the little owl, the cormorant,
the great owl, **18** the white owl, the
desert owl, the osprey, **19** the stork,
any kind of heron, the hoopoe and
the bat.
**20** ' "All flying insects that walk
on all fours are to be regarded as
unclean by you. **21** There are, how-
ever, some flying insects that walk on
all fours that you may eat: those that
have jointed legs for hopping on the
ground. **22** Of these you may eat any
kind of locust, cricket, cicada or grass-
hopper. **23** But all other flying insects
that have four legs you are to regard
as unclean.
**24** ' "You will make yourselves
unclean by these; whoever touches
their carcasses will be unclean till
evening. **25** Whoever picks up one
of their carcasses must wash their
clothes, and they will be unclean till
evening.

**26** ' "Every animal that does not have
a divided hoof or that does not chew
the cud is unclean for you; whoever
touches the carcass of any of them
will be unclean. **27** Of all the animals
that walk on all fours, those that walk
on their paws are unclean for you;
whoever touches their carcasses will
be unclean till evening. **28** Anyone
who picks up their carcasses must
wash their clothes, and they will be
unclean till evening. These animals
are unclean for you.

**29** ' "Of the animals that move along
the ground, these are unclean for
you: the weasel, the rat, any kind of
great lizard, **30** the gecko, the monitor
lizard, the wall lizard, the skink and
the chameleon. **31** Of all those that
move along the ground, these are
unclean for you. Whoever touches
them when they are dead will be
unclean till evening. **32** When one of
them dies and falls on something,
that article, whatever its use, will be
unclean, whether it is made of wood,
cloth, hide or sackcloth. Put it in
water; it will be unclean till evening,
and then it will be clean. **33** If one
of them falls into a clay pot, every-
thing in it will be unclean, and you
must break the pot. **34** Any food you
are allowed to eat that has come into
contact with water from any such
pot is unclean, and any liquid that
is drunk from such a pot is unclean.
**35** Anything that one of their car-
casses falls on becomes unclean; an
oven or cooking pot must be broken
up. They are unclean, and you are to
regard them as unclean. **36** A spring,
however, or a cistern for collecting
water remains clean, but anyone
who touches one of these carcasses
is unclean. **37** If a carcass falls on any
seeds that are to be planted, they
remain clean. **38** But if water has been
put on the seed and a carcass falls on
it, it is unclean for you.

**39** ' "If an animal that you are
allowed to eat dies, anyone who
touches its carcass will be unclean
till evening. **40** Anyone who eats
some of its carcass must wash their
clothes, and they will be unclean till
evening. Anyone who picks up the
carcass must wash their clothes, and
they will be unclean till evening.

**41** ' "Every creature that moves
along the ground is to be regarded
as unclean; it is not to be eaten.
**42** You are not to eat any creature that
moves along the ground, whether it
moves on its belly or walks on all
fours or on many feet; it is unclean.
**43** Do not defile yourselves by any of
these creatures. Do not make your-
selves unclean by means of them

or be made unclean by them. 44 I am the LORD your God; consecrate yourselves and be holy, because I am holy. Do not make yourselves unclean by any creature that moves along the ground. 45 I am the LORD, who brought you up out of Egypt to be your God; therefore be holy, because I am holy.

46 '"These are the regulations concerning animals, birds, every living thing that moves about in the water and every creature that moves along the ground. 47 You must distinguish between the unclean and the clean, between living creatures that may be eaten and those that may not be eaten."'

Leviticus 11 jumps straight into the distinction between pure and impure animals in 11:2–8 and then sea creatures in 11:9–12. There is a pattern that each set of instructions follows. The LORD gives permission for the Israelites to eat (11:3, 9), after which he restricts what the Israelites can eat by prohibiting certain animals or sea creatures (11:4–6, 10–12). With the animals that live on the land, the LORD gives permission in 11:3 to eat 'any animal' with a divided hoof *and* that chews cud. A divided hoof is an animal's foot that is divided into two toes. But 11:3 is very clear that as well as having a divided hoof, the animal must chew cud, which refers to the regurgitation of partially digested food to chew it again and again. For an animal to be in a pure condition, the LORD says that the animal must have *both* characteristics. Similarly, in 11:9, the LORD gives permission to eat *any* sea creatures that have fins *and* scales. Again, sea creatures that the LORD has designated to be in a pure condition have *both* characteristics.

After the permission-giving of 11:2 and 11:9, 11:3–8 and 11:10–12 designate particular animals and sea creatures as being impure, with the consequence that they are prohibited from being eaten. In 11:4, the LORD explains that if an animal displays only one (or none) of the characteristics, then the Israelites are to consider that animal as being 'ceremonially unclean for you'. Again, my language preference is for 'impure' rather than 'unclean' so that we disassociate the ideas in this text from issues of hygiene. Similarly, a more helpful term for 'ceremonial' is 'ritual'. The reason for this language preference is that 'ceremonial' conjures images of elaborate religious events, whereas 'ritual' is how cultures act out their worldview to establish, maintain, celebrate and restore order.[4] In this instance, the ritual of differentiating between animals that are impure from those that are pure is acting out how they make this distinction in the physical and tangible so that they learn how to make the distinction in their attitudes and behaviours in covenant relationship with the LORD. As part of acting out their worldview, all things fall into the category of being pure or impure. By refraining from that which is designated as impure, they learn to refrain from behaviours and attitudes that are impure. Thus, order is maintained within the community and with the LORD by making the distinction between purity and impurity.

It is worth pausing to ask what the LORD is teaching the Israelites about the nature of purity and impurity in the instructions about animals (11:2–8) and sea creatures (11:9–11). In both instances, the animals and sea creatures that represent a pure condition are those that have two characteristics. They have separated hoofs *and* chew cud (animals), or they have fins *and* scales (sea creatures). They must visually be a complete and whole picture. However, where the LORD has chosen to make the distinction between those that are pure and those that are impure is where an animal or sea creature has only one or none of the two characteristics. That is, those animals and sea creatures are visually incomplete and not whole. This distinction teaches the Israelites that purity is associated with completeness and wholeness, whereas impurity is associated with incompleteness and that which is not whole.[5]

4 See Catherine Bell, *Ritual Theory, Ritual Practice* (New York: Oxford University Press, 2009), for further reading about how ritual functions in society.

5 Mary Douglas, *Purity and Danger: An Analysis of Concepts of Pollution and Taboo* (London: Routledge & Paul, 1966), 64–5.

Verses 13–19 consider the distinction between purity and impurity with birds. Rather than identifying characteristics, however, the LORD's instructions simply lists the birds that the Israelites are to consider impure. There are no reasons given for why these birds are to be considered impure. There is one characteristic, however, that is obvious, which is that the majority eat dead creatures of all shapes and sizes.[6] By distinguishing birds that eat carrion as impure, the LORD is associating impurity with death. As we will note below, this theme recurs in Leviticus 11 (see 11:7, 11, 24–25, 26–28, 31–40). However, this is not a 'one-size-fits-all' explanation since osprey, hoopoe and bats rarely eat dead creatures. At this point, Jay Sklar gives permission to say that we do not always know the rationale but the audience for which Leviticus was written would have been able to access the meaning.[7] For now, we note that the osprey, hoopoe and bats are included as impure.

Verses 20–23 address the eating of insects and, from the outset, the LORD declares impure 'all' flying insects that walk on four legs *and* fly (11:20). These insects are creatures of the land *and* of the air. However, he gives permission to eat insects that walk on four legs but where those legs are jointed so that they hop on the ground (11:21). These insects are bound solely to the domain of the land.

So far, every group of creatures belongs to one domain: land, water or air. The echoes of Genesis 1 emerge to the fore.[8] Reading Genesis 1:1–31, the repetition of 'according to their kinds' as God creates sea creatures to teem in the water, birds to fly in the air and animals to move along the ground

6 Wenham, *Leviticus*, 174–5.

7 Sklar, *Leviticus*, 169.

8 The idea that Genesis 1:1–2:4 underpins Leviticus 11 is not a new idea. See G. Geoffrey Harper, *'I Will Walk Among You': The Rhetorical Function of Allusion to Genesis 1–3 in the Book of Leviticus* (Winona Lake: Eisenbrauns, 2018), 118–32.

is repeated to convey that a vital part of created order is that each kind of creature is created according to its kind and within its domain (i.e., ground, air, water). By choosing insects that move on the ground *and* fly in the air to be associated with impurity, the LORD is associating mixing kinds (i.e., by belonging to more than one domain) and this, in turn, is associated with disorder. This is not to suggest that these insects are inherently impure; they are part of God's created order. Instead, as Creator, God has the freedom to choose how he teaches about the nature of impurity by categorising insects in this way so that the Israelites can learn that mixing kinds is associated with impurity.

Verses 24–40 evince the consequence of being in an impure condition by using repetition. In verses 24, 25, 27, 28, 39 and 40, for instance, the consequence emphasised is that the Israelite is impure until evening and they must wash their clothes as an outward sign of being purified. The situation where the Israelite experiences this consequence is when he or she makes him- or herself impure by touching the carcass of any creature declared impure (11:24), as well as that which is declared pure (11:39). In the middle of 11:24–40, 11:29–37 addresses the situation where a carcass falls on an object and the object becomes impure. For these objects to be purified, they too need to be put in water until evening before they can be used again. However, clay pots are a different matter (11:33–35). Clay pots are used to collect water and to cook food, and these are to be broken when they have touched a creature's carcass. Anything in the pot is also considered to be impure and is to be thrown away (11:34). However, in 11:36, a spring or cistern of water is considered differently because water flows continuously and so there is a natural purifying process.

There are three vital points about impurity and its consequences that we can learn from 11:24–40. First, impurity is communicable, that is, the condition of impurity can be transmitted to another (i.e., it is infectious).[9] Second, by emphasising the prohibition against touching the carcass of any creature, the LORD is teaching the Israelites that impurity is associated with death and decay. Third, the consequence of being in an impure condition is exclusion from the LORD's presence. While this consequence is not spelled out in Leviticus 11, the Israelite would know immediately what it means to be impure until evening, even if this information is not obvious to us. Being in a condition of impurity until evening would mean being unable to approach the Tabernacle.[10] They must wait until they are in a condition of purity until they can bring their gifts to the LORD. As we will observe throughout Leviticus 11–15, not all causes of impurity are equal; some causes have longer time periods of exclusion than others. Some causes require sacrifice whereas other situations do not. In Leviticus 11, the LORD is communicating a fundamental idea about the consequence of impurity – exclusion from the LORD's presence – that is to shape their worldview.

There is, however, one final category of creatures that the LORD commands the Israelites to regard as impure in 11:29–31 and 11:41–45. At first, 11:29 suggests that there are specific creatures that move along the ground which the Israelites are to regard as impure. Verses 29–30 contain a list of these creatures. However, 11:41–42 clarifies that *every* creature that moves along the ground is to be considered impure and is not to be eaten.[11] This category of impure creatures stands out from the instructions about other creatures in the rest of the chapter by the addition of 11:44–45.

9 Also, Trevaskis, *Holiness*, 87.

10 Trevaskis, *Holiness*, 88. Harper, *'I Will Walk Among You'*, 133–4, explains how the consequence of impurity (separation from God) echoes the expulsion of Adam and Eve from Eden in 3:23–24.

11 Contrary to Milgrom, *Leviticus 1–16*, 683, who argues that the swarming creatures mentioned in verse 41 are to be detested but are not a cause of impurity. I take the point of view that all that is to be declared as detestable is also to be declared as impure.

In 11:44–45, the LORD commands the Israelites to set themselves apart as a people whose status is holy. The reason they are to embody this status by their obedience is because their covenant God is holy and, as a people who belong to him, they need to conform to his status.[12]

But how does refusing to eat creatures that move on their bellies enable Israel to embody a holy status? To answer this question, we need to bring the logic of the whole chapter together. As noted, the purpose of these instructions is to teach the Israelites to make the distinction between impurity and purity. The LORD is using the tangible and everyday activity of eating to teach how to make this distinction. It is not that these creatures are inherently impure or pure, but that the LORD has the freedom to make this distinction within his own creative work for this purpose. With his instructions about animals and sea creatures, the association with impurity is that which is incomplete or not whole. With birds, the association is with death and decay, and particular insects are to be considered impure when they represent the mixing of creation categories by domains. Thus, in 11:2–22, impurity has been distinguished from purity by the association with three characteristics: incompleteness, death and disorder of creation categories. If impurity is associated with these three characteristics, then purity is associated with the opposite: completeness, life and creation order.[13]

Returning to Genesis 1:24–25, God created 'all the creatures that move along the ground according to their kinds'

---

12 Wenham, *Leviticus*, 24, states, 'Holiness requires that individuals shall conform to the class to which they belong. The Israelites by virtue of the covenant relationship as the goal of the exodus event belong to the LORD and thus must "conform" to the one to whom they belong.' Also, Harper, *'I Will Walk Among You'*, 128–9; Ko, *Leviticus*, 113.

13 This is contrary to Douglas, *Purity and Danger*, 52, who defines holiness, rather than purity, as 'wholeness and completeness'. Douglas, at this point, confuses the distinction between the holy and the pure.

and, moreover, 'God saw that it was good' (1:25). However, all too soon after this majestic picture of God's created order in Genesis 1:1–2:3, a snake emerges into the foreground of the narrative in Genesis 3:1–19 and persuades the woman, and the man through the woman, to rebel against the LORD's command. The consequence for the snake in 3:14 is that the snake will be cursed above all other creatures, and it will crawl on its belly. Significantly, the consequence for the man and the woman is exclusion from God's presence (3:22–24). In Leviticus 11:41–43, we are hearing echoes of Genesis 3 with the category of creatures that move along the ground, and even more so on their bellies. Moreover, the consequence of impurity, which is being excluded from God's presence, reminds us of Adam and Eve's expulsion from the garden as a permanent exclusion from God's presence.[14]

In light of 11:41–43, what the LORD is accomplishing by putting his Tabernacle (i.e., his dwelling place) among his people and giving his people a means to approach his presence is striking. He is providing a temporary solution to the expulsion from Eden. For this temporary solution to be effective, God's people need to be in a condition of purity. This final category of creatures that move along the ground teaches the Israelites that impurity is associated with rebellion and the consequence of rebellion is exclusion. The implication is that purity is associated with obedience to the LORD's instruction. With obedience, there is life in God's presence. Thus, by refusing to be associated with all that impurity represents, especially rebellion, and by embodying all that is associated with a condition of purity, the Israelites are setting themselves apart to conform to the LORD's status of being holy.[15]

---

14 Harper, *'I Will Walk Among You'*, 133–4; Trevaskis, *Holiness*, 89.

15 Similarly, Trevaskis, *Holiness*, 103, notes that the prohibition against becoming impure by the creatures moving on the ground is a 'demand [for] Israel not to

## Moving forward into the New Testament

As Leviticus 11 teaches the distinction between impurity and purity in the physical activity of eating, the goal is for the Israelites to embody what they are learning as they relate to the Lord and within the community (see explanation of Leviticus 20:22–26). With this understanding, we can see how significant Peter's vision and the following scene is within Acts 10:9–23. This whole scene points to three significant developments with Jesus's death, resurrection and ascension. First, there is no longer a distinction between ritual purity and impurity for those who are in Christ. Jesus has declared that all foods are in a condition of purity (see Mark 7:17–23). Second, how the Jews applied the teaching of Leviticus 11 to distinguish between God's people and the nations also no longer applies; the gospel is to go to the ends of the earth. The pouring of the Holy Spirit on both Jewish believers and Gentile believers is evidence that this distinction is to be no more. Third, a vital distinction remains and is implied, which is between those who believe in Jesus and who have received forgiveness for their sin in his name, and those who do not. But this distinction remains so that we can be intentional in sharing the message that there is wholeness and life in Jesus.

One final question remains, however. If Jesus has abolished the distinction between ritual impurity and purity, then why invest time understanding Leviticus 11? Leviticus 11 helps us grasp two key points as Christian believers. The first is what Jesus has achieved for us in his death and resurrection. The Israelites made the ritual distinction between purity and impurity every day so that what they were enacting, they would also embody in their covenant relationship with the Lord. We no longer set

---

act in a way that will result in God's exclusion of them from his immediate presence'.

ourselves apart for God by ensuring we are in a condition of purity because we know we fail and cannot do this by ourselves. The only means by which we can be permanently restored to God's presence is through the blood of Christ that has purified us. If we do not grasp the consequence of our impurity (i.e., exclusion from God's presence), then we cannot truly grasp what it means for Jesus to purify us, for God's Spirit to be poured into our lives as a sign that there is no longer exclusion, and what it means to have a future hope of God's presence being restored among his covenant people (Revelation 21–22).

Second, while Jesus has done away with the ritual distinction, Leviticus 11 teaches us how to make this distinction and to know that impurity is associated with incompleteness, death and disorder, whereas purity is associated with wholeness, life and order. Knowing that God desires us to pursue what is pure and good motivates us to embody wholeness in relationship with God and with one another. Moreover, we constantly make the distinctions that Leviticus 11 teaches us. This is exemplified by Paul as he writes to the believers in Colossae in Colossians 3:5–14. In 3:5–7, he instructs believers to 'put to death, therefore, whatever belongs to your earthly nature: sexual immorality, impurity, lust, evil desires and greed' and charges believers to rid themselves of 'anger, rage, malice slander and filthy language'. Then, in 3:12, he encourages them to 'clothe yourselves with compassion, kindness, humility, gentleness and patience'. Paul is making a distinction between attitudes and behaviours in relationship that are impure and those that are pure. Moreover, he instructs us to desist from what is impure and to 'put on' (that is, embody) what is pure. Just because we no longer have the ritual distinction to train us does not mean that this distinction is abolished completely. Chingota observes, 'African Christians need to be reminded about the dangers of moral impurity [i.e., the attitudes and behaviours that Paul calls us to put off] and the seriousness of sin, which is what truly defiles a person.'[16] This is not just true of African Christians, but global Christians. Every day we are called by God to make this vital distinction between what is impure and what is pure, not so that we can be accepted in God's presence, but so that we are being conformed as God's holy people to the image of Christ.

## 2. *The consequence of impurity after childbirth* • *Leviticus 12*

Childbirth and the postpartum phase are some of the most fearful and messiest times in a woman's life. Those living in the western world have our fears diminished by lower mortality rates. When there is a loss of life, however, it rocks us to the core because it is not our norm. Our low(er) mortality rates do not stop us (women) fearing that between a twelve-week check, a twenty-week check and all the way to giving birth, the life we have carried, protected and nourished may not have survived. Miscarriages are an all too common part of life. Any little thing that suggests that all is not okay sees us immediately at our doctor's door.

However, women in the Global South are too well acquainted with higher mortality rates. There is greater uncertainty as to whether mother and baby will survive. According to the World Health Organization, nearly 800 women died per day in 2020 from complications in pregnancy and childbirth, and this represents a 34 percent drop from the year 2000. About 95 percent of these women were in 'low and lower middle-income countries', and one of the top causes of death is severe bleeding.[17] In Sierra

16 Chingota, 'Leviticus', 149.

17 'Maternal mortality', World Health Organization, 26 April 2024, www.who.int/news-room/fact-sheets/detail/maternal-mortality (accessed 30 September 2024).

Leone, one in seventy pregnancies ends in maternal death, whereas this figure is one in 12,500 women in Europe.[18] There is greater uncertainty in Sierra Leone as to whether a mother will survive, and it is likely that every person will know a family where a mother has died giving birth.

The experience of women in the ancient Near East would have been more akin to women in the Global South. Loss of blood in the birthing process would have been associated with loss of life, even if the mother lived, because of excess maternal mortality rates. Moreover, a woman continues bleeding for anywhere between four to six weeks as the wall of the uterus comes away, and this discharge still bears this association. Whenever blood leaves the body, the association is with illness and death; very rarely, if ever, does blood leave the body and that loss is life-giving.

*Purification after childbirth*

**12** The Lord said to Moses,
2 'Say to the Israelites: "A
woman who becomes pregnant and
gives birth to a son will be ceremo-
nially unclean for seven days, just as
she is unclean during her monthly
period. 3 On the eighth day the boy
is to be circumcised. 4 Then the
woman must wait thirty-three days
to be purified from her bleeding. She
must not touch anything sacred or
go to the sanctuary until the days
of her purification are over. 5 If she
gives birth to a daughter, for two
weeks the woman will be unclean,
as during her period. Then she must
wait sixty-six days to be purified from
her bleeding.

6 ' "When the days of her purifica-
tion for a son or daughter are over,
she is to bring to the priest at the
entrance to the tent of meeting a
year-old lamb for a burnt offering
and a young pigeon or a dove for a
sin offering.[a] 7 He shall offer them
before the Lord to make atone-
ment for her, and then she will be

18 'Maternal Mortality', Our Word in Data, February 2024, ourworldindata.org/maternal-mortality#how-have-maternal-mortality-changed-over-the-long-term (accessed 30 September 2024).

ceremonially clean from her flow of blood.

'"These are the regulations for the woman who gives birth to a boy or a girl. **8** But if she cannot afford a lamb, she is to bring two doves or two young pigeons, one for a burnt offering and the other for a sin offering. In this way the priest will make atonement for her, and she will be clean."'

a 6 Or *purification offering*; also in verse 8

The LORD's instructions about the mother being in an impure condition in the postpartum phase has three small sections: 12:2–5 outlines the consequence of being in an impure condition, 12:6–7b explains the process where the woman is to be restored to the LORD's presence through being purified, and an exception is introduced in 12:7c–8.

In 12:2–5, the LORD first addresses the situation where a son is born. The LORD's command about circumcision to Abraham from Genesis 17 shapes these instructions. In Genesis 17:11–14, the LORD instructs Abraham and all descendants from his line to circumcise their sons when they are eight days old as a sign that they are a part of the covenant community. For this reason, in Leviticus 12:2–5, the mother is to be deemed in an impure condition for seven days after the birth of her son, after which her son is to be circumcised on the eighth day. The consequence of being in an impure condition is implied. The mother is excluded from approaching the LORD for those seven days. However, on the eighth day, she would be present for the circumcision of her son. While temporarily restored for the eighth day, she still needs to wait for another thirty-three days until she is restored to a pure condition from her postpartum bleeding. For the first time, the consequence of being in an impure condition is made explicit. For those thirty-three days, she is not to touch anything holy, and neither is she to approach the LORD's sanctuary.

Verse 5 addresses the situation where the newborn is a

daughter. It is noticeable that the initial period of impurity is double that for a son (i.e., fourteen days rather than seven). Also, the wait time for the postpartum bleeding is also double, that is, sixty-six days instead of thirty-three. We know that the gender of a newborn does not play a part in how long postpartum bleeding lasts, so there must be another explanation for the lengthened time frame for a daughter in comparison with a son. I am not convinced that the sex of the newborn is the reason for the disparity. This is important for the global Christian. In a western context, the tendency is to accuse Leviticus 12 of devaluing the birth of daughters and of being misogynistic. In India, though, where there is a documented cultural devaluing of women evident in the sex-selective abortion rate, for instance, the tendency might be to let the dissonance reinforce the devaluing of female life. For the Chinese Christian, however, who has lived the trauma of China's one-child policy where the preference was for a son, the dissonance between the son and the daughter may cause confusion.[19] As we read 12:2–5, it is good for every Christian to examine how our cultural beliefs shape what we believe about this passage. Generally, a helpful rule of thumb is to seek a generous reading.

So what could account for the difference between the time frames for a newborn son versus a newborn daughter? Curiously, 12:2–4 shapes the consequences for the mother of a son around the eighth day, which is when her son would be circumcised. It is more likely that the shortened time period is due to the son's circumcision where the shedding of the son's blood contributes to the minimising of impurity's consequences. We often read 12:2–5 as though the shorter time frame for the newborn son is the benchmark and then the situation of the newborn daughter represents a lengthening of

19 See Ko, *Leviticus*, 115–6.

the exclusion period because of the newborn's sex. However, a more generous reading is that the time frame for exclusion is shortened after the birth of a newborn son because of the son's circumcision. This would mean that the time frame for the son is halved instead of the time frame for a newborn daughter being doubled.[20] I find this explanation persuasive because we know that, for some women, postpartum bleeding can be heavy for the first two weeks (i.e., for the first fourteen days) and then the bleeding continues beyond this point, albeit changed, for the next four to six weeks. A time of fourteen days plus sixty-six days would ensure that the postpartum bleeding would have stopped before the mother approaches the LORD. It makes sense that this is the standard time frame, which means that the shedding of blood in the act of circumcision diminishes the time frame for impurity associated with postpartum bleeding in the son's case.

This reading halts the western believer's indignation about the time frame difference and encourages a reading of the text that seeks generosity rather than judgment of a culture that is different from our own. Moreover, for a Christian believer in India or China, for instance, this reading emphasises the dignity and worth of both sons and daughters.

With 12:2–5 emphasising the duration of a mother's impurity, the focus is on the consequence of impurity, which is exclusion from the LORD's presence, since impurity cannot encounter the holy.[21] However, exclusion also means waiting. From the mother's perspective, she cannot approach the LORD's presence while she is in the phase of postpartum bleeding because she represents being in an impure condition, so she waits until she can be restored to the LORD's presence by a purification offering. Chingota

20 Also G. Geoffrey Harper, *Teaching Leviticus: From Text to Message* (Fearn: Christian Focus, 2022), 181.

21 Sklar, *Leviticus*, 176.

incorrectly observes that 'a woman's shedding of blood was not deliberate, and was thus one of the unintentional sins requiring purification offering'.[22] While Chingota is right to note that the shedding of blood is not deliberate, that is, outside her control, linking the loss of blood to sin diminishes the idea of impurity and of purification. The purification offering (NIV 'sin offering') addresses all impurity, not solely the impurity of sin. In contrast, Ko highlights, 'Regardless of the reason, the separation of the new mother does not mean that there is anything morally wrong with her as a result of her loss of blood.' [23] So, with the time frame of either the thirty-three or sixty-six days finished, the mother is restored to the LORD's presence by atonement made by a purification offering, which is a joyful moment of devotion and reconciliation.

Significantly, the final section in 12:7c–8 gives a provision for the poverty-stricken mother so that her social-economic status does not prevent her from being restored to the presence of her covenant God. The LORD does not show partiality between those who have wealth and those who are poor; he desires all to be restored to his presence.

It is easy to read Leviticus 12 and have a knee-jerk reaction about how unfair and restricting these instructions appear to be for a mother with a newborn. I wonder, though, if an Israelite woman would have thought about it quite differently. Those first two to three months are some of the hardest for a mother. In the initial two weeks, a mother is trying to encourage a hungry baby to breastfeed, then dealing with vomit and poo, all the while trying to manage her own bleeding and her hurting body from being ripped apart. While her body is healing in weeks three to eight, she is still very sore, and her baby is just as demanding in its wants of feeding, pooing, vomiting, being held and needing

22 Chingota, 'Leviticus', 149.

23 Ko, *Leviticus*, 116.

to sleep. While she is doing life with a newborn, she knows she is excluded from her covenant God's presence because her post-partum blood is a daily reminder of her impure condition, and she must wait to be restored so that she can show her devotion to her covenant God. While she experiences exclusion and the need to wait, she is also experiencing grace as she is given a space to heal and recover. I wonder if there is much wisdom in these instructions that gives mothers of newborns the grace to be kind to themselves in one of the most fearful and messiest phases of life.[24]

## Moving forward into the New Testament

In the opening chapters of Luke's Gospel, the scene of Jesus's birth is astonishing, with the background of Leviticus 12 in mind. The hearer of Luke's Gospel is prepared for who Jesus is from the moment Gabriel reveals to Mary in 1:31–33 that he will be the 'Son of the Most High' and he will inherit the everlasting Davidic kingdom. While 1:31–33 accentuates Jesus's identity as the Davidic king, the phrase 'Son of the Most High' is loaded with additional meaning in 1:35: 'The Holy Spirit will come on you, and the power of the Most High will overshadow you. So the holy one to be born will be called the Son of God.' Jesus is the holy one. It is remarkable how this holy one, in the form of a baby in 2:7 and 2:8–20, is in the presence of his mother who is in an impure condition having given birth. Impurity cannot be in the presence of the holy because there is consequence, but in this scene in Luke's Gospel, the holy is in the presence of impurity and there is no consequence. This suggests from the outset of Jesus's life that there is something about his identity and holiness that overcomes impurity.

As we explore impurity and its consequences in Leviticus 13–15, we will unpack how Jesus's power overcomes ritual

24 Similarly, Ko, *Leviticus*, 116.

impurity. However, there are no instances in the New Testament that speak directly to Leviticus 12 other than Luke 2:22–24 demonstrating that Mary and Joseph fulfilled the requirements of Leviticus 12 after Jesus's birth. To pre-empt the discussion of Leviticus 13–15, where Jesus interacts with those who are in an impure condition and who have no control about the cause of their impurity, Jesus restores each to a condition of purity (e.g., Luke 8:40–48, 49–56; 9:37–43). Each instance foreshadows his work on the cross where Jesus purifies us not only from our sin but from all our impurities. This is one reason the vision of the great multitude in Revelation 7:9–17 is incredible. This great multitude, with representatives from all nations, are wearing white robes that they have washed in the blood of the Lamb, and they are worshipping in fullness of life before the throne of God. The wearing of white robes is symbolic for their complete purification from all impurity, which the blood of Jesus has accomplished on their behalf.

It is because Jesus's blood purifies us that there is no longer exclusion from God's presence when we are in a condition of impurity from, for example, postpartum bleeding. When life is messy with a newborn, we are still able to read God's word and approach the throne of grace. This could not be more different for Muslim women around the globe who, when they see themselves as impure, experience exclusion to the point that they cannot touch the Qur'an. Women who know Jesus and the power of his blood on their behalf have a powerful and life-changing story to speak into the lives of Muslim women around the world. When we are discipling new Christians who are from a Muslim background, it is essential to explore how Jesus's power over ritual impurity is life-giving. The power of Jesus's death and resurrection means they are always able to approach the living God because he has brought them near to him permanently through the blood of Christ.

## *3. The distinction between purity and impurity by appearance • Leviticus 13–14*

Leviticus 13–14 continues to teach the Israelites about the nature of impurity and its consequence through the *appearance* of people, fabric and homes. There is a pattern within Leviticus 13–14 that provides structure to this section. First, 13:1–46 instructs Israel about how they are to determine from a person's appearance when they are in an impure condition. Second, 13:47–59 achieves the same purpose as the first section but with fabrics and materials. Third, 14:1–32 revisits the topic of people affected by impurity based on appearance but with a focus on how people are to be restored to a condition of purity within the community. Finally, 14:33–57 addresses how the Israelites are to purify their homes when mould is a problem. Once the meaning of Leviticus 13–14 has been explored, the final section moves forward to the New Testament.

### *Regulations about defiling skin diseases*

**13** The LORD said to Moses and Aaron, 2 'When anyone has a swelling or a rash or a shiny spot on their skin that may be a defiling skin disease,[a] they must be brought to Aaron the priest or to one of his sons[b] who is a priest. 3 The priest is to examine the sore on the skin, and if the hair in the sore has turned white and the sore appears to be more than skin deep, it is a defiling skin disease. When the priest examines that person, he shall pronounce them ceremonially unclean. 4 If the shiny spot on the skin is white but does not appear to be more than skin deep and the hair in it has not turned white, the priest is to isolate the affected person for seven days. 5 On the seventh day the priest is to examine them, and if he sees that the sore is unchanged and has not spread in the skin, he is to isolate them for another seven days. 6 On the seventh day the priest is to examine them again, and if the sore has faded and has not spread in the skin, the priest shall pronounce

them clean; it is only a rash. They
must wash their clothes, and they
will be clean. 7 But if the rash does
spread in their skin after they have
shown themselves to the priest to be
pronounced clean, they must appear
before the priest again. 8 The priest
is to examine that person, and if
the rash has spread in the skin, he
shall pronounce them unclean; it is
a defiling skin disease.

9 'When anyone has a defiling skin
disease, they must be brought to the
priest. 10 The priest is to examine
them, and if there is a white swelling
in the skin that has turned the hair
white and if there is raw flesh in the
swelling, 11 it is a chronic skin disease
and the priest shall pronounce them
unclean. He is not to isolate them,
because they are already unclean.

12 'If the disease breaks out all over
their skin and, so far as the priest
can see, it covers all the skin of the
affected person from head to foot,
13 the priest is to examine them, and
if the disease has covered their whole
body, he shall pronounce them
clean. Since it has all turned white,
they are clean. 14 But whenever raw
flesh appears on them, they will be
unclean. 15 When the priest sees the
raw flesh, he shall pronounce them
unclean. The raw flesh is unclean;
they have a defiling disease. 16 If the
raw flesh changes and turns white,
they must go to the priest. 17 The
priest is to examine them, and if the
sores have turned white, the priest
shall pronounce the affected person
clean; then they will be clean.

18 'When someone has a boil on
their skin and it heals, 19 and in the
place where the boil was, a white
swelling or reddish-white spot
appears, they must present them-
selves to the priest. 20 The priest is
to examine it, and if it appears to be
more than skin deep and the hair in
it has turned white, the priest shall
pronounce that person unclean. It
is a defiling skin disease that has
broken out where the boil was. 21 But
if, when the priest examines it, there
is no white hair in it and it is not
more than skin deep and has faded,
then the priest is to isolate them for
seven days. 22 If it is spreading in
the skin, the priest shall pronounce
them unclean; it is a defiling disease.
23 But if the spot is unchanged and
has not spread, it is only a scar from
the boil, and the priest shall pro-
nounce them clean.

24 'When someone has a burn on
their skin and a reddish-white or
white spot appears in the raw flesh of
the burn, 25 the priest is to examine

the spot, and if the hair in it has turned white, and it appears to be more than skin deep, it is a defiling disease that has broken out in the burn. The priest shall pronounce them unclean; it is a defiling skin disease. **26** But if the priest examines it and there is no white hair in the spot and if it is not more than skin deep and has faded, then the priest is to isolate them for seven days. **27** On the seventh day the priest is to examine that person, and if it is spreading in the skin, the priest shall pronounce them unclean; it is a defiling skin disease. **28** If, however, the spot is unchanged and has not spread in the skin but has faded, it is a swelling from the burn, and the priest shall pronounce them clean; it is only a scar from the burn.

**29** 'If a man or woman has a sore on their head or chin, **30** the priest is to examine the sore, and if it appears to be more than skin deep and the hair in it is yellow and thin, the priest shall pronounce them unclean; it is a defiling skin disease on the head or chin. **31** But if, when the priest examines the sore, it does not seem to be more than skin deep and there is no black hair in it, then the priest is to isolate the affected person for seven days. **32** On the seventh day the priest is to examine the sore, and if it has not spread and there is no yellow hair in it and it does not appear to be more than skin deep, **33** then the man or woman must shave themselves, except for the affected area, and the priest is to keep them isolated another seven days. **34** On the seventh day the priest is to examine the sore, and if it has not spread in the skin and appears to be no more than skin deep, the priest shall pronounce them clean. They must wash their clothes, and they will be clean. **35** But if the sore does spread in the skin after they are pronounced clean, **36** the priest is to examine them, and if he finds that the sore has spread in the skin, he does not need to look for yellow hair; they are unclean. **37** If, however, the sore is unchanged so far as the priest can see, and if black hair has grown in it, the affected person is healed. They are clean, and the priest shall pronounce them clean.

**38** 'When a man or woman has white spots on the skin, **39** the priest is to examine them, and if the spots are dull white, it is a harmless rash that has broken out on the skin; they are clean.

**40** 'A man who has lost his hair and is bald is clean. **41** If he has lost his

hair from the front of his scalp and
has a bald forehead, he is clean.
**42** But if he has a reddish-white sore
on his bald head or forehead, it is
a defiling disease breaking out on
his head or forehead. **43** The priest
is to examine him, and if the swol-
len sore on his head or forehead is
reddish-white like a defiling skin
disease, **44** the man is diseased and is
unclean. The priest shall pronounce
him unclean because of the sore on
his head.

**45** 'Anyone with such a defiling
disease must wear torn clothes, let
their hair be unkempt,[c] cover the
lower part of their face and cry out,
"Unclean! Unclean!" **46** As long as
they have the disease they remain
unclean. They must live alone; they
must live outside the camp.

### *Regulations about defiling moulds*

**47** 'As for any fabric that is spoiled
with a defiling mould – any woollen
or linen clothing, **48** any woven or
knitted material of linen or wool, any
leather or anything made of leather –
**49** if the affected area in the fabric,
the leather, the woven or knitted
material, or any leather article, is
greenish or reddish, it is a defiling
mould and must be shown to the
priest. **50** The priest is to examine the
affected area and isolate the article
for seven days. **51** On the seventh day
he is to examine it, and if the mould
has spread in the fabric, the woven or
knitted material, or the leather, what-
ever its use, it is a persistent defiling
mould; the article is unclean. **52** He
must burn the fabric, the woven or
knitted material of wool or linen,
or any leather article that has been
spoiled, because the defiling mould
is persistent; the article must be
burned.

**53** 'But if, when the priest exam-
ines it, the mould has not spread
in the fabric, the woven or knitted
material, or the leather article, **54** he
shall order that the spoiled article
be washed. Then he is to isolate it
for another seven days. **55** After the
article has been washed, the priest is
to examine it again, and if the mould
has not changed its appearance,
even though it has not spread, it is
unclean. Burn it, no matter which
side of the fabric has been spoiled.
**56** If, when the priest examines it,
the mould has faded after the arti-
cle has been washed, he is to tear
the spoiled part out of the fabric,
the leather, or the woven or knitted
material. **57** But if it reappears in
the fabric, in the woven or knitted

material, or in the leather article, it is a spreading mould; whatever has the mould must be burned. **58** Any fabric, woven or knitted material, or any leather article that has been washed and is rid of the mould, must be washed again. Then it will be clean.'

**59** These are the regulations concerning defiling moulds in woollen or linen clothing, woven or knitted material, or any leather article, for pronouncing them clean or unclean.

### *Cleansing from defiling skin diseases*

**14** The LORD said to Moses, **2** 'These are the regulations for any diseased person at the time of their ceremonial cleansing, when they are brought to the priest: **3** the priest is to go outside the camp and examine them. If they have been healed of their defiling skin disease,[a] **4** the priest shall order that two live clean birds and some cedar wood, scarlet yarn and hyssop be brought for the person to be cleansed. **5** Then the priest shall order that one of the birds be killed over fresh water in a clay pot. **6** He is then to take the live bird and dip it, together with the cedar wood, the scarlet yarn and the hyssop, into the blood of the bird that was killed over the fresh water. **7** Seven times he shall sprinkle the one to be cleansed of the defiling disease, and then pronounce them clean. After that, he is to release the live bird in the open fields.

**8** 'The person to be cleansed must wash their clothes, shave off all their hair and bathe with water; then they will be ceremonially clean. After this they may come into the camp, but they must stay outside their tent for seven days. **9** On the seventh day they must shave off all their hair; they must shave their head, their beard, their eyebrows and the rest of their hair. They must wash their clothes and bathe themselves with water, and they will be clean.

**10** 'On the eighth day they must bring two male lambs and one ewe lamb a year old, each without defect, along with three-tenths of an ephah[b] of the finest flour mixed with olive oil for a grain offering, and one log[c] of oil. **11** The priest who pronounces them clean shall present both the one to be cleansed and their offerings before the LORD at the entrance to the tent of meeting.

**12** 'Then the priest is to take one of the male lambs and offer it as a guilt offering, along with the log of

oil; he shall wave them before the
LORD as a wave offering. 13 He is to
slaughter the lamb in the sanctuary
area where the sin offering[d] and the
burnt offering are slaughtered. Like
the sin offering, the guilt offering
belongs to the priest; it is most holy.
14 The priest is to take some of the
blood of the guilt offering and put
it on the lobe of the right ear of the
one to be cleansed, on the thumb
of their right hand and on the big
toe of their right foot. 15 The priest
shall then take some of the log of
oil, pour it in the palm of his own
left hand, 16 dip his right forefinger
into the oil in his palm, and with his
finger sprinkle some of it before the
LORD seven times. 17 The priest is to
put some of the oil remaining in his
palm on the lobe of the right ear of
the one to be cleansed, on the thumb
of their right hand and on the big
toe of their right foot, on top of the
blood of the guilt offering. 18 The
rest of the oil in his palm the priest
shall put on the head of the one to
be cleansed and make atonement for
them before the LORD.

19 'Then the priest is to sacrifice
the sin offering and make atone-
ment for the one to be cleansed
from their uncleanness. After that,
the priest shall slaughter the burnt
offering 20 and offer it on the altar,
together with the grain offering, and
make atonement for them, and they
will be clean.

21 'If, however, they are poor and
cannot afford these, they must take
one male lamb as a guilt offering to
be waved to make atonement for
them, together with a tenth of an
ephah[e] of the finest flour mixed with
olive oil for a grain offering, a log of
oil, 22 and two doves or two young
pigeons, such as they can afford, one
for a sin offering and the other for a
burnt offering.

23 'On the eighth day they must
bring them for their cleansing to
the priest at the entrance to the tent
of meeting, before the LORD. 24 The
priest is to take the lamb for the guilt
offering, together with the log of oil,
and wave them before the LORD as
a wave offering. 25 He shall slaughter
the lamb for the guilt offering and
take some of its blood and put it on
the lobe of the right ear of the one
to be cleansed, on the thumb of their
right hand and on the big toe of their
right foot. 26 The priest is to pour
some of the oil into the palm of his
own left hand, 27 and with his right
forefinger sprinkle some of the oil
from his palm seven times before the
LORD. 28 Some of the oil in his palm

he is to put on the same places he
put the blood of the guilt offering –
on the lobe of the right ear of the
one to be cleansed, on the thumb of
their right hand and on the big toe
of their right foot. 29 The rest of the
oil in his palm the priest shall put on
the head of the one to be cleansed,
to make atonement for them before
the LORD. 30 Then he shall sacrifice
the doves or the young pigeons, such
as the person can afford, 31 one as a
sin offering and the other as a burnt
offering, together with the grain
offering. In this way the priest will
make atonement before the LORD
on behalf of the one to be cleansed.'

32 These are the regulations for
anyone who has a defiling skin
disease and who cannot afford the
usual offerings for their cleansing.

*Cleansing from defiling moulds*

33 The LORD said to Moses and
Aaron, 34 'When you enter the land
of Canaan, which I am giving you
as your possession, and I put a
spreading mould in a house in that
land, 35 the owner of the house must
go and tell the priest, "I have seen
something that looks like a defiling
mould in my house." 36 The priest
is to order the house to be emptied
before he goes in to examine the
mould, so that nothing in the house
will be pronounced unclean. After
this the priest is to go in and inspect
the house. 37 He is to examine the
mould on the walls, and if it has
greenish or reddish depressions that
appear to be deeper than the surface
of the wall, 38 the priest shall go out
of the doorway of the house and
close it up for seven days. 39 On the
seventh day the priest shall return to
inspect the house. If the mould has
spread on the walls, 40 he is to order
that the contaminated stones be torn
out and thrown into an unclean
place outside the town. 41 He must
have all the inside walls of the house
scraped and the material that is
scraped off dumped into an unclean
place outside the town. 42 Then they
are to take other stones to replace
these and take new clay and plaster
the house.

43 'If the defiling mould reappears
in the house after the stones have
been torn out and the house scraped
and plastered, 44 the priest is to go
and examine it and, if the mould has
spread in the house, it is a persistent
defiling mould; the house is unclean.
45 It must be torn down – its stones,
timbers and all the plaster – and
taken out of the town to an unclean
place.

**46** 'Anyone who goes into the house
while it is closed up will be unclean
till evening. **47** Anyone who sleeps or
eats in the house must wash their
clothes.

**48** 'But if the priest comes to exam-
ine it and the mould has not spread
after the house has been plastered,
he shall pronounce the house clean,
because the defiling mould is gone.
**49** To purify the house he is to take
two birds and some cedar wood,
scarlet yarn and hyssop. **50** He shall
kill one of the birds over fresh water
in a clay pot. **51** Then he is to take the
cedar wood, the hyssop, the scarlet
yarn and the live bird, dip them into
the blood of the dead bird and the
fresh water, and sprinkle the house
seven times. **52** He shall purify the
house with the bird's blood, the fresh
water, the live bird, the cedar wood,
the hyssop and the scarlet yarn.
**53** Then he is to release the live bird
in the open fields outside the town.
In this way he will make atonement
for the house, and it will be clean.'

**54** These are the regulations for
any defiling skin disease, for a sore,
**55** for defiling moulds in fabric or in
a house, **56** and for a swelling, a rash
or a shiny spot, **57** to determine when
something is clean or unclean.

These are the regulations for defiling skin diseases and defiling moulds.

---

**a** 2 The Hebrew word for *defiling skin disease*, traditionally translated 'leprosy', was used for various diseases affecting the skin; here and throughout verses 3-46.

**b** 2 Or *descendants*

**c** 45 Or *clothes, uncover their head*

**a** 3 The Hebrew word for *defiling skin disease*, traditionally translated 'leprosy', was used for various diseases affecting the skin; also in verses 7, 32, 54 and 57.

**b** 10 That is, probably about 5 kilograms

**c** 10 That is, about 0.3 litre; also in verses 12, 15, 21 and 24

**d** 13 Or *purification offering*; also in verses 19, 22 and 31

**e** 21 That is, probably about 1.6 kilograms

Before exploring the situations of defiling skin diseases in 13:1–46, it is worth noting what this section *is* and *is not* doing. The associations made with impurity and purity in this section are based on *appearance*. There are certain characteristics about how a person looks that determine whether they are pure or are in a condition of impurity. All of the examples of impurity are where the Lord, in his freedom, has chosen to use particular diseases to teach the Israelites about the nature of impurity (14:57).[25] In each instance, we will ask what the Lord is teaching the Israelites about skin disease based on what the text is highlighting about appearance. This passage is not teaching a connection between disease and sin.[26] If anything, this passage helps us see that impurity is a much bigger issue than sin alone. Sin and rebellion are but two aspects of impurity. Also, this passage is *not* making associations with impurity based on medical and scientific reasoning.[27] The reasoning is solely based on *appearance* to teach the Israelites about the nature of impurity and purity (14:57).

## External appearance of people (13:1–46)

The Lord's instructions in 13:2a begin with a situation that, if true, triggers a series of actions and events described in 13:2b–8. This situation is if a swelling, rash or shiny spot appears on the skin, which may be a sign of a 'defiling skin disease'. The phrase in the NIV, 'defiling skin disease', is literally 'a mark of skin disease'. The following actions in 13:2b–8 would determine whether this mark of skin disease is a sign of the person being in an impure condition or whether the person remains in a pure condition. The issue is not that it is a disease but the *appearance* of the disease; the appearance will determine whether the person with the skin disease is considered impure or pure.

In this first situation in 13:2a, verses 3b–5 describe how the

25 Where the NIV mentions 'determine' in 14:57, I would understand the underlying Hebrew to mean 'teach', and the intent of this section would, therefore, be to teach about the nature of impurity and purity. See also Sklar, *Leviticus*, 198.

26 Trevaskis, *Holiness*, 110–19, clarifies what the symbolism of 'defiling skin disease' is *not* doing, which is representing the consequence of a specific sin. This is contrary to Ko, *Leviticus*, 121.

27 Also, Chingota, 'Leviticus', 150.

priest is to determine a mark that is representative of a condition of impurity. For the person to be declared impure, the priest needs to see that the hair in the sore has turned white *and* the mark appears to be more than superficial; it also needs to be deeper than the surface layer of the skin. However, the priest is allowed to suspend making a declaration if the spot is white *and* it is only on the surface of the skin *and* the hair has not turned white (13:4a–c). If a priest postpones his decision, then the person needs to isolate for seven days (13:4d,) and on the seventh day the priest is to examine the mark of skin disease again. There could be one of three outcomes. First, if the mark of skin disease is unchanged, it is neither worse nor better, then the priest directs the person to isolate for another seven days (13:5). Second, if the mark appears better on second examination, that is, it has faded and not spread, then the priest shall declare the person in a pure condition (13:6). They still must wash their clothes, however, as a sign of being in a pure condition. However, with this second outcome, if the mark appears to spread after the person has been declared pure, then the person must return to the priest for examination (13:7). Then the third outcome in 13:8 is that the mark has spread in the skin. The priest then declares the person to be in an impure condition.

The impure skin disease is, therefore, where there is evidence that the skin disease is deeper than the skin. The hair turning white would be understood as evidence of this. Also, evidence of impurity in 13:8 is if the mark has spread. Thus, for the skin condition to be a cause of impurity, it needs to have spread either below the surface of the skin and/or across the surface of the skin.[28] This suggests that the LORD is teaching the Israelites that impurity by nature spreads and corrupts.

Verses 9–17 address the situation where the person knows from

28 Ko, *Leviticus*, 123.

the outset that he or she has a skin disease (13:9a).[29] If the priest sees two characteristics – a white swelling that has turned the hair white *and* raw flesh inside the swelling – then the person is to be declared impure. Verses 12–13 then describe the situation where the skin disease covers the person's entire skin from head to foot and the appearance of the person is white. It is curious that as soon as the skin disease covers the entire person, they can be declared to be in a pure condition. The association at this point is with integrity. While the appearance of the person might be altered, the appearance of the *whole* or *complete* person has been changed.[30] However, if the skin disease disturbs the appearance of the skin partially with evidence that the disease is deeper than the skin, as well as raw flesh appearing, the person is declared impure. The association, as Ko observes, is the 'incompleteness' of the person's appearance.[31] Thus, impurity is not only associated with that which corrupts, but also includes raw flesh. The reason raw flesh is considered impure is that the disease has exposed the flesh. As Ko notes, 'When raw flesh appears on the white surface, this destroys the completeness, and therefore should be considered unclean.'[32]

Verses 18–44 address a further five situations where the Israelites are to make a distinction between a skin disease that is a cause of impurity and a skin condition where the person remains in a pure condition. These five situations follow the same logic as the first two cases, and the distinction between impurity and purity is consistent too. The purpose of teaching the same distinction repeatedly by different situations is so that the Israelites would learn by repetition what is associated with

29 Hartley, *Leviticus*, 191; Trevaskis, *Holiness*, 133.

30 Ko, *Leviticus*, 124–5, 'Since the whole body goes completely white, this turns the person into a state of completeness . . . The state of completeness has been the main indicator for purity, a state without chaos and confusion.'

31 Ko, *Leviticus*, 122, 123.

32 Ko, *Leviticus*, 125.

impurity, which is that which spreads, corrupts and exposes the flesh by disease.

Verses 45–46 conclude this section by drawing attention to the consequence of being declared impure because of a skin disease. The person must wear torn clothes, let his or her hair grow, cover the lower part of his or her face and shout out, 'Impure! Impure!' The instructions about what they are to wear and how they are to appear resemble grieving rituals purposefully. A person declared impure is in a state of grief.[33] They not only have to make everyone aware of their impure condition, that is, it is not a private matter, but they are also commanded to remain alone outside the camp (13:46). They are not only excluded from approaching the LORD's presence, but they are also excluded from the Israelite community.[34] The LORD provides instructions in 14:1–32 to restore those who are healed to the community and to the LORD's presence.

Before we explore the instructions in 13:47–59 about marks of impurity in fabric (i.e., mould), it is worth acknowledging that the instructions about skin disease might seem far removed from our worlds and the consequence quite harsh. However, we now live in a world recovering from the consequences of COVID–19. In my Australian context, our international borders closed first. Then our state borders closed so that no one could travel across state lines, and then our city borders closed, differentiating those who lived regionally with those who lived in the cities. Next, our council areas closed, with everyone required to isolate in their own home. Neighbours could no longer visit neighbours. We understood that this was due to a virus that was highly contagious and, without the population being vaccinated, would leave a significant percentage vulnerable to long-term effects or death. We obeyed our government instructions because we

---

33 Sklar, *Leviticus*, 187. Contrary to Ko, *Leviticus*, 126.

34 Chingota, 'Leviticus', 152; Hartley, *Leviticus*, 200; Trevaskis, *Holiness*, 155.

believed this was the best way to look after our neighbour. While this reflects the experience of many Australians, many countries in the Global South had vastly different experiences, where the devastating consequence of COVID-19 caused widespread grief and long-term effects. While the instructions in 13:1–46 might seem strange, there were aspects to our experiences in 2020 and 2021 that can help us understand infection and isolation. The difference, though, is that while we isolated from an infectious disease, the cause of impurity in Leviticus 13:1–46 is *not* an infectious disease. Rather, it is the impurity associated with those skin diseases that is infectious. Impurity needs to be separated from that which is pure because impurity spreads and corrupts.

## External appearance of fabric (13:47–59)

At the first sign of mould in our house – on walls, on curtains, in our food pantry, on shoes – I immediately reach for the vinegar and bicarbonate of soda mixture and a thorough check for mould begins. The reason I am pedantic about mould is that I know it spreads. Mould spores travel easily, and they are not always visible. Mould destroys when left unchecked in humid climates. However, we do not need to live in a humid climate to know the effects of mould. If bread is not eaten when it is fresh, mould begins to appear, and it does not take long for one spot of mould to spread. This makes mould a helpful topic to teach the Israelites about the nature of impurity and its consequences in 13:47–59.

Leviticus 13:47–59 focuses on mould in fabrics and materials, particularly woven or knitted linen or wool, as well as leather. This could be clothes but also anything within an Israelite household made from these materials, such as curtains. In 13:47–49, an Israelite who notices a spot of mould is instructed to bring the whole piece of material to a priest, who is to examine the mould and then isolate, for example, the piece of clothing for seven days (13:50). Verses 51–54 explore two possible outcomes for the material after the initial seven-day isolation period. First, if the mould has spread (13:51), then the material is to be declared impure by the priest and the priest must burn the affected material (13:52). The second outcome, in 13:53–54, is conditional on the mould not spreading. In this instance, the fabric is to be washed and then isolated for a further seven days. Verses 55–58 describe a further three possible outcomes after this second seven-day period of isolation. By declaring material affected by mould to be in a condition of impurity when the mould has spread on the material or cannot be removed, the LORD is reinforcing the idea that the nature of impurity is such that it spreads and needs to be removed to stop it spreading further.

## Purification from the impurity of skin disease (14:1–32)

As we have explored Leviticus 11–14, we have seen that impurity is associated with decay, death, disorder and rebellion. The person who is declared to be in a condition of impurity because of skin disease is being associated with these ideas too. The LORD's instructions in 14:1–32 teach the Israelites about how they are to be restored to community and to the LORD's presence once a priest confirms that they are healed of their skin disease (14:2–3). Healing does not mean automatic restoration. While the cause of impurity may be gone, the condition of impurity requires a process of purification where a person, after being declared pure, can be restored to relationship with their neighbours and with the LORD. This process occurs in three stages.

During the first stage in 14:3–8, the first bird is killed over 'living' (i.e., flowing; NIV 'fresh') water. Life is associated with purity. This first bird, by being killed over 'living water' (the clay pot is merely the container), is being associated with purity as it is transferred to death and for its blood to be collected. The priest then dips the second bird and the rest of the materials – wood, scarlet yarn and hyssop (marjoram) – into the blood of the first bird (14:6). An assumed piece of information, which the Israelite hearers would know, is that the scarlet yarn would attach the hyssop to the piece of cedar wood before it is all soaked in the bird's blood. In 14:7, the priest uses the cedar wood and hyssop to splatter the bird's blood seven times on the person being purified. Blood is the most powerful purifier, and being splattered seven times represents the complete purification of the person so that they can be restored to the Israelite community. After the person has been soaked in blood, the priest declares the person to be in a pure condition. The living bird, which is covered in blood, is freed as a visual reminder that the condition of impurity has been removed.[35] The newly purified person then washes their clothes, shaves off their hair and washes himself or herself, before the goal of this first stage is realised in 14:8: the person is allowed back into the camp, but they must remain outside their tent for seven days.

The second stage in 14:9 is brief and occurs on the seventh day. The person is to repeat washing their clothes, bathing and shaving off all hair. The purpose of this repetition is to prepare for the third stage. The need to shave in 14:9 might seem strange since this has been done in 14:8. Again, we need to remember what being in a condition of impurity means as opposed to being in a condition of purity. If being in a condition of impurity is being associated with death, decay and disorder, then being in a condition of purity is being associated with life, flourishing and order. Being purified is being associated with rebirth. By shaving off all hair *after* being purified and restored to a condition of purity, the person visually represents the beginning of life (i.e.,

35 Similarly, Ko, *Leviticus*, 129. Also Alter, 'Leviticus', 600; Sklar, *Leviticus*, 191.

life being reborn from death). In this condition, the person is ready for the third stage to begin, which is being restored to the LORD's presence through sacrifice.

While the cause of the person's condition of impurity – skin disease – was outside their control, reparation still needs to be made to the LORD for having been in that condition since impurity among the covenant community affects his presence among his people. For this reason, the third stage begins with the gift of a year-old male lamb for a guilt offering in 14:12–18. However, the instructions for this offering are a bit different from the instructions for the guilt offering in 5:14–6:7. Once the guilt offering is slaughtered, the priest takes the lamb's blood and places it on the lobe of the offerer's right ear, on the thumb of their right hand and on the big toe of the person's right foot (14:14). Then the priest takes the oil (14:15a), pours some onto the palm of his left hand (14:15b), dips his right forefinger into the oil (14:16a) and splatters the oil seven times before the LORD (14:16b). The rest of the oil on the priest's palm is to be placed on the Israelite's right earlobe, thumb of his right hand and big toe of his right foot, as well as on the person's head (14:17–18). These actions may sound familiar to us from the consecration of the priesthood in 8:23–24. However, in this instance, the priest placing blood on the person's right side (earlobe, thumb and big toe) symbolises that the penalty for the impurity of the whole person has been paid and they are restored wholly to a pure condition.[36]

Following the guilt offering, the Israelite also gifts a sin offering (14:19a–b), a burnt offering (14:19c–20) and a grain offering (14:20). As mentioned in the explanation of Leviticus 12, the gift of a sin offering does not suggest that the person's impurity is a result of their sinfulness or that their skin disease is connected with sin. A sin offering can also be called a purification offering,

36 Also, Sklar, *Leviticus*, 192.

and the purpose of this gift more broadly is to purify a person from their impurity, whether that impurity be a result of causes outside their control, like skin disease, or a result of their rebellion against the LORD's instructions (as per 4:1–5:13). Impurity is a much broader category than solely sin. Significantly, after the guilt offering is complete, 14:18 notes that atonement is made for the person being restored back into relationship; similarly, after the sin, grain and burnt offerings are given to the LORD, 14:20 repeats that they are offered to make atonement for the person being purified. With atonement made, the person is restored in their relationship with the LORD.[37]

## Purification from the impurity caused by mould in homes (14:33–57)

Leviticus 14:33–57 returns to the topic of impurity caused by mould, but the mould, in this instance, is in homes. For the first time, the context is forward-looking as the LORD anticipates fulfilling his promise to give the Israelites the land of Canaan (14:34).[38] However, this future situation also anticipates the LORD acting in justice against the Israelites as he puts 'spreading mould' in their homes. In this situation, the LORD instructs the Israelite in 14:35–36 to remove all furnishings, so that they are not affected by the mould, and then to fetch a priest to examine the colour of the mould and whether the impressions are deeper than the surface (14:37). The LORD instructs the priest in 14:38 to close the house for seven days.

After seven days, if the mould has spread on the walls, the affected stones must be torn out from the house's structure (14:39–40). Those stones, along with any clay and plaster, must be taken to

37 Also, Chingota, 'Leviticus', 152.

38 See also Chingota, 'Leviticus', 152–3; Sklar, *Leviticus*, 195–6.

an impure place outside the town. The emphasis is that anything considered impure must be removed. Similarly, if the mould reappears and spreads, it is to be regarded as persistent (14:43–45). The consequence in 14:45 is that the whole house must be destroyed and all materials taken to a place outside the town. Such is the seriousness of persistent impurity after action has been taken to remove it. If it is persistent, then the whole needs to be destroyed.

However, if the mould has gone (14:48), then the house is ready to be purified. The purification process in 14:49–53 follows a similar pattern to the first stage of the person's purification after skin disease (14:3–7). The blood and living water act as a purifier when the priest splatters the whole house seven times to represent the complete purification of the house (14:50–52). The living bird, drenched with blood, is released outside the town to represent the removal of impurity (14:53). Once more, the Israelites learn through these instructions that restoration to a pure condition requires purification through the shedding and splattering of blood, as well as the impurity being removed. However, this restoration can only occur after the mould has disappeared, not when it is still present.

## Moving forward into the New Testament

Understanding Leviticus 13–14, we can grasp the ultimate problem that humanity faces. Each day we wake up to news of war, genocide, famine, bush fires, floods and a global pandemic. Moreover, we are watching the cost of everyday living spike. We can let these events crowd out an even greater problem from our minds and hearts that affects both our present and our eternal futures. This problem is that of impurity. Leviticus 13–14 holds up the mirror so that we can grasp the consequence of being in an impure condition: exclusion from God's presence. For some causes of impurity, the consequence is exclusion from community. This is a microcosm – a small snapshot – of what the whole of humanity experiences, whether we are aware of it or not. We were not created to be excluded from God's presence. We were created to be in relationship (Genesis 1–2). But our decision to choose what is good and evil for ourselves (Genesis 3:1–13), rather than looking to God for the distinction between what is good and evil, disrupted the good, created order of creation, and what was once in a pure condition is now in an impure condition (Genesis 3:14–24). Death, rebellion and sickness spread throughout the world to the point that these are part of our everyday existence (Genesis 4:1–11:9). But this is not how it was meant to be, and neither did God leave us in this condition.

God provided Leviticus 13–14 to help us, through the examples of skin disease and mould, grasp the problem of impurity and to point forward to his permanent solution. The instructions in Leviticus 13–14 to restore a person healed of skin disease is a temporary solution so that the Israelite could be restored to community and to God's presence. However, where one person might be healed and restored, another is still waiting. As we move forward into the New Testament, Luke's portrayal of a man with a skin disease in 5:12–15 is a sign that Jesus is the key to God's permanent solution. After Jesus calls his first disciples in 5:1–11, a man who has a skin disease, which is translated as leprosy in the NIV, approaches Jesus. This man would be calling out, 'Impure! Impure!' and it would be obvious to all that he is in an impure condition and needs to be avoided. However, he falls face down before Jesus and says, 'LORD, if you are willing, you can make me pure.' Remarkably, Jesus touches him. The man's impurity meeting Jesus's holiness does not cause a disastrous consequence. Instead, the reverse is true: Jesus's power heals the cause of his impurity – his skin disease – when he commands, 'Be pure!' (5:13).[39] Jesus not only heals the cause of his impurity, but he also has the power over the distinction between impurity and

---

39 Please note that in these two quotations from Luke, I have changed the NIV's 'clean' to 'pure'.

purity. Immediately, Jesus instructs the man in 5:14 to submit to the offering process as described in Leviticus 14:1–32 as a witness to the priests that he has been healed.

This is one of many healings where Jesus reverses a condition of impurity to a condition of purity. In Matthew's Gospel, Matthew wrote in 8:16–17 that Jesus healed many who were sick, and this was to fulfil what Isaiah wrote: 'He took up our infirmities and bore our diseases' (Isa. 53:4 LXX). That is, he bore the cause of our impurity. Ultimately, this points to the greatest provision where Jesus's sacrifice on the cross purifies us from all our impurities, including our diseases. It is remarkable that he secured our purification before we were healed of our diseases, but he knew the goal to which all things will culminate: a renewed creation where disease and sickness will be no more.

## *4. The consequence of impurity by male and female discharges • Leviticus 15:1–30*

The purpose of Leviticus 11–15 is to demonstrate, using tangible aspects of everyday life, the distinction between impurity and purity. The reason this distinction is critical is that the Israelites are to be set apart to the LORD in a condition of purity and so are to ensure that they separate themselves from conditions of impurity. Leviticus 15 continues to teach the Israelites about the consequence of being in an impure condition with the topic of bodily discharges.

*Discharges causing uncleanness*

**15** The LORD said to Moses
and Aaron, 2 'Speak to
the Israelites and say to them:
"When any man has an unusual
bodily discharge, such a discharge
is unclean. 3 Whether it continues
flowing from his body or is blocked,
it will make him unclean. This is
how his discharge will bring about
uncleanness:
4 '"Any bed the man with a discharge

lies on will be unclean, and anything
he sits on will be unclean. 5 Anyone
who touches his bed must wash their
clothes and bathe with water, and they
will be unclean till evening. 6 Whoever
sits on anything that the man with
a discharge sat on must wash their
clothes and bathe with water, and they
will be unclean till evening.

7 ‘“Whoever touches the man who
has a discharge must wash their
clothes and bathe with water, and
they will be unclean till evening.

8 ‘“If the man with the discharge
spits on anyone who is clean, they
must wash their clothes and bathe
with water, and they will be unclean
till evening.

9 ‘“Everything the man sits on
when riding will be unclean, 10 and
whoever touches any of the things
that were under him will be unclean
till evening; whoever picks up those
things must wash their clothes and
bathe with water, and they will be
unclean till evening.

11 ‘“Anyone the man with a
discharge touches without rinsing
his hands with water must wash
their clothes and bathe with water,
and they will be unclean till evening.

12 ‘“A clay pot that the man touches
must be broken, and any wooden
article is to be rinsed with water.

13 ‘“When a man is cleansed from
his discharge, he is to count seven
days for his ceremonial cleansing;
he must wash his clothes and bathe
himself with fresh water, and he will
be clean. 14 On the eighth day he
must take two doves or two young
pigeons and come before the LORD
to the entrance to the tent of meet-
ing and give them to the priest.
15 The priest is to sacrifice them,
the one for a sin offering[a] and the
other for a burnt offering. In this
way he will make atonement before
the LORD for the man because of his
discharge.

16 ‘“When a man has an emis-
sion of semen, he must bathe his
whole body with water, and he
will be unclean till evening. 17 Any
clothing or leather that has semen
on it must be washed with water,
and it will be unclean till evening.
18 When a man has sexual relations
with a woman and there is an emis-
sion of semen, both of them must
bathe with water, and they will be
unclean till evening.

19 ‘“When a woman has her regu-
lar flow of blood, the impurity of her
monthly period will last seven days,
and anyone who touches her will be
unclean till evening.

20 ‘“Anything she lies on during her

period will be unclean, and anything
she sits on will be unclean. **21** Anyone
who touches her bed will be unclean;
they must wash their clothes and
bathe with water, and they will be
unclean till evening. **22** Anyone who
touches anything she sits on will
be unclean; they must wash their
clothes and bathe with water, and
they will be unclean till evening.
**23** Whether it is the bed or anything
she was sitting on, when anyone
touches it, they will be unclean till
evening.

**24** '"If a man has sexual relations
with her and her monthly flow
touches him, he will be unclean for
seven days; any bed he lies on will
be unclean.

**25** '"When a woman has a discharge
of blood for many days at a time
other than her monthly period or has
a discharge that continues beyond
her period, she will be unclean as
long as she has the discharge, just
as in the days of her period. **26** Any
bed she lies on while her discharge
continues will be unclean, as is her
bed during her monthly period, and
anything she sits on will be unclean,
as during her period. **27** Anyone who
touches them will be unclean; they
must wash their clothes and bathe
with water, and they will be unclean
till evening.

**28** '"When she is cleansed from
her discharge, she must count seven
days, and after that she will be cere-
monially clean. **29** On the eighth
day she must take two doves or two
young pigeons and bring them to the
priest at the entrance to the tent of
meeting. **30** The priest is to sacrifice
one for a sin offering and the other
for a burnt offering. In this way he
will make atonement for her before
the LORD for the uncleanness of her
discharge.

**a** 15 Or *purification offering*; also in verse 30

Leviticus 15 explores the topic of bodily discharges in four sections. The first (15:2b–15) and fourth (15:25–31) sections concentrate on discharges that are not part of normal bodily functions, and the second (15:16–18) and third (15:19–24) sections focus on discharges that are a part of how we are created to function. The structure of the four section and their topics is outlined below.

| Section 1 | 15:2b–15 | When a man has an unusual discharge (atypical) |
|---|---|---|
| Section 2 | 15:16–18 | When a man has an emission of semen (normal) |
| Section 3 | 15:19–24 | When a woman has a discharge of blood (normal) |
| Section 4 | 15:25–31 | When a woman has a discharge of blood for many days (atypical) |

## When a man has an unusual discharge (15:2b–15)

The instructions begin in 15:2b with a situation where a man experiences an 'unusual bodily discharge' and, because the discharge is not part of any normal bodily function, it is a cause of impurity for the man. The discharge is a sign that something is not right, irrespective of whether the discharge flows continuously from his penis or whether the discharge is blocked and so is hindered from flowing out (15:3a–b). Curiously, however, 15:3c is not concerned about the discharge being a cause of impurity for the man, but rather how the man's impurity is a cause of impurity to other things or people, which is the topic of 15:4–11. With each example in 15:4–11, where another person becomes impure either by contact with the man himself or with furniture that he has laid or sat on, the person needs to bathe with water before he or she is restored to a pure condition in the evening (15:5, 6, 7, 8, 10, 11). The emphasis of 15:4–6 is that impurity is contagious. Any person or item that comes into contact with the impure man becomes impure too.[40]

After 15:4–12 highlights the contagious nature of the man's

40 This is a different anthropological basis from the understanding of Lidija Gunjević, 'Leviticus', in *Central and Eastern European Bible Commentary*, edited by Corneliu Constantineanu and Peter Penne (Cumbria: Langham Global Library, 2022), 125, who views the instructions in 15:4–11 to be about 'Counteraction in the form of ritual washing . . . in order to maintain a high standard of personal hygiene and protect the health of community. Everyone in a clean, healthy community had to strive for cleanliness.'

impurity, 15:13–15 changes topic to how the man can be purified. Verse 13 begins with a condition that the rest of the instructions hinge on, which is the healing of the man from his discharge. Once the discharge has ceased, the seven-day wait period represents the completion of his impurity, during which he must wash his clothes and bathe himself with 'living water' (i.e., flowing water; NIV 'fresh water') to represent being restored to a pure condition. Although the man is in a condition of purity, 15:14–15 instructs him to approach the LORD with gifts at the entrance to the Tent of Meeting. The priest offers one bird as a purification offering (NIV 'sin offering') and the other as a burnt offering (15:15). Although the man's discharge is outside his control and his impurity is not a result of his actions, his discharge is still a cause of impurity, and the man needs to ensure that his impurity is removed from God's presence through the shedding of blood (see 4:1–5:13).

## When a man has an emission of semen (15:16–18)

While 15:2–15 addresses a situation where an Israelite man experiences an *unusual* discharge, 15:16–18 focuses on the *normal* bodily function of a man discharging semen.[41] The difference between the cause of discharge (i.e., unusual vs normal) is the reason for the difference in purification instructions. In this situation, the means of purification is washing and waiting until evening (15:16, 17, 18).

Reading these instructions in light of 15:2–15, a question might emerge as to why a normal bodily function that God has created is to be considered a cause of impurity. With the situation of the

41 Contrary to Chingota, 'Leviticus', 154, and Ko, *Leviticus*, 140–41, 15:16–17 address any normal discharge of semen through a sexual act or through an involuntary emission. Verse 18 then narrows the focus solely to the discharge of semen as part of sexual intercourse in continuity with 15:16–17.

unusual discharge, we can understand that the man's discharge is a sign that something is wrong, and we can grasp how this is associated with impurity. It is a sign of bodily disorder, which is contrary to a condition of purity. But God created a man to ejaculate semen so that, as part of his sexual union with his wife, they can fulfil their creation mandate to be fruitful together. This is another instance where God designates a cause of impurity from his created order for a specific reason. As we have noted, 15:16–18 repeats the consequence of impurity, which is being declared impure until the evening. The consequence is that the husband and wife who have had sex, let us say, in the morning cannot approach the LORD's sanctuary that day since they are in an impure condition. They need to wait until the next day to approach the LORD. Therefore, a husband and wife need to be mindful about when they intend to bring gifts to the LORD and the need to abstain from sexual activity until, at least, they have offered their gifts.

The idea that the Israelites needs to abstain from sexual activity in preparation to approach the LORD is not new. In Exodus 19:15, Moses commanded the Israelites to prepare for the third day when the LORD would come down to meet with them on Mount Sinai (see 19:10–13). As part of this preparation, the Israelites were to 'abstain from sexual relations'. It is not that sex is wrong. Rather, the LORD desired the Israelites to abstain from sexual activity before approaching him in his sanctuary.

## When a woman has her regular discharge of blood (15:19–24)

The third cause of impurity addressed in Leviticus 15 is a woman's period. Verse 19 specifies that a woman experiencing her period is to be considered impure for seven days and, moreover, anyone who touches her will share her impurity until evening.

After 15:19c introduces the idea that her impurity is contagious, 15:20–24 gives examples of how the woman's impurity impacts furniture and other people, like the first situation in 15:1–12. Verse 24 addresses the situation where a husband and wife are participating in sexual activity and she begins her period at that time. In this instance, her husband will also be considered impure for the same amount of time as the woman (i.e., seven days).

Again, we might question why a bodily function that is part of how our bodies are created is to be considered impure. I have had students express how unfair these instructions are for women. Women are to be excluded from any activity around and in the LORD's sanctuary for a bodily function they have no control over, and that exclusion is for seven days! Seven days makes sense when we remember the symbolic meaning of seven conveying the idea of completion, that is, the woman's condition of impurity is complete. Also, we need to remember the practical side of seven days, which is that some women's periods can last two or three days but, for others, their bleeding can last up to six days. This instruction is the same for every woman and so seven days encompasses the whole range, as well as theologically representing completion. Is it unfair? The LORD has gifted women with the capacity to bear children, to nourish and protect them until they are ready to meet the outside world. This is a privilege that men are not granted because we each have different functions within a marriage relationship. A part of this privilege is that, every month, when we have not fallen pregnant, the lining of our uterus comes away and it needs to be discharged. This happens so that the lining can renew itself and prepare for the potential of a pregnancy in the coming month. Our bodies do this irrespective of whether we are sexually active or not, and until we reach menopause.

So these instructions are far from being unfair; they are a reminder of the privilege that we have in our marriage relationships to help our babies grow, to nourish and protect them.

This privilege is why not conceiving when women wish to have children is so painful, and when we read Leviticus 12 and 15 as a community we need to be mindful of the women in our midst, both married and single, whose periods come and go each month as a reminder that they are, for whatever reason, unable to conceive and bear children. For many, this is a cause of grief that lasts a lifetime.

The remaining question, then, is why periods are considered impure. To answer this question, we need to put ourselves in the shoes of married women who wish to have children. As noted above, the reason women have monthly periods is because an egg has not started implanting into the uterus. As a result, the uterus lining comes away and needs to be discharged. Women trying to have children are waiting to see if their period comes. If it does not come when expected, anticipation builds because there is the possibility that they could be pregnant! However, when their period does arrive, it is a sure sign that there is not a viable pregnancy, and the process starts again. When a period does not arrive, its absence is a sign of potential new life. So, at the very least, a period coming is a sign of an absence of new life.

However, let us put ourselves in the shoes of a woman in ancient Israel. Women have many vital roles within the household and Carol Meyers paints this picture helpfully in her article, 'The Family in Early Israel'.[42] A cultural assumption in ancient Israel is that a girl of marriageable age will become engaged to a man, she will enter a marriage relationship with him and she will become part of his household with all that this entails. This is not an oppressive patriarchal cultural value at work. A generous view is that girls grow up knowing that to have a place in community is to be part of a household where there is

42 Carol Meyers, 'The Family in Early Israel', in *Families in Ancient Israel*, edited by Joseph Blenkinsopp, John J. Collins, Carol Meyers and Leo G. Perdue (Louisville: Westminster John Knox, 1997), 1–47.

belonging, protection and security. One of her many roles in that household is to bear children so that there is a continuation of the patrilineal line. Having children is a sign of the LORD's blessing on that household. Let us imagine we are one such girl who has joined that household with the hope that she will fulfil *all* her roles, and yet, month after month, her period comes and goes. Can we begin to understand, with all this background, what the coming of her period represents to her and to her household? It represents an absence of new life and an absence of blessing, which is the reason her monthly period is a cause of impurity.[43] This is no fault of her own, and there is much of the process that is outside her control, as every woman knows who waits for at least two weeks to see if her period comes. Although no fault of her own, the consequence of her impurity is that she needs to wait until she is restored to a condition of purity before she can approach the sanctuary of her covenant God.

## When a woman has a discharge of blood for many days (15:25–31)

While 15:19–24 addresses impurity caused by a woman's monthly period, 15:25–31 explores the situation where a woman's bleeding is unexpected. These instructions follow a similar pattern to the previous three sections. Verse 25 declares a woman who experiences unusual bleeding to be impure for as long as her bleeding lasts, then 15:26–27 explores the extent to which her impurity is contagious. Verses 28–30 then explain how she is to be restored to a condition of purity before the LORD. She is to wait seven days, which once again represents completion, beyond when her bleeding has ceased and then she is to bring her gifts to the

43 This is a different understanding from that of Ko, *Leviticus*, 141, who follows Wenham, *Leviticus*, 434.

Lord on the eighth day (15:29). The reason for the offerings is the same as the first situation in 15:1–15. Although the woman's bleeding is outside her control and her impurity is not a result of her actions, her impurity is associated with disorder because it represents something going wrong in her body that is not meant to be and so she needs to ensure that her impurity is removed from God's presence through the shedding of blood.

While the woman's bleeding is not expected and so is associated with disorder, there are other associations at work in this situation that represent impurity. To grasp this, we need to unpack why a woman might suddenly start bleeding. I will name three situations, and each situation is a cause of significant grief within households and marriages.

The first is a miscarriage. There were no seven- or twelve-week scans in ancient Israel. The assumption would be that the baby is progressing and so, when the bleeding begins, a woman knows that this is a loss of new life. While the actual miscarriage can be over in a matter of hours, the lining of the uterus still sheds and is discharged, which means that there is a heavy to light flow of blood for anywhere between a week and three weeks afterwards, depending on the timing of the miscarriage.

The second situation is when a pregnant woman begins haemorrhaging, for instance, when blood collects between the uterus and what is called the chorionic membrane, which forms a hematoma. Sometimes this can cause bleeding and complications if significant. While in the present day, this kind of bleeding can be treated and often resolves itself, at other times it can lead to miscarriage. In ancient Israel, this could have been more common than it is today. Other causes of haemorrhaging during pregnancy include placenta previa and placental abruption. Again, while medical interventions are possible today that mitigate risks, this would not have been the case in ancient Israel. In these examples, the bleeding caused by these conditions could lead to the loss of life.

The third example is unrelated to pregnancy and is uterine or vaginal bleeding caused by an underlying health condition. One such condition is perimenopause, where a woman can experience irregular bleeding due to an imbalance in hormones as she transitions to menopause. Every woman will experience this to some degree as she transitions to a stage beyond her child-bearing years. However, there are other medical conditions that are not normal and which relate to infection or cancer that can cause heavy and prolonged bleeding. In the ancient Near East, this would have led to a great deal of shame culturally and would have been hard to conceal. In any scenario, a woman's ability to have children is affected and it could lead to the loss of that ability.

With any of these three situations, impurity is being associated with loss of life and shame, as well as disorder (i.e., opposite to God's created order). Again, when exploring this passage with others, whether it be in a small group or a sermon, it is likely that there will be women present who have experienced one of these causes. Please be pastorally aware and sensitive when explaining this passage since it is likely that the grief from loss, irrespective of how long ago it happened, may still be a painful reality.

## Moving forward into the New Testament

The four situations described in Leviticus 15 emphasise the infectious nature of impurity and the consequence. We have already observed that Jesus, the holy one who was born to participate in our humanity and to be God with us, overcomes our impurities. Leviticus teaches that death and exile is the consequence when impurity comes into the LORD's presence (see explanation of 15:31–33 below). When impurity comes into contact with Jesus, the same consequence should ensue, but instead of death because of impurity, Jesus restores those who are impure. A remarkable example is narrated in Luke

8:40–56. In 8:40–42, as Jesus walked to Jairus's house, Luke notes that the crowds almost crushed him (8:42b). Jesus felt someone touch him in the throng of the crowd, and power leaving him (8:44–46). The reader is privy to the identity of this person. In 8:43, Luke introduced the woman who had suffered bleeding for twelve years. This would have been twelve years living in a condition of impurity as described in Leviticus 15:25–31 and, because her bleeding had not stopped, she could not approach a synagogue or the Temple, and so she could not participate in any Israelite feast day such as the Day of Atonement. However, in 8:44, she dared to approach Jesus and she touched the edge of his cloak, which would have meant that the cloak was now in a condition of impurity. But Luke observes in 8:44c that she was healed immediately. The woman knew she could not remain concealed when Jesus felt power leave him and she fell at his feet, explaining her actions as though asking for mercy for her audacity. However, Jesus declared that her belief healed her and gave her permission to go in peace (8:48).

Jesus's power is such that his holiness did not destroy but, in a great reversal, the holy one restored the one in a condition of impurity to a condition of purity. Jesus's healings of external impurities, such as the woman's bleeding, foreshadowed a greater healing and restoration that only he could provide: the restoration of all impurity that he achieved through his death and resurrection.

It is not a coincidence that Luke tells the story about this woman before Jesus arrives at Jairus's house, where his daughter has died (8:49). We have already noted that death is associated with impurity and those who are dead are considered impure. The dead were to be taken outside the city gates and buried. Jairus's daughter has not yet been moved. To touch a dead person is a cause of impurity because impurity is a contagion. When Jesus touches her in 8:54, he does not become impure, and neither is there consequence because his holiness is polluted by her impurity. Instead, there is another great reversal. He restores her from death to life in 8:55, from impurity to a condition of purity.

Again, this points to a greater healing and restoration that only he could achieve through his death and resurrection. Through his death, he restored our condition of impurity because of our sin and transgression to a condition of purity where the Holy Spirit can now reside in and among his people. This is the 'already', but he has also defeated death, which is also associated with impurity, so that in a renewed heaven and earth where creation order is fully restored, Jesus can permanently restore his presence among his people. The place where God will dwell among his people in a renewed creation will be in a condition of purity, and all that impurity represents will be no more. This is the good news of the gospel. Jesus offers restoration and healing so that we can have an imperishable hope of life and flourishing in the permanence of God's holy presence. Leviticus 15 holds up the mirror so that we can learn about the consequence of our impurity, and then we are pointed forward to Jesus, in whom lies our only hope for restoration and peace in God's presence.

## *5. Summary: the purpose of separating impurity from purity • Leviticus 15:31–33*

Throughout Leviticus 11–15, we have seen the need for the Israelites to ensure that their impurity does not come into contact with the holy and, when it does, to offer gifts to purify the LORD's sanctuary. We have also seen that the consequence of being in an impure condition is that the Israelites are excluded from the LORD's sanctuary because impurity cannot come into the presence of the holy. Another way to view this exclusion is that impurity prevents the Israelites from approaching the LORD. However, it is not until the end of Leviticus 11–15, in 15:31, that the LORD conveys the reason for this consequence and why impurity cannot come into the presence of the holy.

31 ' "You must keep the Israelites separate from things that make them unclean, so they will not die in their uncleanness for defiling my dwelling-place,[b] which is among them." '

32 These are the regulations for a man with a discharge, for anyone made unclean by an emission of semen, 33 for a woman in her monthly period, for a man or a woman with a discharge, and for a man who has sexual relations with a woman who is ceremonially unclean.

b 31 Or *my tabernacle*

The first part of 15:31 emphasises the command to separate the Israelites from impurity, which has been the concern for the whole of Leviticus 11–15. The second part of 15:31 conveys the reason for this command, which is to protect the Israelites from dying in their impurities because they have desecrated the LORD's dwelling place. That is, as we have seen in the explanation of 10:10, when impurity encounters the holy, impurity defiles the holy. When this happens, the consequence is death. Therefore, this is a matter of life and death for Israel. The only way for the LORD's presence to dwell among the Israelites and for the Israelites' lives to be preserved is to ensure that their impurity is separated from the LORD's dwelling place. If the Israelites allow their impurity to enter the LORD's presence, then death will ensue.

When reading 15:31, it is helpful to remember that the LORD is speaking to Moses and Aaron directly with the intent that they mediate this message to the Israelites (15:1–2a). When the LORD uses the second person 'you' at the beginning of 15:31a, he is addressing Moses and Aaron directly as well as the Israelites. Ensuring that their impurity is separated from the LORD's dwelling place is the responsibility of every Israelite, not just Israel's leadership and priesthood. Furthermore, making the distinction between impurity and purity, so that the Israelites can separate their impurity from the LORD's presence, is a means by which the LORD is glorified and sanctified in their midst (see 10:3).

Given the high stakes for ensuring that Israel's impurities are separated from the LORD's dwelling place that is in their midst, another problem begins to emerge. How can Israel reduce the risk of the nation's impurities coming into the LORD's dwelling place, especially the causes of impurity of which they are unaware? The LORD's provision to resolve this problem in Leviticus 16 is the Day of Atonement. The purpose of the Day of Atonement is to purify the LORD's dwelling place of all kinds of impurities, and so the Day of Atonement is the LORD's provision to protect the life of the nation among whom he dwells. Thus, it is appropriate that the instructions for the Day of Atonement in Leviticus 16 follow the instructions of Leviticus 11–15.

# 4

# The Day of Atonement

## LEVITICUS 16

Leviticus 11–15 concluded with the warning to Moses, Aaron and the Israelites to separate their impurities from the LORD's dwelling place among his people (15:31). In 16:29–34, the LORD instructs Aaron to celebrate the Day of Atonement as a permanent statute for all future generations so that the Israelites *and* the LORD's dwelling place can be purified annually. The Day of Atonement is the LORD's provision to address 15:31. Through the Day of Atonement, the LORD ensures that the Israelites' impurities are removed from his dwelling place so that Israel can live and flourish with God's holy presence in the nation's midst (15:31).[1]

### *1. A warning for Aaron: how Aaron is not to approach the LORD • Leviticus 16:1–2*

In the aftermath of Nadab and Abihu's deaths in Leviticus 10, the narrative was suspended so that the LORD could provide instructions to the Israelites about how to make the distinction between impurity and purity (Leviticus 11–15). Leviticus 16:1 resumes the narrative after the deaths of Nadab and Abihu.

1 Rolf Rendtorff, 'Lev 16 Als Mitte Der Tora', *Biblical Interpretation* 11 (2003): 256.

*The Day of Atonement*

**16** The LORD spoke to Moses after the death of the two sons of Aaron who died when they approached the LORD. **2** The LORD said to Moses: 'Tell your brother Aaron that he is not to come whenever he chooses into the Most Holy Place behind the curtain in front of the atonement cover on the ark, or else he will die. For I will appear in the cloud over the atonement cover.

Leviticus 16 begins with the narrator recalling Nadab and Abihu's deaths in 16:1–2 for two reasons. First, to set the context for the LORD's warning to Aaron in 16:2 and the LORD's instructions about the Day of Atonement in 16:3–34. Verse 1 notes that the LORD's warning to Aaron occurs *after* the deaths of Nadab and Abihu. This purposeful mention of the setting suggests that the LORD's instructions are a response to their deaths. The second reason is to emphasise the seriousness of the LORD's warning to Aaron in 16:2. The narrator reminds hearers of the context in which Nadab and Abihu died: 'when they approached the LORD'. The reason Nadab and Abihu died is that they acted in a way that was not authorised as they approached the LORD (10:1–2). The LORD's warning to Aaron in 16:2 echoes this event when dissuading Aaron from approaching him in the Most Holy Place whenever he chooses.

The Most Holy Place is the inner sanctum of the Tabernacle and is separated from the rest of the Holy Place by a curtain (Exodus 26:31–33). Moreover, the Most Holy Place is where the Ark of the Covenant belongs, which is where the LORD promises to meet with Moses and mediate his commands to him (see Exodus 25:10–22; 26:34). The LORD's presence in the Most Holy Place is not to be entered into lightly or when Aaron feels like it.[2] The LORD warns Aaron that if he disregards this prohibition

2 I understand the prepositional phrase *beḵal eṯ* to mean 'at any time', conveying that Aaron does not have the freedom to choose when he enters the Holy Place. Contrary to Milgrom, *Leviticus 1–16*, 1013.

then he too will die (16:2c). The underlying message is that if Aaron repeats the same actions as Nadab and Abihu, then he will suffer the same fate. The LORD provides a reason for this consequence at the conclusion of 16:2: 'I will appear in the cloud over the atonement cover' (see Exodus 25:17–22).

Thus, Leviticus 16:1–2 depicts how Aaron is *not* to approach the LORD's presence in the Most Holy Place. This is a reminder that the LORD desires to be present among his people, but he must be approached on his terms. For this reason, the LORD provides clear instructions in 16:3–34 about how he is to be approached *solely* on the Day of Atonement and for a particular reason.

## *2. How Aaron is to approach the LORD in the Most Holy Place • Leviticus 16:3–28*

In contrast to the LORD's warning to Aaron in 16:1–2 about how *not* to approach him, 16:3–34 is all about the LORD's permission for Aaron to approach him once a year and for a particular purpose. This twofold purpose is explained in 16:29–34, which is to purify both the priesthood and the people of their impurities, as well as to purify the Tabernacle and so remove Israel's impurities from the LORD's presence. Verses 3–34 outline how Aaron is to approach the LORD to make purification for the priesthood (16:6–14), for the Tent of Meeting (16:15–19) and for the people (16:15, 20–22).

**3** 'This is how Aaron is to enter the Most Holy Place: he must first bring a young bull for a sin offering[a] and a ram for a burnt offering. **4** He is to put on the sacred linen tunic, with linen undergarments next to his body; he is to tie the linen sash round him and put on the linen turban. These are sacred garments; so he must bathe himself with water before he puts them on. **5** From the Israelite community he is to take two male goats for a sin offering and a ram for a burnt offering.

6 'Aaron is to offer the bull for his
own sin offering to make atone-
ment for himself and his household.
7 Then he is to take the two goats
and present them before the LORD
at the entrance to the tent of meet-
ing. 8 He is to cast lots for the two
goats – one lot for the LORD and the
other for the scapegoat.[b] 9 Aaron
shall bring the goat whose lot falls
to the LORD and sacrifice it for a sin
offering. 10 But the goat chosen by lot
as the scapegoat shall be presented
alive before the LORD to be used for
making atonement by sending it into
the wilderness as a scapegoat.

11 'Aaron shall bring the bull for
his own sin offering to make atone-
ment for himself and his household,
and he is to slaughter the bull for
his own sin offering. 12 He is to take
a censer full of burning coals from
the altar before the LORD and two
handfuls of finely ground fragrant
incense and take them behind the
curtain. 13 He is to put the incense
on the fire before the LORD, and the
smoke of the incense will conceal the
atonement cover above the tablets of
the covenant law, so that he will not
die. 14 He is to take some of the bull's
blood and with his finger sprinkle it
on the front of the atonement cover;
then he shall sprinkle some of it with
his finger seven times before the
atonement cover.

15 'He shall then slaughter the goat
for the sin offering for the people and
take its blood behind the curtain
and do with it as he did with the
bull's blood: he shall sprinkle it on
the atonement cover and in front
of it. 16 In this way he will make
atonement for the Most Holy Place
because of the uncleanness and
rebellion of the Israelites, whatever
their sins have been. He is to do the
same for the tent of meeting, which
is among them in the midst of their
uncleanness. 17 No one is to be in
the tent of meeting from the time
Aaron goes in to make atonement
in the Most Holy Place until he
comes out, having made atonement
for himself, his household and the
whole community of Israel.

18 'Then he shall come out to the
altar that is before the LORD and
make atonement for it. He shall take
some of the bull's blood and some of
the goat's blood and put it on all the
horns of the altar. 19 He shall sprinkle
some of the blood on it with his
finger seven times to cleanse it and
consecrate it from the uncleanness
of the Israelites.

20 'When Aaron has finished
making atonement for the Most Holy

Place, the tent of meeting and the altar, he shall bring forward the live goat. **21** He is to lay both hands on the head of the live goat and confess over it all the wickedness and rebellion of the Israelites – all their sins – and put them on the goat's head. He shall send the goat away into the wilderness in the care of someone appointed for the task. **22** The goat will carry on itself all their sins to a remote place; and the man shall release it in the wilderness.

**23** 'Then Aaron is to go into the tent of meeting and take off the linen garments he put on before he entered the Most Holy Place, and he is to leave them there. **24** He shall bathe himself with water in the sanctuary area and put on his ordinary garments. Then he shall come out and sacrifice the burnt offering for himself and the burnt offering for the people, to make atonement for himself and for the people. **25** He shall also burn the fat of the sin offering on the altar.

**26** 'The man who releases the goat as a scapegoat must wash his clothes and bathe himself with water; afterwards he may come into the camp. **27** The bull and the goat for the sin offerings, whose blood was brought into the Most Holy Place to make atonement, must be taken outside the camp; their hides, flesh and intestines are to be burned. **28** The man who burns them must wash his clothes and bathe himself with water; afterwards he may come into the camp.

**a** 3 Or *purification offering*; here and throughout this chapter
**b** 8 The meaning of the Hebrew for this word is uncertain; also in verses 10 and 26.

## Preparation for the Day of Atonement (16:3–5)

To make the contrast clear between the warning in 16:1–2 and the instructions in 16:3–5, verse 3 begins with a declaration giving permission for Aaron to enter the Most Holy Place, but under the conditions that the LORD provides in his instructions. This involves bringing the right animals for sin and burnt offerings first for himself, for his household (16:3b) and then for the Israelite community (16:5). With all preparation complete,

Aaron is ready to offer the gifts on behalf of himself and his household in 16:6–14.

## The sin offering for Aaron and his house (16:6–14)

Aaron's first step in the Day of Atonement, after the preparations in 16:3–5, is to offer a bull for a sin offering to make atonement both for himself and for his household (16:6, 11). The text describes this process in two stages (16:6–10, 11–14). Curiously, however, the focus of the LORD's instructions shifts away from the sin offering in 16:7–10 to describe what Aaron is to do with the two goats being presented before the LORD on behalf of Israel. Verse 8 conveys the reason for casting lots for the goats, which is to designate which goat is for the LORD and which is for the scapegoat. Verses 9–10 describe what this means. The goat chosen by lot to belong to the LORD is to be sacrificed as the sin offering (see 16:15–19), whereas 16:10 then identifies the second goat to be the scapegoat. This scapegoat is the living goat that will be sent out of the camp and into the wilderness to remove the sin of God's people from the camp (16:20–22).[3] As Gunjević explains, the scapegoat is 'a visual aid for the congregation which showed them that their sins were being taken away completely'.[4] For the Day of Atonement to be effective, both aspects of atonement that each goat represents

3 The Hebrew for the word translated in the NIV as 'scapegoat' is *'az'zēl*, and much ink has been spilt over the past decades about what it means and how the word should be understood in English. For example, Milgrom, *Leviticus 1–16*, 1021, observes the significance of the living goat (that is, the 'scapegoat') as a 'vehicle to dispatch Israel's impurities and sins to the wilderness' (see also Levine, *Leviticus*, 106). My understanding is more aligned with Milgrom's suggestion of a 'living goat', and this idea is used in the rest of the commentary from here on in.

4 Gunjević, 'Leviticus', 126.

needs to be complete: a sin offering that purifies both the people and the Tabernacle, and the removal of all Israel's iniquity from the nation.

Verses 11–14 return to Aaron's sin offering for himself and for his household (see 16:6). A vital aspect of the process described in 16:11–14 is Aaron taking a censer full of burning coals from the altar, as well as two handfuls of incense, and carrying both the censer and the incense behind the curtain of the Most Holy Place. By adding the incense onto the fire, the censer creates smoke for the purpose of veiling God's presence over the atonement cover on the Ark of the Covenant (16:13). Aaron's life will be preserved with God's presence being concealed. As Nihan observes, this represents 'an unmistakable contrast' between the fire offered by Nadab and Abihu and the effective obedience of Aaron.[5] Taking the bull's blood, Aaron is to splatter some of the blood *on the front* of the atonement cover and seven times *before* the atonement cover. Again, the number seven represents completion. In this instance, what is being completed is the purification of the Most Holy Place from Aaron's impurities. Once this is done, Aaron is ready to make atonement for God's people in 16:15–22.

## The sin offerings for God's people and the living goat (16:15–22)

The process of making atonement for Israel in 16:15–22 revolves around the two goats. The first goat, which was chosen to belong to the LORD in 16:8, is sacrificed as a sin offering in 16:15a. Verse 15b–c refers to Aaron's actions with the bull's blood from 16:11–14 and commands Aaron to do the same with the blood of the goat. The blood is to be taken behind the curtain, splattered at the front

5 Nihan, *From Priestly Torah*, 101.

of the atonement cover and then seven times before it. Verse 16 gives the reason. By sacrificing the goat and purifying the Most Holy Place, he is making atonement for the Most Holy Place. It is not that the Most Holy Place itself needs atonement, but rather the impurity of Israel's rebellion has reached the LORD's presence in the Most Holy Place and so the place where God's presence dwells among his people needs to be purified so that Israel's impurities can be removed. Verse 16b adds a vital clarification: 'whatever their sins have been'. Impurity is caused by *all* rebellion and sin. There is no kind of rebellion and sin that is exempt from the need for purification. The warning in 15:31 shapes the LORD's provision for *all* Israel's rebellion and sin. The warning is that the Israelites will die if their impurity infiltrates the LORD's holy dwelling place (15:31), and the LORD's provision in 16:15–16 is the death of another (i.e., the goat), whose blood can purify the LORD's dwelling place so that Israel's life can be preserved with God living in the nation's midst.

Verse 16 then instructs Aaron to do the same for the Tent of Meeting, which includes the Tabernacle. Verse 16 supplies the reason once more, which is that the whole of God's dwelling place resides amid Israel and so amid the nation's impurities. Verses 18–19 depict how Aaron is to make atonement for the Tent of Meeting. The outcome in 16:19 is that Israel's impurities are removed and the Tent of Meeting, including the altar, is set apart (i.e., 'consecrated') once more for the purpose that God intended for it.

Once the goat that belongs to the LORD is sacrificed to provide purification for Israel's impurities (16:15–19), 16:20–22 centres on the living goat. The LORD instructs Aaron, as Israel's representative, to press both hands on the head of the living goat and then confess over it all of Israel's wickedness, rebellion and sin.[6]

---

6 Milgrom, *Leviticus 1–16*, 1041, notes that the pressing down on the goat's head with both hands suggests a transference function, 'to convey, by confession, the

The use of these three terms – wickedness, rebellion and sin – is significant as they encompass together the fullness of Israel's relational impurities before the LORD (see Leviticus 17–27).[7] By confessing them over the goat's head, Aaron transfers all of Israel's sins onto the goat, after which the goat is sent into the wilderness outside the camp (16:21). This represents the separation of Israel's wickedness, rebellion and sin from the community and from God's presence by the goat bearing those sins to a place far removed from the Israelite camp (16:22).

## The final stage (16:23–28)

The act of changing clothes often symbolises a transition. In this instance, Aaron changing his clothes from the linen that he wore in 16:6–22 to his usual priestly clothing in 16:23–24b signifies that purification has been made, and so the final stage of the Day of Atonement can now begin. This final stage begins with burnt offerings, both for himself and for the people (16:24). Now that purification for the people and the Tent of Meeting is complete, the Israelites celebrate through the burnt offering that they are now able to approach their covenant God (see the explanation of Leviticus 1:3–16).

## *3. A Day of Atonement for all future generations • Leviticus 16:29–34*

The concluding paragraph in 16:29–34 is a reminder to the Israelites that the Day of Atonement is not just a once-off event in response to the deaths of Nadab and Abihu (10:1–2; 16:1–2).

---

sins of Israel onto the head of the goat'.

7 Hartley, *Leviticus*, 241.

These instructions are the LORD's provision annually for all future generations.

**29** 'This is to be a lasting ordi-
nance for you: on the tenth day of
the seventh month you must deny
yourselves[c] and not do any work –
whether native-born or a foreigner
residing among you – **30** because on
this day atonement will be made for
you, to cleanse you. Then, before the
LORD, you will be clean from all your
sins. **31** It is a day of sabbath rest, and
you must deny yourselves; it is a last-
ing ordinance. **32** The priest who is
anointed and ordained to succeed
his father as high priest is to make
atonement. He is to put on the sacred
linen garments **33** and make atone-
ment for the Most Holy Place, for the
tent of meeting and the altar, and for
the priests and all the members of
the community.

**34** 'This is to be a lasting ordinance
for you: atonement is to be made
once a year for all the sins of the
Israelites.'

And it was done, as the LORD com-
manded Moses.

c 29 Or *must fast*; also in verse 31

Verse 29 begins with a declaration: 'This is to be a lasting ordinance for you,' after which the LORD gives the command that is to shape how every future generation approaches the LORD on the Day of Atonement. This command begins with the timing of the Day of Atonement each year – the tenth day of the seventh month – before the LORD describes what is to happen on this day. The Israelite calendar is a different system from that of the Gregorian calendar that most of the world uses today. The Israelites start their new year with the celebration of the Passover (see Exodus 12:1–6), and so the Day of Atonement is on the tenth day of the seventh month counting from the Passover.

On this day, all within the community must cease their work, as per the Sabbath day, which includes both the Israelite (i.e., the native-born) and the foreigner. The LORD also asks the Israelites to 'deny themselves', which is more helpfully understood as 'humble themselves'. The reason the Day of Atonement is a day of humbling is that the enactment of the sacrifices is a reminder that their impurity has entered the LORD's presence, and this has endangered their lives as a community with their covenant God dwelling in their midst. As they hand over the goats, they know that the only means by which their life as a community can be preserved is by blood being shed on their behalf to purify themselves, the Most Holy Place, and the housing of this holy presence in the Tabernacle (16:30). Being confronted with the reality of the community's wickedness and rebellion, the people of Israel humble themselves before the LORD. They stop their everyday activity to make space for this rest and for reflection on the character of their covenant God who lives among them (16:31).

## Moving forward into the New Testament

Leviticus 15:31–33 left us with a life-and-death quandary by confronting us with the truth that unless Israel's impurity is removed from God's presence, there will be death and not life. As we attend to this truth, we realise the consequence of our impurity. If we wish to know God and have peace with him, then our own impurity needs to be removed if we are to have life. We cannot do this ourselves, and this presents a quandary in a world that prides itself on self-sufficiency. However, God does not leave us in the hopelessness of our impurity. Leviticus 16 points us to God's provision for a once-for-all sacrifice of atonement, but this sacrifice of atonement not only deals with the rebellion of Israel. It also has the power to purify and take away the rebellion of the whole world (John 1:29; 3:16).

As Jesus died on the cross, he accomplished two major acts. First, his blood that was shed can purify us from all our sin, iniquity, transgression and rebellion in our past, present and future (Hebrews 9:14; 1 John 1:7). Second, he bore the penalty of death that we deserved and so has taken away our guilt from us (Romans 6:22–23; Hebrews 9:26). He is both our purification offering and our scapegoat. Yet participating in God's provision of Jesus's sacrifice requires us to depend on the sufficiency of his death for us (John 3:36; Romans 3:22–26). We need to be able to acknowledge that there is nothing in our hands that we can bring to secure this for ourselves. Instead, knowing that Jesus has done for us that which we cannot do for ourselves, we humble ourselves before him, and our experience echoes Augustus Toplady's words:

> Rock of Ages, cleft for me,
> Let me hide myself in thee;
> Let the water and the blood,
> From thy riven side which flow'd,
> Be of sin the double cure,
> Cleanse me from its guilt and pow'r.
>
> Not the labours of my hands,
> Can fulfil thy law's demands:
> Could my zeal no respite know,
> Could my tears forever flow;
> All for sin could not atone,
> Thou must save, and thou alone.
>
> Nothing in my hand I bring,
> Simply to thy cross I cling;
> Naked come to thee for dress,
> Helpless look to thee for grace:
> Foul I to the fountain fly,
> Wash me, Saviour, or I die.

While I draw this fleeting breath,
While my eye-strings break in death;
When I soar to worlds unknown,
See thee on thy judgment throne;
Rock of ages, cleft for me,
Let me hide myself in thee.[8]

We enact our willingness to participate in Jesus's death for us as we celebrate the LORD's Supper together as a community of believers. While we celebrate this meal with joyful thankfulness, we do so humbling ourselves before God as we acknowledge our need for Jesus's atoning sacrifice on our behalf. We remind ourselves that Jesus's body was broken for us, and his blood was shed for us, so that we can have a firm and sure hope of God's presence being permanently restored among his covenant people, where there will be life to the full (Matthew 26:26–28; 1 Corinthians 11:25–26). This is the extraordinary nature of Jesus's sacrifice of atonement. We have an imperishable hope of a future where God's presence is permanently among us, with the crucified and risen Lamb providing light and life for all (Revelation 21–22).

8 Augustus Montague Toplady, *The Works of Augustus M. Toplady* (London: William Baynes and Son, 1825), 6:413–14 (Hymn XXII).

# 5

# Sacrifice Only to the LORD

## LEVITICUS 17

Continuing the theme of atonement, blood and sacrifice from Leviticus 16, chapter 17 emphasises that every sacrifice by the Israelite community must be gifted to the LORD, their covenant God (17:1–9). This is a matter of faithfulness. However, a second reason for this imperative is given in 17:10–16, which is that sacrificial blood has been given to the Israelites, by the LORD, to make atonement. By obeying the LORD's command about sacrifice and blood, the Israelites ensure that they glorify their covenant God who lives among them. Moreover, Leviticus 17 takes us to the heart of the gospel and the radical nature of the LORD's Supper.

### 1. *Every sacrifice is to be gifted to the LORD • Leviticus 17:1–9*

So far in the book of Leviticus, we have heard all kinds of instructions about gifts and offerings to the LORD that all, except for the cereal offering, focus on the sacrifice of animals and birds. The shedding of blood is a visceral reminder that the penalty of our impurity, rebellion and sin is death when the presence of a holy God dwells in our midst. However, at no point within Leviticus has the LORD explicitly commanded the Israelites to bring their gifts solely to him and to no other. Leviticus 17:1–7, however, makes explicit what has been implied throughout Leviticus 1–16 and, by doing so, ensures that the LORD is the only God-King who is sanctified in their midst as a holy people belonging solely to him their covenant God.

*Eating blood forbidden*

**17** The LORD said to Moses,
**2** 'Speak to Aaron and his
sons and to all the Israelites and say to
them: "This is what the LORD has com-
manded: **3** any Israelite who sacrifices
an ox,[a] a lamb or a goat in the camp
or outside it **4** instead of bringing it to
the entrance to the tent of meeting to
present it as an offering to the LORD in
front of the tabernacle of the LORD –
that person shall be considered guilty
of bloodshed; they have shed blood
and must be cut off from their people.
**5** This is so that the Israelites will bring
to the LORD the sacrifices they are
now making in the open fields. They
must bring them to the priest, that is,
to the LORD, at the entrance to the
tent of meeting and sacrifice them as
fellowship offerings. **6** The priest is to
splash the blood against the altar of
the LORD at the entrance to the tent of
meeting and burn the fat as an aroma
pleasing to the LORD. **7** They must no
longer offer any of their sacrifices to
the goat idols[b] to whom they prosti-
tute themselves. This is to be a lasting
ordinance for them and for the gener-
ations to come."

**8** 'Say to them: "Any Israelite or
any foreigner residing among them
who offers a burnt offering or sacri-
fice **9** and does not bring it to the
entrance to the tent of meeting to
sacrifice it to the LORD must be cut
off from the people of Israel.

---

**a** 3 The Hebrew word can include both male and female.
**b** 7 Or *the demons*

Verses 1–7 begin with the familiar introduction where the LORD commands Moses to mediate his words to Aaron, his sons and the Israelites, that is, the whole people of Israel. The addition of the declaration, 'This is what the LORD has commanded,' in 17:2b highlights the importance of the following message. Furthermore, how the message begins accentuates how vital Israel's obedience is, since it is the difference between life and death. The LORD's message begins with an uncompromising command in 17:3–4 that hinges on the situation where an Israelite sacrifices livestock, inside or outside the camp, and fails to bring the animal to the entrance to the Tent of Meeting as a gift to the LORD (17:3–4a).

This introduction does not assume that the slaughter of livestock is offered to another god (this logic is later in 17:7) but encompasses a general situation, regardless of motivation, about the slaughter of livestock at any other location than at the LORD's Tabernacle.[1] The LORD declares in 17:4b–c that the Israelite who does this is guilty of bloodshed. That is, they are guilty of taking a life. The text emphasises this offence by reiterating that 'they have shed blood'.

Previously, in the context of God making a covenant with Noah after the flood (Genesis 9:1–17), God declared in Genesis 9:5 that he would hold to account anyone who sheds the blood of another human, whether the offender is animal or human. Returning to Leviticus 17, the LORD applies the logic of Genesis 9:5–6 to the slaughter of animals outside his instructed purpose of bringing gifts to him at the entrance of the Tent of Meeting. The LORD has provided livestock for the primary purpose of sacrifice, and any blood of livestock shed outside this purpose will be accounted to the person who shed that blood.[2] Ko extends this idea to say that 'the LORD as the Creator has complete lordship over all life. Therefore, those who dare not acknowledge his lordship must be regarded as murderers who are "guilty of bloodshed".'[3] For this reason, at the conclusion of 17:4, the LORD commands that the guilty Israelite is to be cut off from the Israelite community. This does not necessarily mean that the person is to be put to death, but rather the guilty person is to be exiled from Israel without any opportunity for restoration (17:4d).[4]

---

1 Also, Chingota, 'Leviticus', 157–8; Ko, *Leviticus*, 159.

2 As per Jacob Milgrom, *Leviticus 17–22* (New York: Doubleday, 2000), 1456, the logic of 17:4 is that blood will be imputed to the offender because he has spilt blood and so it is an outworking of the *lex talionis* principle. This is a different nuance from Sklar, *Leviticus*, 219, who observes that any use of blood outside of God's command is prohibited and so the offender bears responsibility for the wrongful use of blood.

3 Ko, *Leviticus*, 160.

4 Also, Gunjević, 'Leviticus', 127. Contrary to Chingota, 'Leviticus', 157.

While this initial command in 17:3–4 may seem harsh, the intent is to dissuade the Israelites from sacrificing anywhere other than to the LORD at his dwelling place. The LORD states this motivation positively when he reveals his desire for the Israelites to bring sacrifices to him that 'they are now making in the open fields' (17:5b). Within the Pentateuch's narrative, the Israelites are still at Sinai, having just been formed into a nation under the LORD's kingship after being redeemed from Egypt and from the service of Pharaoh (Exodus 1–18). While the Israelite elders know the LORD as the God of the patriarchs (Exodus 1–6), they are still in the process of learning about the ways in which the LORD, as their covenant God, wishes them to serve him, as these ways would be a contrast to that of Egypt. The LORD reiterates what he desires of his people in 17:5b, which is that they bring their gifts to the priest at the entrance of the Tent of Meeting. It is only within this context that all belonging to the LORD – the blood and the fat – can be given to him (17:6; see 3:17).

Verse 7 accentuates that where the Israelites slaughter their livestock is a matter of faithfulness to the LORD. In the LORD's view, offering gifts to anything or anyone other than to him is prostitution, since Israel is in a covenant of faithful loyalty where he is solely to be their God. Based on the covenant relationship where Israel is to be the LORD's holy people, a people set apart to belong solely to him, they are to desist from offering livestock to idols and to bring their gifts to him at his dwelling place. In this way, the Israelites ensure that the LORD is sanctified and glorified in their midst.

To reiterate that this is a life-and-death matter, 17:8–9 repeats the command from 17:3–4 with the inclusion of the resident foreigner. Any Israelite or foreigner living among the Israelite community who offers any gift or offering, including a burnt offering, and does not bring it before the LORD at the Tent of Meeting is to be cut off, that is, exiled from the Israelite people. The community is pledged in faithful loyalty to their covenant

God, the LORD, and so refusing to bring their gifts to him is essentially saying they do not wish to live in allegiance to him and so they no longer wish to be part of that community. The consequence, therefore, is just. They are to be exiled from the community who have sworn an oath of faithfulness to the LORD.

We might be able to understand this from the viewpoint of the Israelite, but what about the resident foreigner? While the foreigner lives among the Israelites, they are not part of God's people unless they are circumcised (see Exodus 12:48–49), which raises the question as to why they too must adhere to the LORD's command in Leviticus 17:3–8. While the resident foreigner may not be part of God's covenant people, they have chosen to reside among a community that is the LORD's covenant nation, and so they are to 'respect the God without whom the community would not exist'.[5]

## Moving forward into the New Testament

At the crux of 17:1–9 is the matter of covenant faithfulness to the LORD, and an outworking of this was the bringing of gifts to the LORD at the place where he dwelled among his people. He was present because of the provision of gifts and sacrifices, but this was only a temporary provision because of the stubbornness of rebellion. God's people chose repeatedly to bring their gifts to idols rather than to the LORD, and the consequence was the enactment of the covenant curses. Eventually, the LORD's presence left the Jerusalem Temple and the people were exiled (Ezekiel 1–12).

Under the new covenant, we no longer bring physical sacrifices to a particular physical place because Jesus has presented himself as the once-for-all sufficient sacrifice. Our centre of

5 Deborah W. Rooke, 'The Blasphemer (Lev 24): gender, identity, and boundary construction', in *Text, Time, and Temple: Literary, Historical and Ritual Studies in Leviticus*, edited by Francis Landy, Leigh M. Trevaskis and Bryan D. Bibb (Sheffield: Sheffield Phoenix, 2015), 158.

worship now is the Triune God. Moreover, we are urged by the apostle Paul to offer our bodies as 'a living sacrifice' in such a way that is 'holy and pleasing to God' as our 'true and proper worship' (Romans 12:1). We do not do this to maintain good relationship with the LORD, as though the threat of exile is in our future if we fail. Our exile is over (Luke 4:16–19). Jesus's work is finished (John 19:30). We offer ourselves as living sacrifices in faithfulness to Jesus because we know the sufficiency of his death and resurrection on our behalf and now live in service to him (Hebrews 9:14). Our future is not a threat of exile but an imperishable hope of living in the presence of the crucified and risen Lamb in a new creation (1 Peter 1:3–9; Revelation 21–22). Leviticus 17:1–9 reminds us that what God desires of us is faithfulness to Jesus as we offer ourselves as living sacrifices to him *and* only to him in such a way that is holy and pleasing to God.

### *2. Blood is given by the LORD for atonement • Leviticus 17:10–16*

Verses 10–16 focus on the topic of blood. In 17:6, the LORD highlights that one reason the Israelites are to bring their gifts to the priest is so that he can splash blood against the LORD's altar (see 3:13). From our knowledge of Leviticus 1–7, there is one reason for the splashing of blood against the altar in the context of the fellowship offering. When a gift does not have the purpose of atoning for impurity and sin, which the fellowship offering does not, then the blood needs to be given to the LORD as it is not being used for the purpose assigned to it by the LORD (i.e., to make atonement). For this reason, the Israelites have already been warned in 7:26–27 that any Israelite who eats blood in the context of a fellowship offering must be exiled from the Israelite community.

**10** ‘“I will set my face against any
Israelite or any foreigner residing
among them who eats blood, and
I will cut them off from the people.
**11** For the life of a creature is in the
blood, and I have given it to you to
make atonement for yourselves on
the altar; it is the blood that makes
atonement for one’s life.[c] **12** Therefore
I say to the Israelites, ‘None of you
may eat blood, nor may any foreigner
residing among you eat blood.’

**13** ‘“Any Israelite or any foreigner
residing among you who hunts any
animal or bird that may be eaten
must drain out the blood and cover
it with earth, **14** because the life of
every creature is its blood. That is
why I have said to the Israelites,
‘You must not eat the blood of any
creature, because the life of every
creature is its blood; anyone who
eats it must be cut off.’

**15** ‘“Anyone, whether native-born
or foreigner, who eats anything found
dead or torn by wild animals must
wash their clothes and bathe with
water, and they will be ceremonially
unclean till evening; then they will
be clean. **16** But if they do not wash
their clothes and bathe themselves,
they will be held responsible.”’

**c 11** Or *atonement by the life in the blood*

Leviticus 17:10 echoes the LORD’s command from 7:26–27, warning both the Israelite and the resident foreigner, ‘I will set my face against any Israelite or any foreigner residing among them who eats blood, and I will cut them off from the people.’ For the LORD to turn his face towards is a sign of favour and blessing (e.g., Numbers 6:24–26), and so for the LORD to turn his face away is the removal of his favour and blessing. Thus, exile is an outworking of God’s removal of his favour for any Israelite and foreign resident who eats blood. The LORD explains the reason for this penalty in 17:11: ‘For the life of a creature is in the blood, and I have given it to you to make atonement for yourselves on the altar; it is the blood that makes atonement for one’s life.’ Earlier in this commentary, when discussing Leviticus 12 and 15, we noted that the loss of blood was associated with impurity because of its connection with sickness and death, which are not as God created the world to be. However, the reverse is also true. The Israelites knew that blood is pumped around the body by the heart and that this is associated with life. When a heart stops, blood stops flowing around the body and we die. A heart beats, blood circulates and we are alive. When blood is fulfilling its created purpose, which is within the veins and arteries of the body, blood is associated with life, and so is the life of a creature (17:11a).

However, while blood has a created purpose, the LORD has chosen to provide blood for a second purpose, which is to make atonement (17:11b–c).[6] Throughout Leviticus 1–16, we have witnessed the LORD's provision of sacrifice to make atonement through the shedding and splattering of blood in several contexts. Irrespective of the context, however, atonement by the shedding and the splattering of blood functions in at least two ways.

First, in each situation where atonement is required to approach the LORD's presence, the gift-giver is recognising that he or she is not in a condition that is acceptable to God for one of three reasons. The first is a need to restore a broken relationship from sin and guilt. Second, the person has been in a condition of impurity (not related to sin) or, third, because the person is aware that he or she is not without blemish. Therefore, the life of another that represents being without blemish and the condition of purity is needed to be sacrificed in the stead of the gift-giver. It is blood for blood, life for life. In this way, the sacrifice ransoms the life of the Israelite.

Second, once the priest has collected the blood of the sacrifice, which represents the life of the sacrifice, the priest then splatters

6 Curiously, the LORD is giving the blood to the Israelites for the function of atonement, but God gives the blood from that which belongs to him. Thus, there is a mutuality of giving blood (also Schwartz, 'The Prohibition Concerning the "Eating" of Blood in Leviticus 17', in *Priesthood and Cult in Ancient Israel*, edited by Gary A. Anderson and Saul M. Olyan (Sheffield: JSOT, 1991), 49–51). Contrary to Milgrom, *Leviticus 17–22*, 1473, who argues Israel is not to assume that the nation gives blood to the LORD, but rather God gives the blood to Israel.

this blood at various points of the Tabernacle. The purpose of the blood is to purify the LORD's dwelling place from impurity caused by sin, rebellion, wickedness and any other cause that the LORD has designated in Leviticus 11–15. As we have seen from the explanation of Leviticus 11–16, impurity cannot enter God's presence, otherwise death is the consequence. For the lives of the Israelites to be preserved, it is critical that they offer a gift whose blood can purify God's dwelling place after they are aware of a cause of impurity. The LORD's provision for this purification is blood, which represents the unblemished life (i.e., in a pure condition) of another shed on the gift-giver's behalf. Because blood is associated with life, it is a most powerful purifier.

However, an Israelite may ask about how this works in two situations. The first situation, in 17:13–14, is where the animal or bird is hunted and is in a pure condition (17:13). To anticipate this question, the LORD gives a provision for hunting. The second situation, in 17:15–16, is when an Israelite (i.e., 'native-born') or a resident foreigner has found an animal dead or which has been killed by wild animals. While 17:15 gives permission to eat it, the Israelite in this situation would have touched a carcass and so would be considered impure. Consistent with 11:39–40, the Israelite must wash their clothes, bathe and wait until evening until they are restored to a condition of purity. Thus, the consequence of being in an impure condition remains within this second situation and, if this is disregarded, then the Israelite or resident foreigner will be culpable and so held responsible (17:16).

## Moving forward into the New Testament

Leviticus 17:10–16 teaches us that God provided blood for two reasons: to sustain life and to make atonement for our lives. Abstaining from eating blood is a means of honouring the LORD's purposes for blood. It is no wonder, when Jesus declared, 'Unless you eat the flesh of the Son of Man and drink his blood, you have no life in you,' that many of his disciples turned away from following him (John 6:53–66). Jesus was declaring that the opposite of Leviticus 17:10–16 is now true! Previously, drinking blood would have the consequence of exile, which is relational death, but Jesus's words in John 6:53–58 suggest that drinking his blood would have the consequence of life. Rather than being prohibited from participating in the blood of sacrifice, Jesus offers the invitation to drink his blood.

So too as Jesus, during the Last Supper, took the cup and gave it to his disciples saying, 'Drink from it, all you. This is my blood of the covenant, which is poured out for many for the forgiveness of sins' (Matthew 26:27–28), he was inviting his disciples to drink his blood to participate in the forgiveness of sin that the shedding of his blood would bring. The reason is still the same. The shedding of Jesus's blood was his life for our life. His blood has ransomed our lives, paying the penalty of death that our rebellion and guilt deserved, so that we can have peace with God. His blood purified us, the whole of us, and purified the heavenly place where God's presence dwells. For this reason, God's Spirit can dwell in us, and we can approach God's throne of grace.

Because Jesus's blood is a permanent means of atonement for us, Jesus calls us now to participate in his blood as a means to participate in the life everlasting that his blood has secured for us. For this reason, we celebrate the LORD's Supper and this invitation is offered to us: 'Drink from this all of you; for this is my blood of the new covenant, shed for you and for many for the forgiveness of sins,' and then, 'Drink this in remembrance that Christ's blood was shed for you and be thankful.'[7]

---

7 Anglican Church of Australia, *A Prayer Book for Australia: Shorter Edition* (Mulgrave: Broughton Books, 1995), 129, 142. Please note that, in a Reformed Protestant understanding of the LORD's Supper, the reference to wine as blood is symbolic and a spiritual feeding, rather than the wine becoming the blood of Jesus.

# 6

# Be Holy as I, the LORD Your God, Am Holy

## LEVITICUS 18–20

Leviticus 18–20 applies the distinction between impurity and purity from Leviticus 11–15 to Israel's relationships in covenant community. In the introduction to Leviticus 11–15, we observed that the purpose of Leviticus 11–15 is to teach the Israelites the distinction between what is impure and pure by using outward and tangible aspects of life. We observed that impurity is associated with incompleteness, rebellion, disorder and death, whereas purity is associated with the opposite: completeness, order and life. Moreover, the Israelites are to be a holy people to the LORD by being in a pure condition. To be in an impure condition is to be excluded from God's presence. The implication is that they are either to avoid impurity or, when impurity is unavoidable, to wait until they can be restored to a condition of purity and so to God's presence.

Leviticus 18–20 applies this teaching to Israel's relationships where what is impure is associated with the ways of Egypt and the Canaanites. Israel is to avoid embodying the impure ways of Egypt and of Canaan, otherwise death and exile will ensue. In contrast, they are to be in a pure condition by being faithful to the LORD's instructions as they live in good relationships within the household, with their neighbours and with the LORD.

Two phrases are used throughout this section that might be helpful to explain. The first is 'relational order' and the second is 'relational disorder'. In the explanation of Leviticus 11–15, I used similar language of creation order and disorder. In these instances, creation order is that which reflects how God created the world and is associated with a pure condition, whereas disorder is that which reflects the brokenness of God's creation and is associated with being in an impure condition. Similarly, the phrase 'relational order' means living in good relationship with one another and with God in such a way that reflects the LORD's purposes for his world, and living in relational order is associated with purity. The opposite, 'relational disorder', means living in relationship with one another and with God in a way that is contrary to the LORD's purposes for his world and so is associated with impurity. When Israel's relationships within their households, with one another and with the LORD reflect relational order, then there is life and flourishing in the land. However, when the Israelites relate to one another and to the LORD in the same ways as the Egyptians and the Canaanites, then there can only be death and exile. The purpose of Leviticus 18–20 is to persuade the Israelites to avoid impure ways of relating to one another and, instead, to pursue good in relationships within the community and with the LORD.

## *1. A warning to refrain from impure behaviour • Leviticus 18*

Leviticus 18 is a warning for the Israelites to refrain from relational behaviours that reflect the ways of the Egyptians and of the Canaanites. Instead, they are to obey the LORD's instructions because it is by his decrees that they learn how to live as his covenant people. The LORD's instructions begin in 18:2–5 with a sequence of prohibitions (18:3), which are then balanced with a sequence of commands (18:4–5). The purpose of these initial instructions is to dissuade Israel from embodying the ways of the Canaanites and to persuade them to embody the ways of the LORD. Verses 6–23 follow with a list of prohibitions that seek to restrain relational disorder in the household and in community.

### *Unlawful sexual relations*

**18** The LORD said to Moses,
2 ‘Speak to the Israelites
and say to them: “I am the LORD
your God. 3 You must not do as
they do in Egypt, where you used to
live, and you must not do as they
do in the land of Canaan, where I
am bringing you. Do not follow their
practices. 4 You must obey my laws
and be careful to follow my decrees.
I am the LORD your God. 5 Keep my
decrees and laws, for the person who
obeys them will live by them. I am
the LORD.

6 ‘“No one is to approach any close relative to have sexual relations. I am the LORD.

7 ‘“Do not dishonour your father by having sexual relations with your mother. She is your mother; do not have relations with her.

8 ‘“Do not have sexual relations with your father’s wife; that would dishonour your father.

9 ‘“Do not have sexual relations with your sister, either your father’s daughter or your mother’s daughter, whether she was born in the same home or elsewhere.

10 ‘“Do not have sexual relations with your son’s daughter or your daughter’s daughter; that would dishonour you.

11 ‘“Do not have sexual relations with the daughter of your father’s wife, born to your father; she is your sister.

12 ‘“Do not have sexual relations with your father’s sister; she is your father’s close relative.

13 ‘“Do not have sexual relations with your mother’s sister, because she is your mother’s close relative.

14 ‘“Do not dishonour your father’s brother by approaching his wife to have sexual relations; she is your aunt.

15 ‘“Do not have sexual relations with your daughter-in-law. She is your son’s wife; do not have relations with her.

16 ‘“Do not have sexual relations with your brother’s wife; that would dishonour your brother.

17 ‘“Do not have sexual relations with both a woman and her daughter. Do not have sexual relations with either her son’s daughter or her daughter’s daughter; they are her close relatives. That is wickedness.

18 ‘“Do not take your wife’s sister as a rival wife and have sexual relations with her while your wife is living.

19 ‘“Do not approach a woman to have sexual relations during the uncleanness of her monthly period.

20 ‘“Do not have sexual relations

with your neighbour's wife and defile
yourself with her.
**21** '"Do not give any of your child-
ren to be sacrificed to Molek, for you
must not profane the name of your
God. I am the LORD.
**22** '"Do not have sexual relations
with a man as one does with a
woman; that is detestable.
**23** '"Do not have sexual relations
with an animal and defile yourself
with it. A woman must not present
herself to an animal to have sexual
relations with it; that is a perversion.
**24** '"Do not defile yourselves in any
of these ways, because this is how the
nations that I am going to drive out
before you became defiled. **25** Even
the land was defiled; so I punished
it for its sin, and the land vomited
out its inhabitants. **26** But you must
keep my decrees and my laws. The
native-born and the foreigners
residing among you must not do any
of these detestable things, **27** for all
these things were done by the people
who lived in the land before you, and
the land became defiled. **28** And if
you defile the land, it will vomit you
out as it vomited out the nations that
were before you.
**29** '"Everyone who does any of
these detestable things – such
persons must be cut off from their
people. **30** Keep my requirements
and do not follow any of the detest-
able customs that were practised
before you came and do not defile
yourselves with them. I am the LORD
your God."'

The first two prohibitions in 18:3 instruct the Israelites to resist doing as they did in Egypt and not to follow the practices of Canaan.[1] Within the Pentateuch's narrative, Israel is between two lands: between Egypt, where they lived in the past, and Canaan, where the LORD promises to bring them in the future. When they lived among the Egyptians they adopted the ways of the Egyptians, and the LORD instructs the Israelites to desist from those behaviours. Moreover, the LORD warns that when they enter the land, they must be careful not to embody the ways of the Canaanites, and the LORD's motivation for this prohibition is given later in 18:25–30.The third prohibition in 18:3 encompasses

1 Also, Ko, *Leviticus*, 168.

both the ways of the Egyptians and the Canaanites as the LORD commands the Israelites not to follow their ways.

However, the LORD balances whose ways they are *not* to embody (18:3) with whose ways they *are* to embody (18:4–5). Instead of following the ways of Egypt and Canaan, they are to obey the LORD's instructions and follow his decrees with care (18:4).[2] The LORD summarises these two commands from 18:4 in a third, which is to keep his decrees and laws (18:5a). It is by keeping the LORD's instructions and decrees that the Israelites can learn to follow the LORD's ways as their covenant God, rather than falling into past patterns learnt in Egypt or adopting the practices of their future land in Canaan.

After the third command, the LORD gives a motivation, in 18:5b, for obeying his ways. Life is found in their obedience to these instructions. This motivation is not a promise of prosperity or reward for their obedience, but rather that Israel will live *as a consequence* of their obedience.[3] The opposite will be true if Israel follows the ways of Egypt or Canaan: there can only be death and exile (18:24–28).

The three prohibitions (18:3) and the three commands (18:4–5) are book-ended in 18:2c and 18:5c with the refrain, 'I am the LORD your God,' and the shortened version, 'I am the LORD.' This refrain declares the identity of the one speaking and, in this instance, commanding. Because he is their covenant God-King, he has the authority to give instructions to Israel with the expectation that they will follow these instructions out of loyal faithfulness. This refrain is repeated in 18:6 and 18:21.

---

2 I agree with Mary Douglas, 'Justice as the Cornerstone: An Interpretation of Leviticus 18–20', *Interpretation* 53 (1999): 346, that the primary issue is one of covenant faithfulness.

3 See also Hartley, *Leviticus*, 293; Mark F. Rooker, *Leviticus* (Nashville: Broadman & Holman, 2000), 241; Sklar, *Leviticus*, 228. Contrary to Milgrom, *Leviticus 17–22*, 1523, understanding of life as reward and that 'the laws themselves have the inherent power to grant life'.

Verses 6–23 follow with a list of prohibitions where the sexual relationships described are examples of practices from Egypt and Canaan that the Israelites are to resist following. These prohibitions are examples of sexual relationships, first in the family household and second in the community, that reflect relational *disorder* because they are *not* aligned with the LORD's purposes for his people or for the nations. As such, if Israel were to participate in these sexual relationships, they would become impure. The purpose of these prohibitions is to dissuade Israel from these relational behaviours.

The list begins in 18:6 with a general principle, which is that no one is to approach a close relative, that is, someone who shares a kin relationship, to participate in sexual activity.[4] The list of prohibitions in 18:7–18 are examples of how this general principle can be applied within households. Implied is that there is only one relationship in which Israelites have the freedom to engage in sexual activity within a household and which reflects God's purposes for his people, which is between a husband and his wife.

After 18:6–18 exemplifies sexual relationships within the family household that the Israelites are to resist, 18:19–23 exemplifies other sexual relationships that do not represent God's purposes and therefore will cause the Israelites to be in an impure condition. The prohibition in 18:19 assumes that we can recall 15:19–24 where a man and woman become impure if the woman begins her monthly period while they are participating in sexual activity (15:24). There is, however, a difference between 15:24 and 18:19. In 15:24, there is no intention to become impure, whereas a man engages in sexual activity knowing the woman is in an impure condition because of her monthly period in 18:19.

4 Also, Thomas Hieke, *Levitikus 16–27* (Freiburg: Herder, 2014), 667; Ko, *Leviticus*, 169; Rooker, *Leviticus*, 242; Wenham, *Leviticus*, 253. Contrary to Milgrom, *Leviticus 17–22*, 1533.

The prohibition in 18:20 exemplifies the seventh command where an Israelite is prohibited from adultery by the prohibition of sexual relations with a neighbour's wife. A marriage relationship is a form of covenant relationship, and for a man to engage in sexual activity with another man's wife is to transgress this covenant relationship. Verse 23 prohibits a man and a woman from sexual activity with an animal.[5] The final clause of verse 23, 'that is a perversion' (NIV), can be translated as 'that is a confusion'. The LORD is declaring sexual activity between a human and an animal to be a confusion between 'kinds' in his created order and is, therefore, an example of relational disorder.

While most prohibitions in 18:19–23 address examples of sexual relationships that represent relational disorder outside the household (the exception is 18:19), 18:21 is the only prohibition that does not restrain specific sexual conduct. Instead, 18:21 prohibits child sacrifice, which refers to the Canaanite practice of burning children to the Canaanite god, Molek. An adoption of such a practice would profane the name of their covenant God and so Israel must resist the Canaanite practice.[6]

Verses 24–30 prohibit the Israelites from defiling themselves 'in any of these ways' (18:24a), that is, the ways listed in 18:6–23.[7]

---

5 I have explored 18:22 and 18:23 in previous works. See Katherine Smith, 'Belonging to God in Relational Wholeness: A Conservative Perspective on the Old Testament's View of Marriage and Same-Sex Intimate Relationships', in *Marriage, Same-Sex Marriage and the Anglican Church of Australia: Essays from the Doctrine Commission*, edited by M. Stead (Mulgrave: Broughton, 2019), 105–22; Katherine Smith, 'Ordered Relationships in Leviticus', in *Marriage, Family, and Relationships: Biblical, Doctrinal and Contemporary Perspectives*, edited by Thomas A. Noble, Sarah K. Whittle and Philip J. Johnston (London: IVP Academic, 2017), 30–9.

6 Please note that Gunjević, 'Leviticus', 128, links all the prohibitions in 18:19–23 with the polytheistic culture of Egypt and Mesopotamia and so sees a direct link between the behaviour prohibited and idolatry. If this is accurate, then 18:21 would not be out of context.

7 Also, Milgrom, *Leviticus 17–22*, 1578.

Referring to the explanation of 10:10–11, we saw that to defile is to be turned from a condition of purity to a condition of impurity by being in contact with what is impure. In this instance, by following the practices of the Canaanites outlined in 18:6–23, the Israelites would become impure. We know this is a problem because impurity cannot encounter the holy, otherwise death and exile will ensue. As Israel settles into the land, the Tabernacle (later the Temple) will still be the centre of Israel's worship as the LORD dwells in their midst within the land. What we have learnt about life in the camp with the LORD living among them in Leviticus 1–17 is now extended to the whole land.

The LORD conveys the reason for the prohibition in 18:24a. As noted above, Israel at Sinai is between two lands. The LORD has redeemed his people from Egypt and has promised to give the land of Canaan to them (Exodus 3:7–10, 15–17; 6:6–8). As they reside at Sinai, they are preparing to travel to the land of promise so that the LORD can give them the land by driving out the nations who inhabit it (see also Exodus 23:23–33). The LORD reveals in Leviticus 18:24b why he intends to drive out those nations living in Canaan, which is that those nations embodied the practices listed in 18:6–23 and they became defiled. Verse 25 explains that the impurity of the Canaanites impacted the land. Impurity is contagious and so it makes sense that the place where the Canaanites live has been defiled, that is, the land has become impure. Moreover, the LORD announces that he needs to punish the land 'for its sin'. Where the NIV has 'sin', the most accurate rendering is 'guilt'. Because the land became defiled (i.e., became impure), it incurred guilt, and for this reason the LORD needed to bring his justice against the land. The land responded to the LORD's justice by vomiting out the inhabitants. Vomiting is a visceral reaction when our bodies are trying to get rid of something. For the land to vomit out the nations, it is getting rid of the cause of its impurity so that it can be restored to a condition of purity once more.

Rather than defiling themselves and the land by following the ways of the Canaanites, 18:26 commands the Israelites to choose an alternative: they are to keep the LORD's decrees and his laws. Verses 27–28 dissuade the Israelite and resident foreigner from following the practices of the Canaanites by repeating the sentiment of 18:24–25a. Verse 28 then delivers a punch to the guts, so to speak, which is the warning that if they imitate the Canaanites and defile the land, then they too will be vomited out, just as those nations were in the LORD's justice. This warning about consequence is intended to persuade the Israelites to resist adopting Canaanite practices prohibited in 18:6–23.

The conclusion in 18:29–30 is a summary of how Israel is to respond to the LORD's message of warning. Since impurity spreads, if one person or a group of people participates in impure behaviours, this affects the whole nation. Therefore, they are to exile anyone who adopts the practices prohibited in 18:6–23 to protect the Israelites as a people who are to be set apart in a condition of purity in the land. [8]

Reading 18:24–30, we may realise that the consequence for the Canaanites was forced migration by being displaced. Many in the western world migrate for lifestyle and work but know very little about being forced from homes and community because of war, famine or persecution. According to the UNHCR, a total of 117.3 million people were forcibly displaced by the end of 2023, and this estimate has increased to 122.6 million by June 2024.[9] When reading Leviticus 18 across cultures, it is good to

8 There is some contention as to the meaning of being 'cut off'. I am sympathetic to the meaning of exile since the conceptual basis of the text is the offender(s) being cut off from access to God's presence. See also Levine, *Leviticus*, 242, and Milgrom, *Leviticus 17–22*, 1582.

9 '117.3 million people worldwide were forcibly displaced', UNHCR Australia, 13 June 2024, www.unhcr.org/en-au/figures-at-a-glance.html; '117.3 million forcibly displaced people worldwide', UNHCR Global, https://www.unhcr.org/refugee-statistics (accessed 9 October 2024).

acknowledge that the LORD's justice against the Canaanites was forced migration as he drove them out of the land, and many readers may struggle with how a God who desires good can cause people groups to be displaced in foreign lands.[10]

However, we can reflect on three points as we sort through this issue of forced migration. First, it is a misappropriation of this passage to suggest that those who suffer forced migration in today's world are experiencing God's justice. These instructions in 18:24–28 are about the Canaanites at this particular juncture in world history and should not be generalised to every land, nation and time. How the Israelites are to relate to the Canaanites when they enter the land is not how they should relate to the other nations (Exodus 22:21–24; Deuteronomy 4:6–8; 20; 21:10–14). Second, the Israelites are not exempt from the same consequence if they become impure by the same practices and defile the land (Leviticus 18:24–30). There is parity in how God acts in his justice. Third, while God desires good for the nations of this world, part of desiring good is bringing justice. It would not be good for God to turn a blind eye and allow the guilt of the Canaanites to keep increasing, and the same for the Israelites. Part of desiring good is enacting justice and discipline. This does not take away the sting from 18:24–28, but neither are we to soften God's justice to make us more comfortable. God invites us to hear the weight of his justice and then invites his people to follow his ways, where there is life and flourishing.

## Moving forward into the New Testament

It is worth reiterating that this chapter is purposefully shaped with 18:1–5 and 18:24–30 'bookending' the prohibitions in 18:6–23 that restrain relational disorder in the household and in the

---

10 To reflect further on the issue of forced migration in the Bible, see M. Daniel Carroll R., *The Bible and Borders: Hearing God's Word on Immigration* (Grand Rapids: Brazos, 2020).

community. This shape suggests that the prohibitions are examples of what the Israelites are not to replicate from Egypt or from the Canaanites. As we read through the prohibitions, the common theme is how we relate to others with our bodies. The Israelites were between two cultures, having left Egypt and anticipating life in Canaan. They were in a liminal space where they were being transformed into God's covenant people as they prepared to inherit the land of promise. We too are in a liminal space. Just as the Israelites were redeemed from Egypt to be God's covenant community, so too we have been redeemed from the power of sin and death to be God's new covenant community. Just as the Israelites were anticipating life in the land of promise, so too we anticipate entering the rest of the new heaven and the new earth.

However, there are two vital differences between the Israelites at Sinai receiving the LORD's instructions and our situation as a new covenant community. The first key distinction is that we live in 'the already and the not yet'. While we live in the liminal space of being redeemed from the power of sin and have our eyes set on our eternal future, we are guaranteed our inheritance and participate now in the blessings that we have in Christ (Ephesians 1:3–10). We have life to the full in Jesus *now* and his Spirit dwells in and among his people *now* because Jesus has purified us once for all in his atoning sacrifice. Second, Israel could (and did) fail to enter the land of promise (Numbers 11–14) and, as Leviticus 18 and 20 warn, could be exiled from the land if they were to replicate the relational practices of the Egyptians and the Canaanites (2 Kings 21–25). However, the rest we await in the new heaven and the new earth where God will permanently restore his presence among his covenant people has the crucified and risen Lamb present (Hebrews 3–4; Revelation 21–2). His victory is complete. In the new creation, he will permanently separate what is impure from the new covenant community (Revelation 22:15). The new covenant community will be permanently in a pure condition and with a holy status. We will be wholly devoted to the worship of the crucified and risen Lamb (Revelation 21–22). There will be no danger of falling into practices that are opposed to God's purposes for his world, and the threat of exile will be no more.

However, as we live now in 'the already and the not yet', we are still living in a world enslaved by sin, and we live and breathe the relational brokenness of our different cultures. Just as the Israelites were being instructed to desist from the relational brokenness of Egypt and to refuse to adopt the relational brokenness of the Canaanites, so too we are to desist from the relational brokenness of our culture and to pursue God's purposes for relational wholeness in his world. In the Australian western culture in which I live and breathe, we have a 'do what is right for you' cultural value. We choose who we follow for ourselves, and what we do with our bodies is what pleases solely us as individuals. No one outside ourselves has the right to influence who we worship and what we do with our bodies. There is also a lot of freedom to gaze on the bodies of others, except for the bodies of children, and this freedom is not restrained by an acknowledgment that other peoples' bodies do not belong to us. This boundary only kicks in when talking about sexual consent, and even then we are confused about sexual consent because of the freedom we perceive ourselves as having. These cultural values, however, are contrary to God's purposes for his people in his world. He desires us to relate sexually within a covenant marriage relationship between a man and a woman, and not outside it (1 Corinthians 7:1–5). If we are not married, then he asks us to desist from sexual activity and to devote ourselves wholly to him (1 Corinthians 7:8–9). However, irrespective of our marital status, Jesus seeks our wholehearted worship and that we desist from patterns of idolatry (1 Corinthians 10:14).

Moreover, Jesus asks us to acknowledge that he has the

authority to call us to follow him according to the patterns that reflect his purposes because he is our Redeemer, Saviour and King (Matthew 16:24–26). If we participate in his death and resurrection by faith, then we belong solely to him, and he calls us to embody our holy status of belonging solely to him. For this reason, we desist from the patterns of our culture and of the world and we seek to put on relational wholeness that reflects Jesus's purposes for his covenant community, such as compassion, kindness, humility, gentleness, patience and love (Colossians 3:12–14).

## *2. Relational order in the land of promise • Leviticus 19*

*Various laws*

**19** The LORD said to Moses,
**2** 'Speak to the entire assembly of Israel and say to them: "Be holy because I, the LORD your God, am holy.

The refrain, 'I am the LORD your God,' is a declaration of identity as the LORD reminds Israel that he has the authority to command because he is their covenant God who redeemed them from Egypt to belong to him as his people. This refrain recurs throughout Leviticus 19 in verses 3, 4, 10, 12, 14, 16, 18, 25, 28, 30, 31, 32, 33, 36 and 37, to accentuate who the LORD is that he can command the Israelites. Moreover, the LORD's message to the Israelites in Leviticus 19 is prefaced with the command in 19:2c, 'Be holy'. Verse 2d relates the reason for this command: 'because I, the LORD your God, am holy.' This command is for Israel to embody their status as a holy people because they are to conform to the status of their covenant God to whom they belong. The following instructions in 19:3–37 describe how Israel is to conform to the LORD's status of being holy. These instructions are shaped into four sections: 19:3–19, 20–22, 23–32 and 33–37.

## An exposition of the Decalogue (19:3–19)

Some of the commands and prohibitions in 19:3–19 might sound familiar because they echo the Decalogue (i.e., the Ten Commandments) from Exodus 20:1–17.[11] The purpose of 19:3–19 is to exposit the Decalogue to persuade the Israelites to pursue relational conduct that reflects God's purposes for his covenant people and to refrain from relational conduct that is contrary to those purposes.[12] By embodying relational behaviour that reflects God's purposes for his world, they conform to his status as being holy.

**3** ' "Each of you must respect your mother and father, and you must observe my Sabbaths. I am the LORD your God.

**4** ' "Do not turn to idols or make metal gods for yourselves. I am the LORD your God.

**5** ' "When you sacrifice a fellowship offering to the LORD, sacrifice it in such a way that it will be accepted on your behalf. **6** It shall be eaten on the day you sacrifice it or on the next day; anything left over until the third day must be burned. **7** If any of it is eaten on the third day, it is impure and will not be accepted. **8** Whoever eats it will be held responsible because they have desecrated what is holy to the LORD; they must be cut off from their people.

**9** ' "When you reap the harvest of your land, do not reap to the very edges of your field or gather the gleanings of your harvest. **10** Do not go over your vineyard a second time or pick up the grapes that have fallen. Leave them for the poor and the foreigner. I am the LORD your God.

**11** ' "Do not steal.

---

11 The relationship between the Sinaitic Decalogue and Leviticus 19 has generated much discussion. See Gunjević, 'Leviticus', 128; Hartley, *Leviticus*, 308–12; Ko, *Leviticus*, 176–9; Levine, *Leviticus*, 124–5; Milgrom, *Leviticus 17–22*, 1596–602; Nihan, *From Priestly Torah*, 479.

12 Contrary to Milgrom, *Leviticus 17–22*, 1601, who states strongly, 'Thus I disagree . . . that the Decalogue is embodied in this chapter.'

'"Do not lie.

'"Do not deceive one another.

12 '"Do not swear falsely by my name and so profane the name of your God. I am the LORD.

13 '"Do not defraud or rob your neighbour.

'"Do not hold back the wages of a hired worker overnight.

14 '"Do not curse the deaf or put a stumbling-block in front of the blind, but fear your God. I am the LORD.

15 '"Do not pervert justice; do not show partiality to the poor or favouritism to the great, but judge your neighbour fairly.

16 '"Do not go about spreading slander among your people.

'"Do not do anything that endangers your neighbour's life. I am the LORD.

17 '"Do not hate a fellow Israelite in your heart. Rebuke your neighbour frankly so that you will not share in their guilt.

18 '"Do not seek revenge or bear a grudge against anyone among your people, but love your neighbour as yourself. I am the LORD.

19 '"Keep my decrees.

'"Do not mate different kinds of animals.

'"Do not plant your field with two kinds of seed.

'"Do not wear clothing woven of two kinds of material.

**a** 20 Or *be an enquiry*

As 19:3–19 teaches how the Decalogue is to be applied to the life of God's people in community, it progresses from relationships with parents (19:3a) to the Israel–God relationship (19:3b–8, 12, 19) and then to relationships within the community (19:9–18).[13] However, some of the commands from the Decalogue are not repeated word for word. Rather, some of the commands demonstrate how the prohibitions in the Decalogue are to be applied in everyday life. For instance, 19:16b–18 prohibits the Israelite from endangering his or her neighbour's life, followed by prohibitions against hating their fellow Israelites or seeking

13 Please note that this is a different order from the Decalogue, which progresses from the Israel–God relationship (19:2–11) to relationships within the household (verses 12, 14) and then to relationships within the community (19:13, 15–17).

revenge. At no point is the prohibition against murder from Exodus 20:13 repeated in Leviticus 19, but rather 19:16b–18 teaches the Israelites about what this prohibition looks like for every Israelite as they seek to be a holy people set apart for the LORD. However, there is one command in the Decalogue that is missing from 19:3–19, which is the seventh command against adultery. This omission is purposeful since 18:6–23 has already prohibited sexual behaviour that does not reflect God's purposes, including adultery.

However, there are also additional emphases, such as respecting what is holy to the LORD (19:5–7), providing for the poor in community (19:9–10), not cursing the deaf or putting a stumbling block in front of the blind (19:14), not perverting justice (19:15) and refraining from mixing different kinds of animals, seed and materials (19:19). With this last example in 19:19, the prohibitions against mixing kinds of animals, seed and materials is to teach the Israelites that part of respecting God's creation order is not mixing *within* the kind.[14] That is, the Israelites need to maintain distinctions within kinds (i.e., within animals or seeds), not just between the different kinds (i.e., between animals and humans). The reason 19:3–19 extends the commands and prohibitions beyond the topics addressed in the Decalogue is to accentuate that being holy to the LORD by how they relate to one another in community is not limited by the relational boundaries in the Decalogue. Instead, how they relate to one another must extend further than the Decalogue to include, for instance, honouring what is holy, caring for the vulnerable in community and ensuring that the community embodies justice in all relationships.

---

14 Ko, *Leviticus*, 181, who follows Milgrom, *Leviticus 17–22*, 1659; Sklar, *Leviticus*, 247–8.

## Repairing sexual offence against a neighbour (19:20–22)

Verses 20–22 depict a situation that resembles adultery. This situation may cause discomfort for readers as the case involves a slave and seems to devalue her. For this reason, this situation is placed into context so that we can grasp the intent of the instructions.

**20** ' "If a man sleeps with a female slave who is promised to another man but who has not been ransomed or given her freedom, there must be due punishment.[a] Yet they are not to be put to death, because she had not been freed. **21** The man, however, must bring a ram to the entrance to the tent of meeting for a guilt offering to the LORD. **22** With the ram of the guilt offering the priest is to make atonement for him before the LORD for the sin he has committed, and his sin will be forgiven.

The situation begins in 19:20 with a man engaging in sexual relations with a female slave (i.e., a concubine). There are five assumptions within this situation. First, the man is an Israelite. Second, the slave is not an Israelite and is a foreigner (see 25:44–46). Third, the slave belongs to the household of the Israelite man. The situation continues to unfold in 19:20 with the added complication that the slave woman is promised in marriage to another man. For this marriage to take place, the slave needs to be freed, but this redemption has not yet taken place since the Israelite has not received the ransom payment. A fourth assumption is that the marriage is not to a slave within the same household. Finally, a fifth assumption is that the guilt offering in 19:21–22 includes a financial penalty to the offended neighbour. Curiously, there is no penalty for the woman. This is a vital observation. As a slave, her agency is diminished in this situation.[15]

15 Also, Ko, *Leviticus*, 182.

There is much in this situation that could cause discomfort, irrespective of our cultural background. For instance, we are often confused as to why the LORD does not prohibit slavery in the Israelite community. Moreover, this situation suggests that the LORD permits sexual relations between an Israelite man and a slave woman who belongs to his household when she is not promised in marriage to another. The offence in this instance is that his sexual engagement transgresses her future marriage relationship.

With regard to the first issue, the explanation of Leviticus 25 discusses further the issue of slavery and the LORD's purposes in permitting slaves in Israel. However, to address the second issue, it is good for us to understand the kind of law that 19:20–22 represents. It is a different kind of law from, for example, 19:18. Verse 18 is made up of two prohibitions and one command. The two prohibitions, which are not to seek revenge or bear a grudge, are not dependent on a situation being true. They are principles of law that are black and white, and their purpose is to communicate what is and what is not acceptable. However, the consequence described in 19:20–22 is dependent on the situation at the beginning being true, which is that a man sleeps with a concubine who is promised in marriage to another man. This initial situation is descriptive and explains the particulars of the situation that determines the consequence of the offence. When a situation is described like this, the intent of the law is not to give permission, but rather the purpose is to restrain harm when a situation like this arises because God's covenant people are still a people stained by sin. God's instructions are often very real about the extent of his people's brokenness in order to restrain further harm by instructing consequence when that situation arises. In this instance, the harm being restrained is the enactment of the death penalty. In other case law within the Pentateuch where a woman *willingly* engages in a sexual relationship with a man who is not her husband and where she is betrothed to another, both are to be put to death (Deuteronomy 22:22–24). This case law protects the woman, who has diminished agency in this situation, from the death penalty, and so the purpose of this case is to mitigate harm. While 19:20 restrains the use of the death penalty in this particular situation, there is an acknowledgment that there must be a just punishment. Rather than the death penalty, the man is to bring a guilt offering to the LORD so that there is reparation for the wrongful sexual relation that has offended the man's neighbour.

## Honouring the Lord in the land of promise (19:23–32)

The LORD's instructions in 19:23–32 focus on honouring the LORD as their covenant God as they enter and settle into the land.

**23** ' "When you enter the land and
plant any kind of fruit tree, regard its
fruit as forbidden.[b] For three years
you are to consider it forbidden;[b] it
must not be eaten. **24** In the fourth
year all its fruit will be holy, an
offering of praise to the LORD. **25** But
in the fifth year you may eat its fruit.
In this way your harvest will be
increased. I am the LORD your God.
**26** ' "Do not eat any meat with the
blood still in it.
' "Do not practise divination or seek
omens.
**27** ' "Do not cut the hair at the sides
of your head or clip off the edges of
your beard.
**28** ' "Do not cut your bodies for the
dead or put tattoo marks on your-
selves. I am the LORD.
**29** ' "Do not degrade your daughter
by making her a prostitute, or the
land will turn to prostitution and be
filled with wickedness.
**30** ' "Observe my Sabbaths and have
reverence for my sanctuary. I am the
LORD.
**31** ' "Do not turn to mediums or
seek out spiritists, for you will be
defiled by them. I am the LORD your
God.
**32** ' "Stand up in the presence of the
aged, show respect for the elderly
and revere your God. I am the LORD.

b 23 Hebrew *uncircumcised*

The topics addressed in 19:23–32 are far ranging. Verses 23–25 instruct the Israelites not to eat the produce from the fruit trees for the first three years, after which all the fruit is to be given to the LORD as a gift of praise (19:24) in the fourth year (19:23). Following the fourth year, they are free to eat fruit from the trees (19:25). Verses 26–29 and 31 prohibit practices that are characteristic of the Canaanites, and which are often connected with idolatry. Verse 29 is connected to this topic since prostitution is commonly integrated within Canaanite worship. An Israelite is not to give his daughter over to prostitution since to do so would be to ruin the condition of the land, and it is implied that there will be consequence since the LORD cannot dwell amid a land filled with wickedness. In this context, 19:30 and 31 accentuate how the Israelites are to honour the LORD as their covenant God. They are to observe his Sabbaths and have respect for his sanctuary that dwells in their midst. Verse 32 repeats the verb 'to reverence' when relating the command to respect the elderly with revering their covenant God. How the Israelites relate to their elderly directly reflects how they relate to their God.

## Israel's relational conduct is to be shaped by their redemption (19:33–37)

In this final paragraph, the LORD grounds his commands in Israel's memory of Egypt (19:34) and in his identity as their covenant God who redeemed them from slavery (19:36). These commands address two areas of Israel's relational conduct as they live in the land of promise: how they relate to resident foreigners (19:33–34) and justice (19:35–36).

**33** ' "When a foreigner resides among you in your land, do not ill-treat them. **34** The foreigner residing among you must be treated as your native-born. Love them as yourself, for you were foreigners in Egypt. I am the LORD your God.

**35** ' "Do not use dishonest standards

when measuring length, weight or
quantity. **36** Use honest scales and
honest weights, an honest ephah[c]
and an honest hin.[d] I am the LORD
your God, who brought you out of
Egypt.
**37** ' "Keep all my decrees and all
my laws and follow them. I am the
LORD." '

c 36 An ephah was a dry measure having the capacity of about 22 litres.
d 36 A hin was a liquid measure having the capacity of about 3.8 litres.

The focus in 19:33–34 is how Israel is to relate to resident foreigners. This topic begins in 19:33 with a prohibition about what the Israelites are not to do, which is followed by a command about what they are to do (19:34). A resident foreigner is someone from another nation (other than Canaan) *and* who is living among the Israelite community. In the situation of the resident foreigner, Israel is their host culture and so they are among a people not their own. Moreover, the ancient Near East is an honour/shame culture where it is honourable for a people group to extend hospitality to free people living among them. What the Israelites experienced in Egypt was a failure of hospitality (Exodus 1–2). Leviticus 19:33–34 is grounded in this memory of being enslaved. The prohibition in 19:33 is a command for Israel not to repeat the failures of Egypt by mistreating and oppressing resident foreigners living among them in the land of promise. Instead of oppression, 19:34 commands the Israelites to treat resident foreigners as though they are Israelites. They are to love them as Israelites because 'you were foreigners in Egypt'. The Israelites know what it is like to live in a host culture and so they are to love the resident foreigner as though they were one of their own (i.e., 'native-born').

Verses 35–36 follow the same pattern as 19:33–34, which is a prohibition followed by a command focusing on justice in community. In an agrarian context where crops and livestock are food on the table for your household, there would be a temptation to adjust the weights so that less is given for the money paid. Alternatively, a farmer might be selling grain or livestock to a merchant and the merchant might be tempted to take more than he would pay the farmer. Verse 35 prohibits such behaviour so that people are paid what they are fairly owed and that others get what they pay for. For this reason, 19:36 instructs the Israelites to use honest scales and weights. Verse 36 concludes with the refrain declaring the LORD's identity as their covenant God ('I am the LORD') who redeemed the Israelites out of Egypt. They were redeemed by justice and so they are to be a people whose behaviour is just. How the Israelites relate to others within their wider community is to reflect the character and work of the God to whom they belong.

## Moving forward into the New Testament

I was strolling to a café midmorning on a Sunday. My eyes were drawn to a homeless man sitting ten metres from a church entrance, his back against a metal fence, legs drawn up and his head on his knees. Then I heard the lyrics, 'He lifted me up from the miry clay.' There was something broken about this scene. A homeless man, who was hungry and whose body language cried out 'hopelessness', was hearing the words of the gospel through song, yet he did not walk through the doors of the church to be enveloped in warmth and to be given a hot drink and food to eat. As I walked through those same church doors later that day for the evening gathering, I was heartbroken by what I heard. It was mission Sunday, and the lead pastor was clear: the purpose of the church was to proclaim the gospel; it was not to engage in feeding the homeless in the local community.

In the west, the conservative Evangelical Church has prided itself on the ministry of the word and the proclamation of the gospel. Yet it has diminished the gospel in action through radical hospitality and justice shaped by the remembrance of Jesus's death and resurrection. I wonder if we emphasise words over gospel-embodied action in community because we have a partiality towards reaching the educated middle and upper classes where there is no need to sit on dusty pavements, against an uncomfortable fence, offering a hot drink to a man who has not showered for months and who might not be polite. We struggle to find people in our churches to visit and to sit with the elderly in homes that are within striking distance of our buildings. Our foster care agencies are desperate to find homes for vulnerable children when most of us have spare rooms and seats at our family tables. We wonder if the Sabbath still applies today because we harbour a culturally acceptable idol: busyness. My plea to the church in the Global South is not to become like the western church in these ways. Embody just hospitality that is cross shaped and which conforms to the holiness of our LORD.

The message of Leviticus 19 is as true for the community in Christ as it was for the Israelite community waiting to enter the land of promise. We have been redeemed by justice in the death and resurrection of Jesus and we are called to conform to the holiness of our LORD in all that we are – our character, our actions, our desires and our speech. We are to ensure that the LORD Jesus is sanctified by our actions in community and in the world.

How do we do this? The same ways as in Leviticus 19, which is ensuring that our actions embody his purposes for his covenant people. This means embodying the principles of loving God, loving our neighbour and going further than the ten commands in the Decalogue to embody hospitality and justice in community. Why do we do this? For the same motivation, which is the memory that Jesus is our God whose life ransomed us from the powers of darkness to belong to him as his people. His blood formed us as a community to serve him under his kingship.

What might this community look like? A community that serves from rest; where outsiders are regularly invited to share meals at family tables; where foster children are present and belong in kids' and youth programmes; where our elderly are remembered, belong and are respected within community; where outsiders can find refuge and welcome; where members of the church are known in their work contexts for dealing fairly; and where neighbours are loved just as we love people within our own church community. Jesus does not call solely our words to embody the gospel, but our whole lives as a community as a means of loving God and loving our neighbour (see Matthew 22:36–40), which is at the very crux of Leviticus 19.

## *3. Consequences of relational disorder • Leviticus 20*

Leviticus 18–19 instructed the Israelites about how to conform to the holy status of their covenant God through their relational behaviour in the household, within community and with the LORD. In this context, the purpose of Leviticus 20 is to list the penalties for relational offences that are a cause of relational impurity and which follow the ways of the Canaanites. Leviticus 20 unfolds in three stages of logic: penalty for idolatry (20:1–8), penalties for relational offence (20:9–21) and Israel's responsibility to make the distinction between relational purity and relational impurity (20:22–27).

*Punishments for sin*

**20** The LORD said to Moses,
**2** 'Say to the Israelites: "Any
Israelite or any foreigner residing in
Israel who sacrifices any of his chil-
dren to Molek is to be put to death.
The members of the community are
to stone him. **3** I myself will set my
face against him and will cut him
off from his people; for by sacrificing
his children to Molek, he has defiled
my sanctuary and profaned my
holy name. **4** If the members of the
community close their eyes when
that man sacrifices one of his chil-
dren to Molek and if they fail to put
him to death, **5** I myself will set my
face against him and his family and
will cut them off from their people
together with all who follow him in
prostituting themselves to Molek.

**6** ' "I will set my face against anyone

who turns to mediums and spiritists
to prostitute themselves by following
them, and I will cut them off from
their people.

7 ‘“Consecrate yourselves and be
holy, because I am the LORD your
God. 8 Keep my decrees and follow
them. I am the LORD, who makes
you holy.

9 ‘“Anyone who curses their father
or mother is to be put to death.
Because they have cursed their
father or mother, their blood will be
on their own head.

10 ‘“If a man commits adultery with
another man's wife – with the wife of
his neighbour – both the adulterer
and the adulteress are to be put to
death.

11 ‘“If a man has sexual relations
with his father's wife, he has dishon-
oured his father. Both the man and
the woman are to be put to death;
their blood will be on their own
heads.

12 ‘“If a man has sexual relations
with his daughter-in-law, both of
them are to be put to death. What
they have done is a perversion; their
blood will be on their own heads.

13 ‘“If a man has sexual relations
with a man as one does with a
woman, both of them have done
what is detestable. They are to be
put to death; their blood will be on
their own heads.

14 ‘“If a man marries both a woman
and her mother, it is wicked. Both
he and they must be burned in the
fire, so that no wickedness will be
among you.

15 ‘“If a man has sexual relations
with an animal, he is to be put to
death, and you must kill the animal.

16 ‘“If a woman approaches an
animal to have sexual relations with
it, kill both the woman and the ani-
mal. They are to be put to death;
their blood will be on their own
heads.

17 ‘“If a man marries his sister, the
daughter of either his father or his
mother, and they have sexual rela-
tions, it is a disgrace. They are to be
publicly removed from their people.
He has dishonoured his sister and
will be held responsible.

18 ‘“If a man has sexual relations
with a woman during her monthly
period, he has exposed the source of
her flow, and she has also uncovered
it. Both of them are to be cut off from
their people.

19 ‘“Do not have sexual rela-
tions with the sister of either your
mother or your father, for that would
dishonour a close relative; both of
you would be held responsible.

**20** ' "If a man has sexual relations
with his aunt, he has dishonoured
his uncle. They will be held respon-
sible; they will die childless.

**21** ' "If a man marries his brother's
wife, it is an act of impurity; he has
dishonoured his brother. They will
be childless.

**22** ' "Keep all my decrees and laws
and follow them, so that the land
where I am bringing you to live
may not vomit you out. **23** You must
not live according to the customs
of the nations I am going to drive
out before you. Because they did
all these things, I abhorred them.
**24** But I said to you, 'You will possess
their land; I will give it to you as
an inheritance, a land flowing with
milk and honey.' I am the LORD your
God, who has set you apart from
the nations.

**25** ' "You must therefore make
a distinction between clean and
unclean animals and between
unclean and clean birds. Do not
defile yourselves by any animal or
bird or anything that moves along
the ground – those that I have set
apart as unclean for you. **26** You are
to be holy to me because I, the LORD,
am holy, and I have set you apart
from the nations to be my own.

**27** ' "A man or woman who is a
medium or spiritist among you must
be put to death. You are to stone
them; their blood will be on their
own heads." '

Without introduction, the LORD launches straight into the penalty for idolatry in 20:2b. Applied to both the Israelite and the resident foreigner alike, the LORD declares that anyone in the community that sacrifices their children to Molek is to be put to death (see also 18:21). Verses 2c–5 accentuate the responsibilities of the community and of the LORD when the death penalty for idolatry is to be enacted. The community is to stone the offender (20:2c) and the LORD will revoke his favour from him (20:3). Verses 4–5 then address community failure to acknowledge the offence committed within Israel: the LORD will revoke his favour from the community and cut them off from Israel. Those who fail to enact the penalty will suffer the same consequence as the offender. By refusing to acknowledge the offence of child sacrifice to Molek, the community is complicit in the offence and so are guilty too.

Verse 3c evinces why child sacrifice cannot be tolerated. Such a practice causes the LORD's dwelling place to be 'defiled' to a condition of impurity, and the holy cannot be in the presence of impurity. Moreover, the LORD's holy name is profaned by such a practice. Both priests and Israelites have the responsibility to ensure that the LORD is glorified and sanctified in the midst of Israel, and the practice of child sacrifice to Molek is contrary to this responsibility as the LORD's covenant people. Similarly, any Israelites who participate in the Canaanite practice of ancestral worship, through mediums and spiritists, are actively being unfaithful to the LORD and so are acting in such a way that is contrary to their identity as a people set apart to belong to the LORD. For this reason, 20:6 declares a penalty for anyone who participates in this practice.

Verses 7–8 shift focus from the prohibited practices associated with idolatry (20:2b–6) to who they are to be as a people belonging to the LORD. Verse 7 begins with two commands: 'Consecrate yourselves and be holy.' The reason the Israelites should adhere to these commands is that the one commanding is the LORD their God. As we saw in Leviticus 8–10, to consecrate is to be set apart and, in this context, Israel is to be set apart to belong to the LORD. As a people who are holy to the LORD, they are to conform who they are and what they do to the LORD's status – of being holy. Verse 8 then follows with a further two commands, which are the imperatives to keep the LORD's decrees and to follow them. The motivation for their obedience is that the giver of these instructions is their covenant God who makes them holy. Thus, it is not solely Israel's responsibility to conform to the LORD's status of being holy by following the LORD's ways, but it is also God's work as he sets them apart, which he did as he redeemed them from Egypt (Exodus 7–18), made a covenant with them (Exodus 19–24) and set his dwelling place in their midst (Exodus 25–40).

The list of penalties for relational offences in 20:9–21 begins with two fundamental relationships within the household and which are a major cause of relational disorder when those relationships go awry: children and parents (20:9) and husband and wife (20:10).[16] The first command in 20:9 instructs the Israelites to put to death anyone who curses their father or mother. Previously, in 19:3, the LORD has commanded the Israelites to respect their mother and father, which echoes the fifth command in the Decalogue. To curse is to wish harm on another, and this is the opposite of respect and honour. Thus, anyone in the Israelite community who speaks words of harm against their parents is to experience what they desired: death. The clause, 'their blood will be on their own head', conveys that the offender will bear the penalty for their own guilt. There is no sacrifice that will bear the penalty on behalf of the offender. The second command in 20:10 then addresses the consequence of adultery where a man engages in consensual sexual activity with a woman who is not his wife. The consequence is that both are to be put to death (see also Deuteronomy 22:22–29).

Verses 11–21 declare penalties for relational offences of a sexual nature and where those sexual offences affect the cohesion of the household. There are, however, a couple of exceptions interspersed throughout the list, such as 20:13 and 20:15, where the former declares the death penalty for men engaged in same-sex sexual activity and the latter declares the same for the Israelite who engages in sexual activity with an animal. Within the list, the majority of penalties are the death penalty, and while the cumulative effect of the declarations can be overwhelming for the hearer, these declarations are a reminder that there is no provision of sacrifice for these offences.[17] Another will not die to take the guilt of those who participate in causing relational

16 Milgrom, *Leviticus 17–22*, 1745, observes, 'Without respect for parents, all other family relationships are liable to collapse.' To this, I would add that family relationships are 'liable to collapse' when marriage relationships are dishonoured.

17 The way in which the instructions are grouped suggests that the type of penalty shapes the arrangement, rather than the kind of offence or the identity of the offenders. See also Milgrom, *Leviticus 17–22*, 1742; Sklar, *Leviticus*, 254.

disorder among God's people, and neither will another life die to purify those who caused impurity by their actions. There is no restoration to God's presence. Such is the seriousness of relational offence that is a cause of impurity in the Israelite community. Thus, the death penalty and the penalty of exile (see 20:18) have a purifying purpose. By shedding the blood of those responsible, or removing them into exile where that is permitted, the Israelite community is removing the cause of impurity from their midst.

After the list of penalties in 20:9–21, 20:22–24 persuades the Israelites to follow the LORD's instructions and to resist following Canaanite practices. The first reason is to avoid being vomited from the land. That is, a motivation towards obedience is ensuring that they, as a nation, do not suffer the same penalty of death and exile that the Canaanites suffered (see explanation of 18:24–30). The second reason is that the LORD 'abhorred' the Canaanites because of their actions (20:23b). The implied warning of 20:23 is that if they do not resist, then the LORD will abhor them too.

At the conclusion of 20:24, the LORD declares who he is and what he has done for the Israelites. The LORD has not set Israel apart from the nations to become like them by following their practices. Instead, he has set Israel apart from the nations to conform to his status of being holy, and this requires the Israelites to follow his ways. A practical outworking of what conforming to the LORD's status looks like is making the distinction between purity and impurity. Verse 25 refers to Leviticus 11:43–45 with the command to make the distinction between pure and impure animals and birds, as well as the prohibition not to defile themselves with the animals, birds and crawling things that the LORD has set apart as impure. Remembering Leviticus 11, the purpose of this distinction in the domain of food was to teach the Israelites about what is associated with purity and impurity so that the Israelites will learn to choose what is pure and avoid what is impure.[18] This is exactly the teaching goal of Leviticus 18–20, which is to instruct the Israelites to choose what is pure, to follow the LORD's instructions and to avoid impurity – the practices of the Canaanites. By choosing what is pure and resisting that which is impure, the Israelites are set apart to belong to the LORD as a holy people. For this reason, the LORD reminds the Israelites in 20:26, 'You are to be holy to me because I, the LORD, am holy, and I have set you apart from the nations to be my own.' The LORD redeemed Israel not to be free, but to be set apart to belong to him as his covenant people.

Some readers might wonder why 20:27 occurs at the end of the chapter. It seems out of place considering 20:22–26 provides a fitting conclusion not only to Leviticus 20 but also to Leviticus 18–20. Old Testament authors tend to like bookends where the conclusion of a passage shares a thematic connection with the passage's introduction (see Leviticus 18). It is likely that the reason 20:27 appears at the conclusion is to form this concluding bookend and so make a thematic connection to the speech's beginning in 20:2–8.

## Moving forward into the New Testament

The list of penalties in Leviticus 20 is confronting. There is no provision for atonement for these offences. The guilty must bear the penalty for their own guilt and they must be removed to purify the community. The very nature of these penalties makes us uncomfortable. One reason for our discomfort is that the list confronts us with the penalty that our own actions deserve.

---

18 The food laws then become an analogy for how the LORD separated Israel from the nations to embody a pure condition (e.g., by following God's instructions) and by separating themselves from that which is associated with impurity (i.e., the ways of the Egyptians and the Canaanites). See also Walter Houston, 'Towards an Integrated Reading of the Dietary Laws of Leviticus', in *The Book of Leviticus: Composition and Reception*, edited by Rolf Rendtorff and Robert A. Kugler (Leiden: Brill, 2003), 158.

The apostle Paul is very clear in Romans 6:23: 'the wages of sin is death'. None of us is blameless, especially in light of Jesus's teaching in the Sermon on the Mount that accentuates our guilt for so much as lusting after another (Matthew 5:27–30). Guilt is not just incurred by actions but by our desires too. If it all depended on us, we are all dead in our sin, and there would be no hope of reconciliation with God.

But God does not leave us in the hopeless position of being guilty. In his generous mercy, he provided a means of atonement where there was none under the law in Leviticus, through the blood of Jesus shed for us. His sacrifice atoned for the penalty we deserve and purifies us from our impurity. The second part of Romans 6:23 says, 'but the gift of God is eternal life'. As new covenant believers we do not need to carry around guilt and shame, because Jesus invites us to unburden ourselves and find refuge in him. He can do this because he is both our sacrifice and our great high priest. By trusting in the sufficiency of Jesus's blood for our sinfulness, we can have confidence before the throne of God because the crucified and risen Lamb is present. What do we need to do? Approach the throne of grace trusting in the sufficiency of Jesus's blood for us, confessing how we have desired and acted contrary to God's purposes, and turn away from those desires towards desiring the purposes of the living God. For those in Christ, your penalty is forgiven and you have peace with God.

# 7

# The Holy Shall Not Be Profaned

## LEVITICUS 21–22

Leviticus 21–22 is the second part to Leviticus 18–20. Leviticus 18–20 instructed Israel about how they are to conform to the LORD's status of being holy by ensuring that their relational conduct aligns with God's purposes for his people. Leviticus 21–22 continues this theme but with a very specific focus. While Leviticus 18–20 addressed relational conduct within the whole community, Leviticus 21–22 instructs the priesthood about how they are to embody their holy status and avoid profaning the LORD's sanctuary where they are privileged to serve.

### *1. The priesthood shall be holy to the LORD • Leviticus 21:1–15*

While the priests are expected to embody the LORD's instructions in Leviticus 18–20, there are additional expectations because they alone serve the LORD in his sanctuary.[1] Leviticus 21:1–15 addresses these expectations for the relational conduct of priests when they are bereaved (21:1–6, 10–12) and who they are to marry (21:7–8, 13–15). The theme that ties the two topics together is that of the family household.

---

1 Ko, *Leviticus*, 193.

### *Rules for priests*

**21** The LORD said to Moses,
'Speak to the priests, the
sons of Aaron, and say to them: "A
priest must not make himself cere-
monially unclean for any of his people
who die, **2** except for a close relative,
such as his mother or father, his son or
daughter, his brother, **3** or an unmar-
ried sister who is dependent on him
since she has no husband – for her
he may make himself unclean. **4** He
must not make himself unclean for
people related to him by marriage,[a]
and so defile himself.

**5** ' "Priests must not shave their
heads or shave off the edges of their
beards or cut their bodies. **6** They
must be holy to their God and must
not profane the name of their God.
Because they present the food offer-
ings to the LORD, the food of their
God, they are to be holy.

**7** ' "They must not marry women
defiled by prostitution or divorced
from their husbands, because priests
are holy to their God. **8** Regard them
as holy, because they offer up the
food of your God. Consider them
holy, because I the LORD am holy –
I who make you holy.

**9** ' "If a priest's daughter defiles
herself by becoming a prostitute,
she disgraces her father; she must
be burned in the fire.

**10** ' "The high priest, the one
among his brothers who has had the
anointing oil poured on his head and
who has been ordained to wear the
priestly garments, must not let his
hair become unkempt[b] or tear his
clothes. **11** He must not enter a place
where there is a dead body. He must
not make himself unclean, even for
his father or mother, **12** nor leave the
sanctuary of his God or desecrate it,
because he has been dedicated by
the anointing oil of his God. I am
the LORD.

**13** ' "The woman he marries must
be a virgin. **14** He must not marry
a widow, a divorced woman, or a
woman defiled by prostitution, but
only a virgin from his own people,
**15** so that he will not defile his
offspring among his people. I am the
LORD, who makes him holy." '

[a] 4 Or *unclean as a leader among his people*
[b] 10 Or *not uncover his head*

The LORD's instructions to Aaron and his sons begin with the topic of bereavement in 21:1–6. Verse 1 introduces the general principle.[2] By being in contact with the dead, even if related by marriage, a priest would knowingly make himself impure (21:4), which he is not to do since he serves the LORD in his presence in the sanctuary. Verses 2–3, however, make an exception for his mother, father, brother or unmarried sister. Yet while there is permission to participate in the funeral rites of close relatives (21:2), there are cultural practices for grieving that the priest must not follow. These practices would alter the appearance of his body, which is contrary to his status as holy to his God. By participating in these practices, the priest would profane the LORD's holy name, that is, he would be treating the LORD as though he were common rather than holy.

The priests must maintain their holy status, which is needed to fulfil their role of mediating Israel's food gifts to the LORD in his presence (21:8). However, 21:10–12 restricts the high priest from being in the same physical space as a dead body. He has a greater responsibility to ensure he avoids impurity (21:12).

The second topic addressed is the issue of whom the priests and high priest can marry (21:7–8, 13–15). Verse 7 prohibits a priest from marrying a woman who is divorced or who has become impure by prostitution, and the reason for this prohibition is his status as being holy to God.[3] Verse 8 repeats the reason they are to maintain their holy status: 'because they offer up the food of your God'. The LORD has conformed them to his holy status and so the priesthood are to embody being holy. The instructions for the priesthood more broadly are concluded in 21:9 with a tangent connected by the issue of prostitution.

2 Ko, *Leviticus*, 193.

3 Please note that this explanation of 21:7 is based on the Hebrew text. The NIV suggests that the woman who is divorced is also defiled, not just the woman who has been a prostitute. However, in the Hebrew text, it is solely the woman who has participated in prostitution that is defiled. For this reason, the explanation above reverses the order of prostitution and then divorce so that there is clarity and avoids confusion.

Verse 9 addresses the situation where a priest's daughter becomes impure by becoming a prostitute. While the NIV translates the impact on the priest (i.e., her father) as 'she disgraces her father', the idea of the Hebrew is that she has profaned her father. To profane is to be transformed from a holy status to being common. The impact of his daughter's conduct is that she has undone his consecration as a priest holy to the LORD and he now has the status of every Israelite, which is common. The penalty for the daughter is that she must be burned by fire, which is an act of purification.

The instructions for the high priest, however, differ from those for the other priests (21:13, 14b–c). He is to marry a girl who is of a marriageable age, who has not engaged in sexual activity with another and who must be a Levite. The implication of this command is that the high priest is forbidden in 21:14a to marry a widow, as well as a divorced woman. By marrying a virgin from his own people, the high priest ensures that future generations remain pure because the LORD has made him holy. The reason prostitution is emphasised both in 21:7–8 and 21:13–15 is that cultic prostitution is a significant Canaanite practice, and so it is implied that the priests and the high priests are not to replicate the practices of Canaanite priests.

While 21:1–15 sounds demanding and restrictive, these instructions accentuate the serious responsibility of the priesthood as they offer the Israelites' gifts before the LORD and in his presence. The LORD desires to be near his people, but to enable this to happen with the life of God's people preserved, he has appointed a priesthood to serve him and to mediate between himself and the Israelites so that God's covenant people can approach him. A vital part of the privilege of mediating Israel's gifts to the LORD is that they are holy because the LORD has made them holy.

## *2. The blemished priest shall not serve before the LORD • Leviticus 21:16–24*

Throughout the gift instructions in Leviticus 1–7, a crucial characteristic for a gift to be acceptable before the LORD is that the offering needed to be without blemish. That is, it needs to have physical integrity. Having explored Leviticus 11, we can understand the reason for this characteristic since being in a pure condition is associated with what is complete and whole. However, what happens when a priest, who serves before the LORD, has a disability that affects his physical appearance? Verses 16–24 address this situation.

**16** The LORD said to Moses, **17** 'Say
to Aaron: "For the generations to
come none of your descendants
who has a defect may come near to
offer the food of his God. **18** No man
who has any defect may come near:
no man who is blind or lame, disfig-
ured or deformed; **19** no man with a
crippled foot or hand, **20** or who is a
hunchback or a dwarf, or who has
any eye defect, or who has festering
or running sores or damaged testi-
cles. **21** No descendant of Aaron the
priest who has any defect is to come
near to present the food offerings to
the LORD. He has a defect; he must
not come near to offer the food of
his God. **22** He may eat the most holy
food of his God, as well as the holy
food; **23** yet because of his defect,
he must not go near the curtain or
approach the altar, and so desecrate
my sanctuary. I am the LORD, who
makes them holy." '
**24** So Moses told this to Aaron and
his sons and to all the Israelites.

The LORD's instructions begin in 21:17 with the general principle, which is that none of Aaron's descendants, whose birthright would be to serve as a priest, may offer gifts before the LORD if he has a physical disability. To emphasise this principle, the command is repeated in 21:18a and 21:21. The NIV translates the Hebrew term as 'defect'. In the discussion of the gift instructions, we noted that a more helpful term is 'blemish'.[4] The idea is that the priest's body does not appear as God created the human body. Examples of these 'blemishes' are given in 21:18b–20. From these instructions, the idea is reinforced that only the complete and the whole can approach God's presence, that is, those whose outward appearance represents a pure condition are accepted before the LORD.[5] This is the reason the priest's presence would desecrate the LORD's sanctuary (21:23b). His physical appearance represents an impure condition because of the association with incompleteness or a body that is not whole. The assumption is that he would still be consecrated as a priest but would serve in the role of a Levite. By being consecrated as a priest, he has access to the priestly food portions (21:22).

For the person with a physical disability, especially a disability named in 21:18–20, this passage might be quite difficult. He or she is all too aware that their disability is not something they have control over and so may feel uncomfortable with the idea that a priest would be excluded from serving in God's presence because of their disability. In today's western world, where culturally there is a social imperative to make accommodation for people with disabilities so that there is inclusion (and rightfully so!), 21:16–24 seems discordant and at odds with western culture. It is vital, however, to remember two aspects of this passage. First, these instructions pertain to the priests who are a small subsection of the Israelite community. Where they have access and how they serve the LORD is only open to a few. There is already inclusion and exclusion even among the Levites. Second, apart from this few, every Israelite is excluded from this kind of access and service. The boundary marking where 'every Israelite'

4 See discussion of Leviticus 1:3–16.

5 As both Chingota, 'Leviticus', 162, and Ko, *Leviticus*, 196–7, clarify, the incompleteness of the priest's outward appearance is not about the moral character of the priest.

can enter is a reminder that no one is without blemish, and it takes the death of an animal without blemish for an Israelite to enter the outer court. Even with this sacrifice, 'every Israelite' can go no further. This knowledge is what makes Jesus's work on the cross even sweeter. When the curtain tore in two, with God accepting his atoning sacrifice on our behalf, everyone who is washed in the blood of the Lamb can now approach the LORD, and moreover the Spirit is given without distinction between those with a disability and those without. God has given his Spirit as a down payment of our imperishable inheritance where God will permanently restore his presence among his covenant people, and there will be no more barriers to the joy of being in God's presence (Revelation 21–22).[6]

### *3. Respect the holy • Leviticus 22:1–16*

A shared responsibility between the Israelite people and the priesthood is to ensure that the LORD's name is glorified in the midst of the community. A critical way for the priesthood to fulfil this responsibility is by treating the holy gifts of the Israelites with respect and by refraining from profaning the name of the LORD.

**22** The LORD said to Moses,
**2** 'Tell Aaron and his sons
to treat with respect the sacred offer-
ings the Israelites consecrate to me,
so that they will not profane my holy
name. I am the LORD.
**3** 'Say to them: "For the generations
to come, if any of your descendants is
ceremonially unclean and yet comes
near the sacred offerings that the

6 For a more in-depth exploration of 21:16–24 as a person with a disability, see Katherine Smith, 'Should the Local Church Resist Texts in Scripture that Clash with Western Culture? The Test Case of Leviticus 21:16–24', *Themelios* 45.1 (2020).

Israelites consecrate to the LORD, that person must be cut off from my presence. I am the LORD.

**4** '"If a descendant of Aaron has a defiling skin disease[a] or a bodily discharge, he may not eat the sacred offerings until he is cleansed. He will also be unclean if he touches something defiled by a corpse or by anyone who has an emission of semen, **5** or if he touches any crawling thing that makes him unclean, or any person who makes him unclean, whatever the uncleanness may be. **6** The one who touches any such thing will be unclean till evening. He must not eat any of the sacred offerings unless he has bathed himself with water. **7** When the sun goes down, he will be clean, and after that he may eat the sacred offerings, for they are his food. **8** He must not eat anything found dead or torn by wild animals, and so become unclean through it. I am the LORD.

**9** '"The priests are to perform my service in such a way that they do not become guilty and die for treating it with contempt. I am the LORD, who makes them holy.

**10** '"No one outside a priest's family may eat the sacred offering, nor may the guest of a priest or his hired worker eat it. **11** But if a priest buys a slave with money, or if slaves are born in his household, they may eat his food. **12** If a priest's daughter marries anyone other than a priest, she may not eat any of the sacred contributions. **13** But if a priest's daughter becomes a widow or is divorced, yet has no children, and she returns to live in her father's household as in her youth, she may eat her father's food. No unauthorised person, however, may eat it.

**14** '"Anyone who eats a sacred offering by mistake must make restitution to the priest for the offering and add a fifth of the value to it. **15** The priests must not desecrate the sacred offerings the Israelites present to the LORD **16** by allowing them to eat the sacred offerings and so bring upon them guilt requiring payment. I am the LORD, who makes them holy."'

---

**a** 4 The Hebrew word for *defiling skin disease,* traditionally translated 'leprosy', was used for various diseases affecting the skin.

If a priest offers Israel's gifts to the LORD while knowing he is in an impure condition, this would be dishonouring the holy because the priest knows that to be impure requires temporary exclusion from the sanctuary. Impurity cannot come into the presence of the holy. A vital way in which a priest can respect the holy is by offering Israel's gifts solely when he is in a pure condition. Leviticus 22:1–16 addresses this topic by exhorting the priesthood not to approach with gifts offered by the Israelites (22:3) and not to eat the food portions (22:4–9) while they are in an impure condition. The topic of eating continues in 22:10–16 with instructions prohibiting anyone to eat the priestly food portions other than those that the LORD has permitted. The theme that ties the whole section together is summarised in 22:2: 'treat with respect the sacred offerings the Israelites consecrate to me, so that they will not profane my holy name'.

## 4. *Offering gifts that are acceptable on behalf of the gift-giver* • *Leviticus 22:17–30*

So far, the LORD's message in 21:1–22:16 has focused solely on the priesthood. However, 22:17–30 addresses the Israelite community more broadly. The theme of the passage is connected to 21:1–22:16 in two ways. First, 22:17–30 continues the theme of respecting the holy that has been developed throughout 21:1–22:16. Second, 22:17–30 focuses on the topic of Israel's gifts for the LORD, which was the topic of 22:1–16.

*Unacceptable sacrifices*

**17** The LORD said to Moses,
**18** 'Speak to Aaron and his sons and
to all the Israelites and say to them:
"If any of you – whether an Israelite
or a foreigner residing in Israel –
presents a gift for a burnt offering to
the LORD, either to fulfil a vow or as a
freewill offering, **19** you must present
a male without defect from the cattle,
sheep or goats in order that it may
be accepted on your behalf. **20** Do
not bring anything with a defect,
because it will not be accepted on
your behalf. **21** When anyone brings
from the herd or flock a fellowship

offering to the LORD to fulfil a special
vow or as a freewill offering, it must
be without defect or blemish to be
acceptable. **22** Do not offer to the
LORD the blind, the injured or the
maimed, or anything with warts or
festering or running sores. Do not
place any of these on the altar as a
food offering presented to the LORD.
**23** You may, however, present as a
freewill offering an ox[b] or a sheep
that is deformed or stunted, but it
will not be accepted in fulfilment of
a vow. **24** You must not offer to the
LORD an animal whose testicles are
bruised, crushed, torn or cut. You
must not do this in your own land,
**25** and you must not accept such ani-
mals from the hand of a foreigner
and offer them as the food of your
God. They will not be accepted
on your behalf, because they are
deformed and have defects." '

**26** The LORD said to Moses,
**27** 'When a calf, a lamb or a goat is
born, it is to remain with its mother
for seven days. From the eighth day
on, it will be acceptable as a food
offering presented to the LORD. **28** Do
not slaughter a cow or a sheep and
its young on the same day.

**29** 'When you sacrifice a
thank-offering to the LORD, sacri-
fice it in such a way that it will be
accepted on your behalf. **30** It must
be eaten that same day; leave none
of it till morning. I am the LORD.

**b** 23 The Hebrew word can include both male and female.

Verse 18 introduces a situation where an Israelite or resident foreigner draws near with a gift for a burnt offering to the LORD. The motivation for the gift is either to fulfil a vow (e.g., Hannah's offering in 1 Samuel 1:11–25) or as a freewill offering. The LORD reminds the Israelites in 22:19 about the characteristics of the gift that are required for acceptance:[7] it needs to be

7 Please note that the issue at stake is not that the characteristic of 'without defect' (NIV) is a central attribute of holiness, but rather that the criterion for acceptance into God's presence is that which is 'complete' or 'whole'. It is more likely that the Hebrew term translated by the NIV as 'without blemish' is central to the domain of purity as a condition rather than holiness, which is about status. Contrary to Douglas, *Purity and Danger*, 64–5; Milgrom, *Leviticus 17–22*, 1873.

male, 'without defect' and from specific kinds of livestock. Verse 19 repeats the LORD's instructions for the burnt offering from 1:2–3, 10. In the explanation of 1:3–9, we noted that the NIV's translation 'without defect' is not helpful. The Hebrew term *tāmim* is a positive term meaning 'whole' and 'to have integrity'.[8] The gift must be complete as opposed to being broken, marked or having a blemish. The gift-giver must actively choose a gift that embodies these characteristics, a bull that is whole, so that the gift can be accepted on the gift-giver's behalf.[9]

While the Hebrew of 22:19 describes the characteristics positively – male, whole and from livestock – that the gift must embody, 22:20 presents the same idea but as a prohibition about what the gift must not be. The Israelite must not bring anything that has a blemish (NIV 'defect'). Similarly, 22:21 applies the same logic from 22:19–20 to the fellowship offering. This time, however, both descriptions are used: it must be whole (*tāmim*) and therefore without blemish. The term translated as 'blemish' in 22:20 and here in 22:21 is the Hebrew *mûm*, which means 'spot, blemish, injury'. Again, the NIV's translation is not helpful as it has certain connotations within the English language (e.g., what is defective is to be rejected). The thrust of the prohibition is a command for the Israelites to avoid bringing what is injured. Verse 22 gives an example of these injuries, which include blindness, injury that maims, warts or festering sores. Verse 22 then repeats the sentiment of 22:19–21: livestock, which have these conditions, must not be placed on the altar as a food offering for the LORD. Verses 23–25 continue this theme

8 Also, Ko, *Leviticus*, 200.

9 Ko, *Leviticus*, 200, also brings the idea of economic inefficiency into the discussion of being with blemish/being without blemish. Again, this passage is not about economic efficiency but rather only that which is in a pure condition (i.e., complete and whole) is acceptable in the LORD's holy presence. We must take care, even in contextual readings, not to inadvertently bring our cultural bias into the meaning of the text.

of injuries or conditions for a gift that are either acceptable (22:23) or unacceptable (22:24–25).

While language such as 'defect' and 'blemish' may be uncomfortable, the repetition and ideas in this passage are significant. The LORD is teaching the Israelites about the nature of what is acceptable before him: that which is complete and whole. Anything less than what is complete and whole is not acceptable. The reason this is stressed is that the gift is to be sacrificed on behalf of the gift-giver. By giving over to death an animal that is complete and whole on behalf of the gift-giver, there is recognition that the animal is what the gift-giver is not: complete and whole. With the death of an animal that is whole, the gift-giver can approach the LORD. Moreover, by respecting the LORD's requirements for approaching him, the Israelite reveres the LORD as holy.

## *5. Honouring the LORD who is in the midst of Israel • Leviticus 22:31–33*

**31** 'Keep my commands and follow
them. I am the LORD. **32** Do not
profane my holy name, for I must
be acknowledged as holy by the
Israelites. I am the LORD, who made
you holy **33** and who brought you out
of Egypt to be your God. I am the
LORD.'

Verses 31–33 form a conclusion to Leviticus 21–22. The repetition of the self-declaration, 'I am the LORD,' is a reminder to the Israelites that he has the authority to set his instructions among them and to expect faithful obedience because of all that his name means and embodies. Verse 32a exhorts the Israelites not to profane his holy name, that is, to treat his name as common, because of who the LORD is. Verse 32b gives the reason for revering the LORD's name: 'for I must be acknowledged as holy by the Israelites'. The Hebrew can also be translated another way, 'for

I will be sanctified in the midst of Israel'. Israel's responsibility is to ensure that the Lord is sanctified in their midst, otherwise the consequence will be that the Lord will sanctify himself. Verse 32 concludes by highlighting the mutuality of the Israel–Lord relationship.[10] Israel is to ensure the Lord is sanctified in their midst in response to the Lord having made Israel holy.

## Moving forward into the New Testament

As a people gathered under the new covenant, we no longer ensure that God's name is sanctified by treating priests and sacrifices as holy, but rather by treating the body of Christ, the priesthood of believers, as holy. This is more so because we no longer need to ensure that a physical tabernacle remains holy as God's dwelling place; the body of Christ is God's tabernacle, with his Spirit dwelling among us. Moreover, we are to treat the body of Christ as holy because Jesus has made his church holy. So the same teaching from Leviticus 21–22 applies, which is that we can by our words and actions treat the body of Christ as common by not respecting the body's holy status. We can allow, for instance, conflict to cause chaos, we can adopt doctrine that conforms to the culture around us instead of conforming to Jesus's ways, or we can be lukewarm about being part of the body. For example, we fit gathering together around our children's activities as though it is just another thing that we do in our week that needs to be juggled. This is treating the body of Christ as common. The same warning applies. If we fail to treat the body of Christ as holy, then God will act in discipline to sanctify himself, and we see this is true from the seven churches addressed in Revelation 1–3.

10 See Reinhard Müller, 'The Sanctifying Divine Voice: Observations on the אני יהוה-Formula in the Holiness Code', in *Text, Time, and Temple: Literary, Historical and Ritual Studies in Leviticus*, edited by Francis Landy, Leigh M. Trevaskis and Bryan D. Bibb (Sheffield: Sheffield Phoenix, 2015), 82.

While we are a people saved by grace, this does not mean that we treat lightly what God has made holy. By ensuring that we uphold the holy status of the people to whom we belong, we are ensuring that Jesus's name is sanctified in the midst of the body of Christ and in the midst of a watching world.

# 8

# Israel's Celebrations and Feasts

## LEVITICUS 23

Continuing the theme of respecting the holy, the LORD exhorts the Israelites in Leviticus 23 to observe five festal days: the Sabbath (23:3), the Passover (23:5–8), the firstfruits of the harvest (23:9–22), the Day of Atonement (23:23–32) and the Feast of Booths, or Shelters (23:33–36). The four festivals in 23:5–36 form the shape of Israel's calendar.[1] Ko writes:

> Rather than determining feasts because of natural phenomena, such as the phases of the moon or the changing of the tides, the sacred calendar helps Israelites to remember God's salvific acts, his covenant and divine grace. Since these acts and concepts reflect the collective memory of the whole Israelite nation, the calendar is fixed among Jews.[2]

### *1. The Sabbath* • *Leviticus 23:1–3*

Leviticus 23 has two introductions. The first in 23:2 announces that the following festal days are appointed by the LORD and are to be proclaimed as holy. The Sabbath instructions follow afterwards in 23:3. A second introduction in 23:4 introduces the other four festal days in 23:5–36. A likely reason that

1 Ko, *Leviticus*, 203.
2 Ko, *Leviticus*, 203.

the Sabbath is set apart from the other festal days by having its own introduction is that the Sabbath is a recurring festal day throughout the Israelite year. The following four feasts, however, occur once a year and are arranged in 23:4–44 in chronological order.[3]

*The appointed festivals*

**23** The LORD said to Moses, **2** 'Speak to the Israelites and say to them: "These are my appointed festivals, the appointed festivals of the LORD, which you are to proclaim as sacred assemblies.

*The Sabbath*

**3** ' "There are six days when you may work, but the seventh day is a day of sabbath rest, a day of sacred assembly. You are not to do any work; wherever you live, it is a sabbath to the LORD.

The LORD exhorts the Israelites in 23:3 to work for six days and then rest as a Sabbath on the seventh day (Exodus 20:8–11; 31:15; 35:2–3). While we take it for granted that the seventh day is the last day of the week, the idea is that the seventh day signifies completion. The Israelites are to cease work to mark the completion of the week's cycle, just as God rested on the seventh day to mark the completion of his creative activity (Genesis 2:2–3). By resting to culminate the week, the Israelites depend on their covenant God for provision rather than relying on their own efforts and labours.

## 2. *The LORD's Passover • Leviticus 23:4–8*

Verses 4–8 summarise the instructions for the Passover Feast from Exodus 12–13. In Exodus 12, future generations are exhorted to celebrate the Passover annually. The purpose of the Passover is to remember how the LORD preserved the life of the Israelite

3 Sklar, *Leviticus*, 277, 284; Wenham, *Leviticus*, 300.

firstborns by passing over the households where blood was on the entrance, while he brought justice against the Egyptians (12:24–30).

*The Passover and Unleavened Bread*
**4** ' "These are the LORD's appointed
festivals, the sacred assem-
blies you are to proclaim at their
appointed times: **5** the LORD's
Passover begins at twilight on the
fourteenth day of the first month.
**6** On the fifteenth day of that month
the LORD's Festival of Unleavened
Bread begins; for seven days you
must eat bread made without yeast.
**7** On the first day hold a sacred
assembly and do not do any of your
ordinary work. **8** For seven days
present a food offering to the LORD.
And on the seventh day hold a sacred
assembly and do not do any of your
ordinary work." '

In Leviticus 23:5, the LORD reminds the Israelites that they are to share the roasted lamb, bitter herbs and unleavened bread as a household at twilight on the fourteenth day of the first month as the Passover Feast (see Exodus 12:1–8). The next day, the Israelites are to begin celebrating the Feast of Unleavened Bread, where they remember how they were hurried by the Egyptians so that they had to carry dough before it had an opportunity to rise. To remember how they left Egypt, the Israelites are instructed to eat bread where there is no rising agent added, such as yeast, for seven days (Leviticus 23:6).

## *3. The firstfruits of each harvest • Leviticus 23:9–22*

The Sabbath (verse 3) and Passover (23:9–22) are festal days that can be celebrated irrespective of where the Israelites are geographically – when they are at Sinai, when travelling to the land or when they have settled in the land of promise. However, the third festival is dependent on the LORD giving the Israelites the land of promise (23:10). In anticipation of the LORD making good on his promise, 23:19–21 instructs the Israelites to give to the LORD the firstfruits of their harvest. This harvest celebration occurs in two stages, 23:10–14 and 23:15–21, and is a costly festival for the Israelites.

*Offering the Firstfruits*

**9** The LORD said to Moses, **10** 'Speak to the Israelites and say to them: "When you enter the land I am going to give you and you reap its harvest, bring to the priest a sheaf of the first grain you harvest. **11** He is to wave the sheaf before the LORD so it will be accepted on your behalf; the priest is to wave it on the day after the Sabbath. **12** On the day you wave the sheaf, you must sacrifice as a burnt offering to the LORD a lamb a year old without defect, **13** together with its grain offering of one fifth of an ephah[a] of the finest flour mixed with olive oil – a food offering presented to the LORD, a pleasing aroma – and its drink offering of a quarter of a hin[b] of wine. **14** You must not eat any bread, or roasted or new grain, until the very day you bring this offering to your God. This is to be a lasting ordinance for the generations to come, wherever you live.

*The Festival of Weeks*

**15** ' "From the day after the Sabbath, the day you brought the sheaf of the wave offering, count seven full weeks. **16** Count fifty days up to the day after the seventh Sabbath, and then present an offering of new grain to the LORD. **17** From wherever you live, bring two loaves made of one fifth of an ephah of the finest flour, baked with yeast, as a wave offering of firstfruits to the LORD. **18** Present with this bread seven male lambs, each a year old and without defect, one young bull and two rams. They will be a burnt offering to the LORD, together with their grain offerings and drink offerings – a food offering, an aroma pleasing to the LORD. **19** Then sacrifice one male goat for a sin offering[c] and two lambs, each a year old, for a fellowship offering. **20** The priest is to wave the two lambs before the LORD as a wave offering, together with the bread of the firstfruits. They are a sacred offering to the LORD for the priest. **21** On that same day you are to proclaim a sacred assembly and not do any ordinary work. This is to be a lasting ordinance for the generations to come, wherever you live.

22 ' "When you reap the harvest of your land, do not reap to the very edges of your field or gather the gleanings of your harvest. Leave them for the poor and for the foreigner residing among you. I am the LORD your God." '

a 13 That is, probably about 3.2 kilograms; also in verse 17

b 13 That is, about 1 litre

c 19 Or *purification offering*

The first stage, in 23:10–14, begins with a sheaf of the first grain being given to the priest so that it can be waved before the LORD (23:10b–11). Offering a whole sheaf of the first harvest is not a small amount. A sheaf is a bundle of grain stalks, including ears of grain, tied so that each can be stacked to dry. As well as the bundle of grain, the Israelite is instructed to present a burnt offering (23:12), a cereal offering and a drink offering (23:13). The explanation of this first stage is concluded in 23:14 with a prohibition not to eat from the harvest of the new grain until they bring this gift of the new harvest to the LORD. This acknowledges that the harvest ultimately is provided by the LORD and belongs to him.

The second stage revolves around the offering of a second gift of new grain to the LORD on the ninety-ninth day (seven weeks plus fifty days) after the first stage (23:16). This time, however, the grain has been dried and processed, ready to be made into bread. In 23:17, the LORD instructs the Israelites to present the gift of new grain as two loaves of bread, each made with one-fifth of an ephah and with yeast. An ephah is approximately ten days' food and so one-fifth is the food equivalent of two days. Again, this is not an insignificant gift. Moreover, the costliness is further emphasised by the instruction to present seven male lambs as burnt offerings (23:18), a male goat for a sin offering (23:19a) and two lambs for a fellowship offering (23:19b–20). Offering gifts from the new harvest is costly as the Israelites acknowledge that their provisions ultimately belong to the LORD and are also given by him.

While on the topic of firstfruits, 23:22 instructs the Israelites to leave the edges and their gleanings as provision for others in the wider community.[4] In an agrarian economy where land ownership is essential for food supply to the household, there will be those in the wider community who do not own land to harvest and who are likely to be vulnerable. Verse 22 names two such groups. The first are the poor, who are unlikely to be reaping their own harvest, and the second are the resident foreigners who are immigrants permanently settled among the Israelites. This final instruction for the harvest is a reminder not to ignore the physical needs of those who are vulnerable within the community but to offer hospitality by making food provision available.

## 4. *The Day of Atonement* • *Leviticus 23:23–32*

The fourth festal day in 23:23–32 is the Day of Atonement. These instructions do not repeat the particulars from Leviticus 16, nor the meaning of the holy festival day. Rather, 23:23–32 seeks to ensure that the Israelites respect the Day of Atonement as a day set apart for the Lord.

*The Festival of Trumpets*

**23** The Lord said to Moses, **24** 'Say to
the Israelites: "On the first day of the
seventh month you are to have a day
of sabbath rest, a sacred assembly
commemorated with trumpet blasts.
**25** Do not do any of your ordinary
work, but present a food offering to
the Lord." '

*The Day of Atonement*

**26** The Lord said to Moses, **27** 'The

4 Please note that 23:22 is a repetition of 19:9–10 and this repetition emphasises God's provision for the poor and the resident foreigners among the Israelites. See also Hartley, *Leviticus*, 374; Ko, *Leviticus*, 210; Milgrom, *Leviticus 23–27*, 2010; Sklar, *Leviticus*, 284.

tenth day of this seventh month is the Day of Atonement. Hold a sacred assembly and deny yourselves,[d] and present a food offering to the LORD.
**28** Do not do any work on that day, because it is the Day of Atonement, when atonement is made for you before the LORD your God. **29** Those who do not deny themselves on that day must be cut off from their people. **30** I will destroy from among their people anyone who does any work on that day. **31** You shall do no work at all. This is to be a lasting ordinance for the generations to come, wherever you live. **32** It is a day of sabbath rest for you, and you must deny yourselves. From the evening of the ninth day of the month until the following evening you are to observe your sabbath.'

**d** 27 Or *and fast*; similarly in verses 29 and 32

Verse 23 begins with the command to have a Sabbath rest on the first day of the seventh month, which is to be marked with trumpet blasts. While no reason is given explicitly for this Sabbath, the implied reason is to acknowledge that this is the month where atonement will be made for the whole community.

Verse 27 echoes 16:29–31 to impress on the Israelites that the Day of Atonement is a holy festal day where they are to humble themselves before the LORD, bringing a food offering to him as they gather with the community for the Day of Atonement sacrifices. A part of humbling themselves before the LORD is that they cease work from the evening of the ninth day to the evening of the tenth day so that they can focus on the significance of atonement being made for the community (23:28, 31–32). The act of resting from work is of such importance that the failure to do so results in a double penalty: the Israelites are to exile the offending Israelite from the community (23:29) and the LORD himself promises to act against the person by causing them to perish from among their people (23:30).

## 5. *The Feast of Shelters • Leviticus 23:33–36, 39–43*

Leviticus 23:33–44 is the first time within the Pentateuch that the Lord provides instructions for the Feast of Shelters. I have chosen to translate the Hebrew name for this festival as the 'Feast of Shelters' rather than preferring the NIV's translation 'Feast of Tabernacles', for two reasons. First, when we read 'Tabernacles', this translation is already associated with the Lord's dwelling place from Exodus 25–40. Second, the Hebrew term for 'tabernacle' is different from that which is used in 23:33–44 to refer to the temporary shelters that the Israelites made when they travelled out of Egypt and into the wilderness on their way to Sinai (Exodus 12–19). These shelters are not mentioned within the Exodus narrative. However, the Lord's explanation for this festival in Leviticus 23:42–43 makes this connection when he instructs the Israelites, who are members of the community, to live in shelters for seven days during the festival. This command reminds the first and future generations how they lived in shelters when the Lord brought them out of Egypt. As Ko notes, 'They in effect re-experience their life of temporary dwelling in order to remember their history as God's covenantal people and also God's gracious salvation.'[5]

*The Festival of Tabernacles*

**33** The Lord said to Moses, **34** 'Say
to the Israelites: "On the fifteenth
day of the seventh month the Lord's
Festival of Tabernacles begins, and it
lasts for seven days. **35** The first day
is a sacred assembly; do not do any
of your ordinary work. **36** For seven
days present food offerings to the
Lord, and on the eighth day hold a
sacred assembly and present a food
offering to the Lord. It is the closing
special assembly; do not do any of
your ordinary work.

**39** ' "So beginning with the fifteenth
day of the seventh month, after you

5 Ko, *Leviticus*, 211.

have gathered the crops of the land,
celebrate the festival to the LORD for
seven days; the first day is a day of
sabbath rest, and the eighth day also
is a day of sabbath rest. **40** On the first
day you are to take branches from
luxuriant trees – from palms, willows
and other leafy trees – and rejoice
before the LORD your God for seven
days. **41** Celebrate this as a festival to
the LORD for seven days each year.
This is to be a lasting ordinance for
the generations to come; celebrate
it in the seventh month. **42** Live in
temporary shelters for seven days:
all native-born Israelites are to live in
such shelters **43** so that your descen-
dants will know that I made the
Israelites live in temporary shelters
when I brought them out of Egypt. I
am the LORD your God." '

**44** So Moses announced to the Isra-
elites the appointed festivals of the
LORD.

Leviticus 23:34–36 and 23:39 focus on the duration of the festival (seven days plus one day). The first part of the festival lasts seven days from the fifteenth day of the seventh month, only five days after the Day of Atonement. Like the Passover, the first day of the festival is to be declared holy and the Israelites are to cease from doing work on that first day (23:35, 39). While the Israelites are permitted to resume work for the following six days of the festival, they are instructed to bring drink offerings to the LORD leading up to the eighth day (the second part of the festival), which is also to be declared as holy. Work is to be ceased on that eighth and final day (23:36, 39).

Leviticus 23:40–43 explains what is to happen during the first seven days of the festival. In 23:40, the LORD describes how they are to take branches from majestic trees that are leafy and green, and rejoice for seven days before the LORD. The mention of trees with abundant leaves echoes Exodus 15:22–27 where, after their experience at Marah with bitter water, the Israelites camped at Elim with its twelve springs of water and seventy palm trees. The Festival of Shelters is a celebration of the LORD's provision as they travelled out of Egypt and towards Sinai.

## *6. Concluding summaries • Leviticus 23:37–38, 44*

**37** (' "These are the LORD's
appointed festivals, which you are
to proclaim as sacred assemblies
for bringing food offerings to the
LORD – the burnt offerings and grain
offerings, sacrifices and drink offer-
ings required for each day. **38** These
offerings are in addition to those
for the LORD's Sabbaths and[e] in
addition to your gifts and whatever
you have vowed and all the freewill
offerings you give to the LORD.)

**44** So Moses announced to the Isra-
elites the appointed festivals of the
LORD.

e 38 Or *These festivals are in addition to the LORD's Sabbaths, and these offerings are*

A conclusion to the chapter in 23:37–38 suddenly occurs in the middle of the instructions for the Feast of Shelters. Verse 37 announces that 'these are the LORD's appointed festivals', which refers to all four festivals described in 23:4–43. Each is to be proclaimed as holy for the bringing of food gifts to the LORD. The message to the Israelites is that they are to adhere to these festivals as an outworking of respecting the holy. However, a second conclusion to the chapter occurs in 23:44 where the narrator notes that Moses obediently announced all these instructions to the first generation of Israelites and for the sake of all future generations too.[6]

### MOVING FORWARD INTO THE NEW TESTAMENT

Let us be honest. Reading Leviticus 23, we might be a bit stumped about how we look forward into the New Testament and to the 'here and now'. We are reading instructions for festivals that

6 See also Rooker, *Leviticus*, 281, who states, 'The chapter closes (23:44) with the declaration that Moses had announced the appointed feasts to the Israelites. Clearly the chapter is a unified whole.'

are no longer mandated by our LORD to observe. So how do we embody these instructions as God's new covenant people? There are three big picture points to note.

First, we are no longer required to celebrate the Passover and the Day of Atonement because each is fulfilled in Jesus's crucifixion and resurrection.[7] However, we are instructed by the LORD Jesus to observe the LORD's Supper as our feast (Matthew 26:17–30), which remembers Jesus as our Passover Lamb and our Sacrifice of Atonement. The instructions for the Passover and the Day of Atonement remind us that when we approach the LORD's Supper, we are remembering Jesus's work on our behalf (past) that shapes our identity in the present and our future. Therefore, it is a holy feast where we joyfully humble ourselves in obedience to the LORD Jesus.

Second, while we are no longer commanded to observe the Sabbath day or the firstfruits festival, as Jesus is LORD of both (see Mark 2:23–28), it is good for us to observe the spirit of both the Sabbath and the firstfruits. Both festal days are about cultivating spiritual disciplines. With the Sabbath, it is good for us to set apart a day in our week to rest from work and to remember that God is sovereign, and we are not. This requires us to trust God with our work, with what is done and with what is not finished. In western culture, we prize hurriedness, busyness and productive efficiency, which cultivates self-dependence and the belief that what we earn is entirely due to our own productivity. While it is true that we get paid a salary for the job we do, ultimately our job and the food on our table is God's provision for us. Setting apart a Sabbath day is an antidote to our hurried

---

7 For a reading of how the Day of Atonement is fulfilled in Jesus's work on our behalf, see the explanation of Leviticus 16 in this commentary. For the Passover, see my forthcoming Exodus commentary in the Zondervan Exegetical Commentary on the Old Testament series: Katherine Davis, *Exodus: A Discourse Analysis of the Hebrew Bible* (Grand Rapids: Zondervan, 2027).

busyness and reminds us that we are dependent on our Sovereign God who superintends over all. This is like the firstfruits festival. The firstfruits festival is all about the Israelites recognising that their harvest is God's provision. It is a giving back to God what ultimately belongs to him and which he has given us. While some readers may live in an agrarian context, many of us do not. While I have fruit, vegetables and herbs growing in my garden, this is not our livelihood; our salaries are our livelihood.

In the spirit of the firstfruits festival, it is good for us to give a part of our livelihood (i.e., our salaries) to God by supporting gospel work in both the local and the global church. Moreover, a related habit that we could cultivate for those readers who experience plenty is to purposefully make leftover meals, freeze them and make them available through our local church for households that would be blessed by them. This too is a way of providing for those in our community who are struggling. Again, this is countercultural to our western values, but embodying the instructions of the firstfruits festivals helps us embody a different belief, which is that our daily provision ultimately belongs to God and he has given it to us. By cultivating this spiritual discipline, we are also embodying the LORD's Prayer: 'Give us today our daily bread,' where we acknowledge our dependence on God for daily provision.

Third, as we move forward into the New Testament, Paul also reinterprets the firstfruits festival as being fulfilled in Jesus's resurrection: 'But Christ has indeed been raised from the dead, the firstfruits of those who have fallen asleep' (1 Corinthians 15:20). In this reinterpretation by the apostle Paul, the firstfruits is a promise of what is to come. That is, Jesus as the first risen from the dead is the promise and guarantee that we will all be made alive in Christ (1 Corinthians 15:22). The festival of firstfruits, therefore, teaches us to have confidence that just as Jesus is the firstfruits from the dead, those who belong to him will also be raised to life through death.

# 9

# A Remembrance of Presence

## LEVITICUS 24:1–9

Leviticus 24:1–9 is a significant turning point in the book. Since Leviticus 11, the book has been concerned with how the Israelites are to conform to the holy status of their covenant God as the means by which they ensure his name is sanctified in their midst. Leviticus 24:1–9, however, changes direction as a signal that the book is ending. The focus of 24:1–9 is the presence of the LORD in the midst of Israel. The entirety of Leviticus is shaped by this holy presence and how the Israelites are to ensure this holy presence is glorified and sanctified. Verses 1–9 centre on God's continual presence (24:1–4) and how the LORD is to remember the Israelites among whom he is present (24:5–9).

*Olive oil and bread set before the LORD*

**24** The LORD said to Moses,
2 'Command the Israel-
ites to bring you clear oil of pressed
olives for the light so that the lamps
may be kept burning continually.
3 Outside the curtain that shields the
ark of the covenant law in the tent of
meeting, Aaron is to tend the lamps
before the LORD from evening till
morning, continually. This is to be a
lasting ordinance for the generations
to come. 4 The lamps on the pure
gold lampstand before the LORD
must be tended continually.
5 'Take the finest flour and bake
twelve loaves of bread, using one
fifth of an ephah[a] for each loaf.
6 Arrange them in two piles, six in
each pile, on the table of pure gold
before the LORD. 7 By each pile put
some pure incense as a memorial[b]
portion to represent the bread and
to be a food offering presented to
the LORD. 8 This bread is to be set out

before the LORD regularly, Sabbath after Sabbath, on behalf of the Israelites, as a lasting covenant. **9** It belongs to Aaron and his sons, who are to eat it in the sanctuary area, because it is a most holy part of their perpetual share of the food offerings presented to the LORD.'

a 5 That is, probably about 3.2 kilograms
b 7 Or *representative*

The LORD's instructions in 24:2–4 begin with a command to the Israelites to bring pressed olive oil so that it can be used to keep the light of the lamps burning continually (24:2). These lamps are placed on gold lampstands just outside the curtain that separates the sanctuary from the Most Holy Place where the LORD promises his presence will appear over the atonement cover on the Ark of the Covenant. For this reason, the lamps are described in 24:3 as being 'before the LORD'. Each verse repeats that the lamps need to be kept burning 'continually', and this is significant for understanding the reason for these instructions. These lamps, kept burning by oil that has been pressed to ensure its purity, represent the LORD's holy presence that is in Israel's midst.[1] Because the light symbolises the LORD's permanent presence among his people, the light of the lamps is always to be kept burning, and this is part of the high priest's responsibility.

Verse 5 shifts topic to the twelve loaves of bread. In 24:6–7, these twelve loaves are to be arranged before the LORD in two piles of six loaves (i.e., twelve loaves) and with incense

1 See also Gunjević, 'Leviticus', 134; Nobuyshi Kiuchi, *Leviticus* (Nottingham: Apollos, 2007), 437; Sklar, *Leviticus*, 287. Please note that this is a different understanding from that of Ko, *Leviticus*, 216–7: 'Light is the first thing that God creates (Gen 1:3–5), and it symbolizes God as the life-giver of all creation. When the priests bring the clear oil of pressed olives (i.e., fresh oil) to maintain the burning lamp (24:2), this ritual act acknowledges God as the creator of light that drives our anti-divine forces. This is symbolically compatible with the theology of God's name, which affirms the LORD's exclusive claim of sanctuary, where it will become dark if there is no light.'

placed before each pile. Each loaf represents an Israelite tribe. As the incense burns, the aroma of burning frankincense causes the LORD to remember the twelve tribes of Israel.[2] Verse 8 instructs the priesthood to set out these twelve loaves regularly before the LORD, on behalf of the Israelites, as an enduring covenant.

While 24:1–4 reminds the Israelites about the LORD's pure and holy presence in their midst, 24:5–9 describes how the LORD is to remember that he dwells among his covenant people, the twelve tribes of Israel. These two ideas within 24:1–9 shape the whole book. The whole book is established on the idea that the LORD dwells among his people. This is to shape Israel's identity and how they relate to one another in community with the LORD in their midst.

## Moving forward into the New Testament

Within the Old Testament, God's people neglected the truth time and again of the LORD's pure and holy presence in their midst. They either tried to use this presence as a magic talisman guaranteeing their triumph against their enemies (e.g., 1 Samuel 4) or they forgot that the LORD is pure in his holiness. They sought to place idols in the very place that bears his presence among them (Ezekiel 8–9). Either way, they profaned the purity of the LORD's holy presence among them. The consequence is as Leviticus 15:31 and 18:24–30 pre-empted. The LORD removed his presence from among his people (Ezekiel 10) and then he removed them from the land into exile, first the northern kingdom by the Assyrians (Amos 5; 2 Kings 17) and then the southern kingdom of Judah by the Babylonians (Ezekiel 11:1–13; 2 Kings 25). While the exiles

2 Also, Chingota, 'Leviticus', 164; Ko, *Leviticus*, 217; Jacob Milgrom, *Leviticus 23–27* (New York: Anchor, 2001), 2095. Contrary to Kiuchi, *Leviticus*, 438–9. This remembrance for the twelve tribes is so that the LORD will remember them favourably, as per Sklar, *Leviticus*, 290.

from Judah were restored to Jerusalem by the Persians and the Temple was rebuilt (Ezra–Nehemiah; Haggai), God's presence did not return to dwell among them as it once did (Ezra 6:13–18). This caused a dissonance between the beautiful vision in Ezekiel of the LORD's presence permanently dwelling among his people (Ezekiel 40:1–47:12) and their reality. This dissonance grew a conviction among the Jews that God would one day gloriously restore his presence among his people.

However, God's presence tabernacling among his people in the form of a human was not the spectacle the Jews were anticipating (John 1:1–18). Jesus was Immanuel, God with us, who, in the form of a servant, was crucified, yet was raised from the dead to break the power of death and sin. Because of Jesus's work as God with us, we who participate in his death and resurrection have an imperishable hope of God's covenant people being gathered in a new heaven and new earth with God's presence being permanently restored among us (Revelation 21–22). We experience a foretaste of this permanent dwelling with God's presence dwelling in and among us by his Spirit (Ephesians 1:13; 2:19–22). God's presence that dwells among us by his Spirit is that same pure and holy presence. This truth is to shape our present. It shapes how we conduct ourselves in the 'already and not yet', which is exemplified in Leviticus's instructions. It also shapes how we anticipate the imperishable future that God has prepared for us by honouring this holy presence in our midst as we live and work in the world.

Leviticus 24:5–9 also points to a need for a permanent reminder in God's presence of whom he dwells among, and this is the role of Jesus our Great High Priest. As our representative before God's throne of grace, he is the reminder, in God's heavenly throne room, of his covenant people whom Jesus has purified through his own blood (Hebrews 9:11–15).

10

# Warning: Cursing the Name of the LORD

## LEVITICUS 24:10–23

The message that has shaped Leviticus to this point is summarised in 10:3 and 22:32, which is that the LORD is to be sanctified and glorified amid the Israelite community. Leviticus 17–22 emphasised that both the priesthood and the Israelites are to ensure that they do not profane the LORD's holy name. They are not to treat the LORD, with all that his name embodies, as common.

But what happens if the LORD's name is not only profaned but worse – cursed? After being reminded that the LORD's holy and pure presence is among them in 24:1–9, this is a critical question that needs to be resolved before the book concludes. Leviticus 24:10–23 addresses this question and uses the opportunity to instruct the Israelites about the nature of justice within the community.

### *1. The penalty for cursing the LORD's name • Leviticus 24:10–16*

As the Israelites were leaving Egypt in Exodus 12:37–39, the narrator comments that 'many other people went up with them', that is, those who left were not only Israelites. While they resided in Egypt, it is likely that the Israelites intermarried with those outside the Israelite community and Israelite women were treated like slaves within Egyptian households. With the latter scenario, the Israelite women would have diminished agency over their bodies, and they may have borne children as concubines. In 24:10, we are introduced to a son of an Israelite mother and an Egyptian father. The narrator does not comment on whether the son's mother and father are married, whether the father joined the Israelites in their exodus out of Egypt or if the mother bore the son in a concubine relationship in Egypt. The text focuses solely on the status of the son as half Israelite and half Egyptian as he gets into a fight with an Israelite, blasphemes the LORD's name and utters a curse.

*A blasphemer put to death*

**10** Now the son of an Israelite
mother and an Egyptian father went
out among the Israelites, and a fight
broke out in the camp between him
and an Israelite. **11** The son of the
Israelite woman used the Name
blasphemously with a curse; so they
brought him to Moses. (His mother's
name was Shelomith, the daughter
of Dibri the Danite.) **12** They put him
in custody until the will of the LORD
should be made clear to them.
**13** Then the LORD said to Moses:
**14** 'Take the blasphemer outside the
camp. All those who heard him are
to lay their hands on his head, and
the entire assembly is to stone him.
**15** Say to the Israelites: "Anyone who
curses their God will be held respon-
sible; **16** anyone who uses the name
of the LORD blasphemously is to be
put to death. The entire assembly
must stone them. Whether foreigner
or native-born, when they use the
Name blasphemously they are to be
put to death.

We are not told in 24:11 whom the son uttered a curse against, and neither are we privy to how precisely the son blasphemed. However, 24:15 suggests that the act of blaspheming and the act of cursing were the same by depicting the son cursing God. By uttering a curse against God, the son profaned the name of the LORD in the midst of the community. The immediate consequence in 24:11–12 is that the son is brought to Moses and placed under custody until Moses gains clarity about the nature of the penalty to be incurred by the son's offence. The issue is not the kind of penalty for the offence, but rather the penalty in light of the offender's status of being half Israelite and half Egyptian.

The LORD clarifies the penalty in 24:14–16 and how this should be applied to the Israelite and the resident foreigner. The penalty is by stoning outside the camp (24:14) and, before he is stoned, those who heard him blaspheme are to press their hands on his head. By virtue of hearing God's name being cursed, they have been impacted by his offence and so by pressing their hands on the offender's head, they are identifying with him as he is stoned. The LORD conveys the guiding principle for anyone who curses God, whether the person be Israelite or resident foreigner, which is that they are to be put to death by stoning (24:15–16). Verses 15–16 have two purposes: first, to make explicit that there will be accountability for anyone who blasphemes God's name, and second, they will bear responsibility personally. That is, there will be no sacrifice bearing the responsibility of their guilt for them.

## 2. *Life for life: the* lex talionis • *Leviticus 24:17–22*

Verses 17–22 might appear odd for the reader. Verse 17 instructs the Israelite community to put to death anyone who takes the life of another human, which we might find bemusing. Is not stoning to death taking the life of a human? The apparent contradiction in 24:17 might jar. However, the death penalty in 24:10–16 is directed by God and so carries God's authority as the one who solely is sovereign over life and death. Only God can rightfully determine whether a person lives or dies. The command in 24:17, however, addresses the situation where a human has determined to take the life of another human and this incurs guilt, which in turn results in a penalty where life is taken for a life.[1] The scenario of the death penalty motivates the instructions in 24:17–22.

17 ' "Anyone who takes the life of a human being is to be put to death. 18 Anyone who takes the life of someone's animal must make restitution – life for life. 19 Anyone who injures their neighbour is to be injured in the same manner: 20 fracture for fracture, eye for eye, tooth for tooth. The one who has inflicted the injury must suffer the same injury. 21 Whoever kills an animal must make restitution, but whoever kills a human being is to be put to death. 22 You are to have the same law for the foreigner and the native-born. I am the LORD your God." '

The commands in 24:17–22 are based on the general principle of life for life. The penalty for taking a human life is death (24:17). If a person in the community kills a neighbour's animal, then the offender must make reparation in the form of life for life. This could be understood two ways. Either the person makes reparation by giving his or her neighbour an animal of equal value as a replacement, or an animal of equal value belonging to the offender is killed as a penalty. Since the idea of reparation is to make peace, the first option is most likely, where the offender offers an animal of an equal value and condition to his or her neighbour as reparation.

Verses 19–20 then address the situation where a person injures their neighbour. The consequence to the person injuring his or her neighbour is that the same injury is done to them. Verse 22 is clear that the principle of law being taught in 24:17–22 is the same for the Israelite and for the resident foreigner; there is to be no distinction.

1 The purpose of the *lex talionis* is to mitigate excessive penalties. Also, Bibb, *Ritual Words*, 155; Chingota, 'Leviticus', 164; Ko, *Leviticus*, 220; Milgrom, *Leviticus 23–27*, 2141; Wenham, *Leviticus*, 311–2.

### *3. Obedience modelled • Leviticus 24:23*

After 24:17–22 clarifies the penalties for those who harm others, 24:23 briefly resumes the narrative from 24:10–16.

**23** Then Moses spoke to the Israelites, and they took the blasphemer outside the camp and stoned him. The Israelites did as the LORD commanded Moses.

The hearer has been privy to the instructions that the LORD gave Moses in 24:14–16, but the question as to whether the Israelite community will take responsibility and carry out the death penalty remains unclear until 24:23. In 24:23, Moses mediates the LORD's instructions to the Israelites and they do as the LORD has commanded. Before the book concludes in Leviticus 25–27, the Israelites are portrayed as responding faithfully to the LORD's instructions. They take responsibility for enacting the death penalty when the LORD's name has been profaned, and implied is that all future generations are to adhere similarly to the LORD's instructions when his name is profaned in the Israelite community.

## Moving forward into the New Testament

As we move forward into the New Testament, the sinfulness of blaspheming Jesus's name, or blaspheming the Holy Spirit dwelling among God's people (Matthew 12:30–32), has not changed. It is still a deadly matter among the new covenant community. However, there is a significant development within biblical theology and under the new covenant. God's people are no longer bearers of executing God's justice against those who endanger the pure and holy status of God's people. We are called to trust that God will enact his justice, and this could be when Jesus returns, when he will hold to account all who slander God's name.

However, the new covenant community still has responsibility in the 'already and not yet' to discipline those in the body of Christ who malign the truth of the gospel, which I would also include in this category of blaspheming Jesus's name and blaspheming the Spirit, especially if the believer remains unrepentant. Although Jesus has paid the penalty of the law for us, this does not mean that we should let those among the new covenant community continue to curse, blaspheme or malign Jesus's name. This is where we can enact Jesus's instruction in Matthew 18:15–19, where we are to approach the believer about their sin on a one-to-one basis first and, in the instance where there is no repentance, then we are to bring witnesses to call the person to repentance. If there is no repentance, then the person is to be separated from the new covenant community until there is repentance in line with the truth of the gospel.

However, since the focus of the narrative is also on the resident foreigner blaspheming God's name, we need to consider those who are among the body of Christ and yet who are not believers cursing or maligning the name of Christ. This is not about the person on the street. This is someone who does not believe in Jesus and yet is present among the new covenant community maligning Jesus's name. On one hand, we need to extend grace as we do not wish to demand patterns of behaviour consistent with the gospel before they believe in Jesus. However, we can gently ask the person to desist from maligning Jesus's name as it is a name that is precious to the new covenant community. It is about respecting what the community respects and upholds. If done in both grace and truth, then we can model being saved by grace while maintaining the precious name of Jesus among the body of Christ.

However, between the beginning (24:10–16) and end of the narrative about the blaspheming son (24:23), we have instructions in 24:17–22 about enacting justice among the community when someone takes the life of another, whether it be another human or a neighbour's animal. Irrespective of the situation addressed, we learn about the seriousness of causing harm to our neighbour, and this should deter us from causing harm. However, when we are the injured party in a similar situation, Jesus calls us to surrender justice to God and not to take justice into our own hands. Moreover, a significant part of submitting to our governments is letting the secular legal process to be carried out without trying to enact justice ourselves. It is not a coincidence that Paul instructs the church in Rome not to repay evil for evil, but instead to rely on God's justice (Romans 12:17–21) just before he exhorts believers to submit to governing authorities (13:1–7). Part of being faithful as a covenant community is entrusting retributive justice to God when harm has been done.

## 11

# The Land and People Belong to the LORD

## LEVITICUS 25–26

The central message of Leviticus is that the LORD is to be glorified and sanctified in the midst of the Israelite community. One reason this is imperative is that the LORD's holy and pure presence dwells among them. While this reason remains a vital motivation, there are two other theological truths as to why it is imperative that the Israelites ensure that the LORD is glorified and sanctified in their midst as they live in the land. First, the land belongs to the LORD, and second, Israel belongs to the LORD. Leviticus 25 expounds these two theological truths and Leviticus 26 outlines the implications for Israel's obedience and their rebellion.

### 1. *The land belongs to the LORD • Leviticus 25:1–34*

Verses 2–34 anticipate the Israelites entering the land after God fulfils his promise to gift the land to his people (25:2b). This situation sets the context for the LORD's instructions in 25:2–34.

*The Sabbath Year*

**25** The LORD said to Moses
at Mount Sinai, 2 'Speak
to the Israelites and say to them:
"When you enter the land I am
going to give you, the land itself
must observe a sabbath to the LORD.
3 For six years sow your fields, and
for six years prune your vineyards
and gather their crops. 4 But in the

seventh year the land is to have a year of sabbath rest, a sabbath to the LORD. Do not sow your fields or prune your vineyards. **5** Do not reap what grows of itself or harvest the grapes of your untended vines. The land is to have a year of rest. **6** Whatever the land yields during the sabbath year will be food for you – for yourself, your male and female servants, and the hired worker and temporary resident who live among you, **7** as well as for your livestock and the wild animals in your land. Whatever the land produces may be eaten.

*The Year of Jubilee*

**8** ' "Count seven sabbath years – seven times seven years – so that the seven sabbath years amount to a period of forty-nine years. **9** Then sound the trumpet everywhere on the tenth day of the seventh month; on the Day of Atonement sound the trumpet throughout your land. **10** Consecrate the fiftieth year and proclaim liberty throughout the land to all its inhabitants. It shall be a jubilee for you; each of you is to return to your family property and to your own clan. **11** The fiftieth year shall be a jubilee for you; do not sow and do not reap what grows of itself or harvest the untended vines. **12** For it is a jubilee and is to be holy for you; eat only what is taken directly from the fields.

**13** ' "In this Year of Jubilee everyone is to return to their own property.

**14** ' "If you sell land to any of your own people or buy land from them, do not take advantage of each other. **15** You are to buy from your own people on the basis of the number of years since the Jubilee. And they are to sell to you on the basis of the number of years left for harvesting crops. **16** When the years are many, you are to increase the price, and when the years are few, you are to decrease the price, because what is really being sold to you is the number of crops. **17** Do not take advantage of each other, but fear your God. I am the LORD your God.

**18** ' "Follow my decrees and be careful to obey my laws, and you will live safely in the land. **19** Then the land will yield its fruit, and you will eat your fill and live there in safety. **20** You may ask, 'What will we eat in the seventh year if we do not plant or harvest our crops?' **21** I will send you such a blessing in the sixth year that the land will yield enough for three years. **22** While you plant during the eighth year, you will eat from the old crop and will continue to eat from

it until the harvest of the ninth year
comes in.

**23** ' "The land must not be sold
permanently, because the land
is mine and you reside in my
land as foreigners and strangers.
**24** Throughout the land that you hold
as a possession, you must provide for
the redemption of the land.

**25** ' "If one of your fellow Israelites
becomes poor and sells some of their
property, their nearest relative is to
come and redeem what they have
sold. **26** If, however, there is no one
to redeem it for them but later on
they prosper and acquire sufficient
means to redeem it themselves,
**27** they are to determine the value
for the years since they sold it and
refund the balance to the one to
whom they sold it; they can then go
back to their own property. **28** But
if they do not acquire the means to
repay, what was sold will remain in
the possession of the buyer until the
Year of Jubilee. It will be returned
in the Jubilee, and they can then go
back to their property.

**29** ' "Anyone who sells a house in
a walled city retains the right of
redemption a full year after its sale.
During that time the seller may
redeem it. **30** If it is not redeemed
before a full year has passed, the
house in the walled city shall belong
permanently to the buyer and the
buyer's descendants. It is not to be
returned in the Jubilee. **31** But houses
in villages without walls round them
are to be considered as belonging
to the open country. They can
be redeemed, and they are to be
returned in the Jubilee.

**32** ' "The Levites always have the
right to redeem their houses in the
Levitical towns, which they possess.
**33** So the property of the Levites is
redeemable – that is, a house sold
in any town they hold – and is to be
returned in the Jubilee, because the
houses in the towns of the Levites are
their property among the Israelites.
**34** But the pasture-land belonging to
their towns must not be sold; it is
their permanent possession.

The LORD announces in 25:2c that the land is to observe a Sabbath to the LORD. Verses 3–7 describe what this Sabbath is to look like for the land. Just as the Israelites are to refrain from work on the seventh day of the week as a day set apart for the LORD, so too the land is to set apart the seventh year for the LORD as an 'expression of its relationship to Yahweh'.[1] Allowing the land to rest requires trust from the Israelites that the LORD will provide what they need for the seventh year, just like they need to trust the LORD that he will provide for the six days leading to their Sabbath rest on the seventh day. As an outworking of this trust, the Israelites are to refrain from planting seed or pruning vineyards during this seventh year (25:4b).

While the Israelites may not purposefully plant seeds or prune their vines, the land itself may grow some harvest and the vines may produce grapes. Verse 5 prohibits the Israelites from harvesting during the seventh year for economic gain. Sandra Richter explains:

> What is being described here is the practice of 'fallowing' – allowing a ploughed and tilled field to remain unseeded during a growing season. Not only does this ancient practice aid the recovery of soil fertility, but it also breaks the natural cycle of species-specific pests and diseases that result when a single crop is repeatedly cultivated in that same field . . . the Sabbath mandate in Israel's agricultural system limited short-term yield but helped to ensure long-term productivity.[2]

However, 25:6–7 gives permission for the Israelites to eat within the community whatever the land yields within that seventh year. There are no exceptions to who can eat of the produce; there is to be provision for everyone in the community.[3] No one is to be stopped from sharing in the land's abundance.

---

1 Christopher J. H. Wright, 'What Happened Every Seven Years in Israel? Old Testament Sabbatical Institutions for Land, Debts and Slaves Part 1', *Evangelical Quarterly* 56 (1984): 132.

2 Sandra L. Richter, *Stewards of Eden: What Scripture Says About the Environment and Why it Matters* (Downers Grove: IVP, 2020), 22, 23.

3 Contrary to Ko, *Leviticus*, 228.

Related to the topic of the land's Sabbath, 25:8–12 introduces the Jubilee for both the land and the Israelites. The LORD instructs the Israelites in 25:8–9 to count seven Sabbath years for the land (i.e., forty-nine years; 25:8) and to blow a trumpet on the tenth day of the seventh month (see 23:23–32), which is the Day of Atonement, to mark that the following year is to be a Jubilee (25:9). This fiftieth year is to be set apart for the LORD, and the purpose of the Jubilee is to restore people to their tribes and to release property back to its owners (25:10). The outcome is that land is redistributed among the people of Israel and there is a release from the burden of debt.

Since a central part of the Jubilee is the restoration of land, a question emerges as to how this happens fairly for both the original owners and for those to whom the land is sold between Jubilees. The purpose of 25:13–17 is to exhort the Israelites to act fairly. Verse 13 assumes that some Israelites have needed to sell property while others have needed to work for another Israelite to pay back debt and have needed to relocate. Verse 13 announces a reset of property ownership and debt release so that land can be restored to those to whom God has given it as their inheritance. Verses 14–16 then address the situation where an Israelite needs to sell their land or they wish to buy land to expand their harvest. The Israelites can buy land from other Israelites with the valuation based on how many years are left to the Jubilee year. Although the system of valuation in 25:15–16 is fair, there could be some among the Israelites who might, when selling land, try to profit by setting the valuation higher than it should be, or by bullying their way to a lower valuation if they are trying to buy land. To anticipate this injustice, the LORD repeats in 25:14b and 25:17 the prohibition against the Israelites taking advantage of one another. They are to treat one another fairly.

After 25:14–17 persuades the Israelites to deal fairly as they trade land, 25:18–23 exhorts the Israelites to follow the LORD's instructions. Verse 18 begins with a series of three verbs that can be translated, 'You shall do my statutes and obey my judgments, and you shall do them.' The repetition emphasises that the Israelites are to action the LORD's instructions. Verses 18c–19 then highlights the outcome of their obedience by repeating the same consequence: 'and you will live there [in the land] safely'. This repetition has two functions. The first is to accentuate that they will live securely in the land (i.e., will not be invaded or removed into exile) if they follow the LORD's instructions. The second purpose is to bookend 25:19a–b that describes the abundance of the land in providing food to satisfy the Israelite community. There will not only be security but also plentiful provision.

What happens, though, if the land does not produce enough food by itself without purposefully being harvested? Verses 20–22 pre-empt this objection from the Israelites by posing the rhetorical question in 25:20. Verses 21–22 provide the answer. The LORD clarifies in 25:21 that he will provide such abundance in crops in the sixth year that they will have plenty for three years. That is, the LORD will ensure that the Israelite community will have enough to stockpile, rather than just having sufficient provision for that harvest year. This will ensure they will have food provisions for the Sabbath year *and* also for the next two years while they wait for the grain stores to be replenished (25:22).

Verse 23 acts as a transition from the topics of the Sabbath and the Jubilee (25:2–22) to the topic of the redemption of land (25:24–34).[4] Verse 23 expresses the theological idea that shapes the instructions in 25:2–22 and also in 25:24–34, which is that the land belongs to the LORD.[5] The LORD can give the land a

---

4 Milgrom, *Leviticus 23–27*, 2188.

5 Milgrom, *Leviticus 23–27*, 2185, explains, 'The larger implication of "the land is mine" is that the land is holy. In the priestly system whatever belongs to God is sacred. Whereas P [Leviticus 1–16] restricts the sacred sphere to the sanctuary, H [Leviticus 17–26] extends its borders to embrace the entire land.'

Sabbath rest every seven years because the land belongs to him, and similarly he can reset the sale of property every fifty years because, again, ultimately he is the landowner. While the LORD is giving the land to the Israelites as a gift, they are resident foreigners in the land. For this reason, 25:23a declares that the land must not be sold permanently. This declaration makes sense of the instructions about the restoration of land during the Jubilee year in 25:14–17 and the instructions for the redemption of land in 25:24–34.

The instructions for the redemption of land begin in 25:24a by acknowledging that the land is given as an inheritance to the Israelites. Because the LORD has given the Israelites their allotments of land, 25:24b instructs the Israelites to make provision for the redemption of land, which 25:25–34 explains by giving example situations. These instructions conclude in 25:32–34 with a focus on property belonging to the tribe of Levi. The Levites as a tribe are not given a tribal allotment of land, but instead are given villages and land within other tribal allotments (see Numbers 34:1–35:5). The reason for this distinction between the tribe of Levi and the other eleven tribes is that the Levites are set apart to belong to the LORD (see Numbers 3:1–20). It is from the tribe of Levi that the priestly line has been chosen. Since the Levites do not have an allotment of land like the other tribes, the instructions about the selling and redeeming of land is different. In 25:32–33, the LORD gives permission for Levites to have a permanent right to redeem their houses in the Levitical towns and, if not redeemed, they are to be returned to the Levites at the Jubilee. However, in 25:34, any farming land that belongs to a Levite town cannot be sold as it remains a permanent possession and inheritance for the Levite tribe.

## 2. *Israel belongs to the* LORD • *Leviticus 25:35–55*

Verses 2–34 explain what it means for the Israelites to live in the land as their possession where the land ultimately belongs to the LORD. Similarly, 25:35–55 evince what it means for the Israelites to belong to the LORD.

**35** ‘“If any of your fellow Israel-
ites become poor and are unable to
support themselves among you, help
them as you would a foreigner and
stranger, so that they can continue
to live among you. **36** Do not take
interest or any profit from them,
but fear your God, so that they may
continue to live among you. **37** You
must not lend them money at interest
or sell them food at a profit. **38** I am
the LORD your God, who brought you
out of Egypt to give you the land of
Canaan and to be your God.

**39** ‘“If any of your fellow Israelites
become poor and sell themselves
to you, do not make them work as
slaves. **40** They are to be treated as
hired workers or temporary resi-
dents among you; they are to work
for you until the Year of Jubilee.
**41** Then they and their children are to
be released, and they will go back to
their own clans and to the property
of their ancestors. **42** Because the
Israelites are my servants, whom I
brought out of Egypt, they must not
be sold as slaves. **43** Do not rule over
them ruthlessly, but fear your God.

**44** ‘“Your male and female slaves are
to come from the nations around you;
from them you may buy slaves. **45** You
may also buy some of the tempo-
rary residents living among you and
members of their clans born in your
country, and they will become your
property. **46** You can bequeath them
to your children as inherited property
and can make them slaves for life, but
you must not rule over your fellow
Israelites ruthlessly.

**47** ‘“If a foreigner residing among
you becomes rich and any of your
fellow Israelites become poor and
sell themselves to the foreigner or
to a member of the foreigner’s clan,
**48** they retain the right of redemp-
tion after they have sold themselves.
One of their relatives may redeem
them: **49** an uncle or a cousin or
any blood-relative in their clan may
redeem them. Or if they prosper, they

may redeem themselves. **50** They
and their buyer are to count the
time from the year they sold them-
selves up to the Year of Jubilee. The
price for their release is to be based
on the rate paid to a hired worker
for that number of years. **51** If many
years remain, they must pay for their
redemption a larger share of the price
paid for them. **52** If only a few years
remain until the Year of Jubilee, they
are to compute that and pay for their
redemption accordingly. **53** They are
to be treated as workers hired from
year to year; you must see to it that
those to whom they owe service do
not rule over them ruthlessly.

**54** ' "Even if someone is not
redeemed in any of these ways, they
and their children are to be released
in the Year of Jubilee, **55** for the Isra-
elites belong to me as servants. They
are my servants, whom I brought out
of Egypt. I am the LORD your God.

Verse 35 introduces a situation where an Israelite, and most likely his household, becomes poor and their income is not enough to sustain the whole family household. In this instance, 25:35 instructs the wider Israelite community to show hospitality to this family as they would to a foreigner residing among them. This hospitality may be the provision of food, shelter or financial help. Either way, 25:36 and 37 repeat the same idea, which is that the Israelites who offer help are not to profit in any way, especially by charging interest. Instead, the Israelite community is to fear their God, which would restrain any temptation to profit from another household's distress. Verse 38 reminds the Israelites of whom they fear. The God they fear is the LORD their covenant God who brought them out of slavery in Egypt to give them the land of promise. The Israelites know what it is like to live in a context of injustice. Moreover, the LORD redeemed Israel by justice. For these reasons, the Israelites are to be just in their relationships in community, especially when they are helping those who are poor among them.

However, some households may reach a certain level of debt where they see no other option than to sell themselves into slavery. Verse 39 restricts this from happening. Rather, 25:40

provides an alternative, which is to treat the Israelite and, most likely, his household as hired workers. In this situation they have agency, provision of shelter and food, and status. The Israelite and his household are then to work to the Jubilee year, after which they are to be released from their debt and their obligation to work for another landowner (25:41).

Verses 42–43 convey the reason for the instructions in 25:35–41, which centres on identity. The Israelites are servants belonging to the LORD. When he redeemed them from slavery in Egypt, he transferred the Israelites from the service of Pharaoh to being in his service as a people belonging in covenant relationship with him (see Exodus 1–15; 19:1–6). Since the Israelites belong to the LORD as his servants, they cannot belong as a servant (or slave) to another, including an Israelite. The Israelites are not to return to their state of being enslaved as they were in Egypt. Instead, they have permission to be hired workers and so retain their status as servants belonging to the LORD. This is not the first time we have come across the concept of Israelites being servants to the LORD. We have noted that the priesthood are servants to the LORD and that the priesthood are a small snapshot of Israel's identity as they live in the land; as a people, they are servants to the LORD as they mediate the LORD and his ways to the nations.

Verses 44–46, however, are tricky pastorally. Israel's role as servants belonging to the LORD is to mediate the LORD to the nations. Yet, in 25:44, the LORD states that Israel's slaves are to come from the other nations (25:44a) and then gives permission for the Israelites to buy slaves. Moreover, 25:45–46 gives permission for these slaves to be passed on to future generations as inherited property.

As we reflect on these verses, we could be frustrated that the LORD did not choose to abolish slavery from the beginning. We think that a lot of pain could have been avoided, and perhaps reform could have come about sooner, if the LORD had refused permission for the Israelites to take slaves from the other nations.

Our thinking often assumes, consciously or unconsciously, our own societal provisions (if we are from the western world), such as a central government maintaining a welfare system that seeks to protect the vulnerable within society. There was none in the ancient Near East. The welfare system was the household.

With this said, it is worth thinking through three contexts in which slaves are gained: through war, by foreigners living among the Israelites needing a livelihood and protection, and by the sale of a person through merchants. With war, slaves are gained by defeating a people group and taking captives. What is the alternative to taking captives in the ancient Near East? Putting the people group to death. Taking captives, even as slaves, is a means by which lives are preserved. In ancient Near Eastern culture, survival is seen as vital since life continues and so does the family and people group to whom the captives belong. Alternatively, when foreigners are displaced from their land and people groups, they would often have no means to survive and would need the protection of another household. To abolish slavery among the Israelites would deny foreigners needing this kind of protection when there is, for instance, no such thing as government provisions for refugees.

However, the focus of Leviticus 25:35–55 is not on the foreigner. Rather, the focus is on the Israelites belonging as slaves to the LORD. Simply, they are not to belong to another, and they are also not to be treated cruelly by another Israelite because they know what it is like to be treated brutally as slaves. The Israelites must not return one another to the same condition that they experienced in Egypt.

But does that mean they are permitted to treat foreign slaves brutally as they were treated in Egypt? No. There are two reasons for this answer. The first is implied and the second is explicit. A pattern within biblical theology is that how God relates to his people is how they are to relate to others. The Israelites belong as slaves to the LORD and are honoured by him. They are not mistreated, coerced or abused. They are disciplined by the LORD, as we find in Leviticus 26, yet discipline is not intended to be coercive but corrective for their own good. As the LORD teaches the Israelites that they belong to him as his servants and as he gives permission for the Israelites to have foreign slaves of their own, implied is that they are to relate to their servants as the LORD relates to them.

The second reason is that there are instructions, such as Leviticus 19:33–34, where the Israelites are instructed not to oppress a foreigner living among them (this includes slaves), and they are to be treated helpfully in community, like Israelites. The motivation for relating to foreigners with dignity and with a spirit of hospitality is that the Israelites were once foreigners in Egypt and were forced into harsh slavery. They are not to replicate the harm done by the Egyptians to foreigners living among them. This mitigates the potential for much harm as God gives permission to the Israelites to own slaves from generation to generation.

So, all this is to say, the Israelites belong as slaves to the LORD and the Israelites can have foreigners as slaves belonging to their household, but this does not mean they have *carte blanche* permission to treat their slaves as they wish. They are to relate to their slaves as the LORD relates to the Israelites as his slaves.

What happens, though, if the person the Israelite approaches is not another Israelite but rather a wealthy resident foreigner within the Israelite community? Verses 47–55 address this issue. After 25:47 describes this scenario, 25:48a clarifies that the Israelite still retains the capacity to be redeemed and 25:48b–54 describes the responsibilities of the Israelite community in this situation. The community is to ensure that the poor Israelite and his household are to be treated as hired workers and not as slaves (25:53a). While the Israelite may have sold himself and his family to the resident foreigner, there is still a boundary as to how they are to be treated. While 25:53a states this positively, 25:53b expresses this in the negative. The Israelite community is to ensure that the Israelite and his household are *not* ruled over harshly or with cruelty by a resident foreigner. Milgrom evinces the significance of 25:53: 'Its implication is clear: as God redeemed you from Egypt in the time of your national need, should you not do the same when your brothers find themselves in slavery in the time of their individual need?'[6]

The emphasis on the Israelites belonging to the LORD as his servants concludes in 25:54–55. Verse 54 refers to all the instructions about redeeming an Israelite and his household and states that if an Israelite cannot be redeemed, then the Israelite and his household must be released in the Year of Jubilee. It is not too hard to imagine a situation where another Israelite or a resident foreigner may refuse to release an Israelite if no one has redeemed him and his household. Verse 54 protects the vulnerable Israelite from this situation by stating clearly that there is to be release and restoration in the Jubilee year. Verse 55 then conveys the reason, which is that the Israelites belong to the LORD as his servants (25:55a). When God secured their release from slavery in Egypt, the Israelites were transferred to the LORD's service to belong to him as servants (25:55b). As previously noted in 25:42, since they belong to the LORD, they are not to belong to others as slaves and, if this situation cannot be avoided, then they must not belong to another in perpetuity. They must experience release and restoration to the land that the LORD has given to them because they are ultimately servants belonging to him.

### *3. Israel's response to the LORD • Leviticus 26:1–2*

After Leviticus 25 explores what it means for the land and people to belong to the LORD, 26:1–2 emphasises Israel's relational

6 Milgrom, *Leviticus 23–27*, 2241.

response to the LORD. Verse 1 expresses this response by two prohibitions centring on idolatry, while 26:2 expresses this same relational response positively through two commands.

*Reward for obedience*

**26** 1 "Do not make idols or set up an image or a sacred stone for yourselves, and do not place a carved stone in your land to bow down before it. I am the LORD your God.

2 "Observe my Sabbaths and have reverence for my sanctuary. I am the LORD.

The three prohibitions in 26:1 ask the Israelites to refrain from making idols, setting up images and placing stones in the land that represent a deity with the intent to bow down to it. They have solely one God and that is the LORD. His presence among his people is represented by the Tabernacle amid the Israelite community. Their worship of the LORD is to be centred in this Tabernacle and, for this reason, 25:1b prohibits the Israelites from setting up any images or carved stones.

Verse 2 then provides balance by providing two commands that express how the Israelites should respond as they refrain from idolatry. The first command in 26:2a is that they are to keep the LORD's Sabbaths. These Sabbaths encompass the seventh day (see 23:3), the Sabbaths as part of the firstfruits festival (23:9–22), the Sabbath associated with the Day of Atonement (23:23–25) and the land's Sabbath every seventh year (25:3–7).

The second command in 26:2b is for the Israelites to have reverence for the LORD's sanctuary. All that Leviticus has instructed – from the bringing of gifts (Leviticus 1–7; 17), to approaching the LORD in a condition of purity (Leviticus 11–16) and by ensuring that how they relate to one another honours the LORD's name (Leviticus 18–22) – is connected to respecting the LORD's sanctuary. By fearing the LORD's sanctuary, the Israelites are fearing the presence of their holy covenant God who dwells in their midst.

## Moving Forward to the New Testament

As we look forward into the New Testament, a significant development transforms how we view this passage. Because of Jesus's death, resurrection and ascension, the new covenant community is called to be a scattered people among the nations as we embody and speak the good news of Jesus (Acts 1–2). The reason for this development is that Israel living in the land was meant to be a preview of God's blessing that he intended to go to the ends of the earth under the new covenant.[7] Leviticus 25:1–26:2 teaches that the land belongs to the LORD and Israel belongs to him as his servants. Now, under the new covenant, we have a global focus: the whole earth belongs to God, and the new covenant community, redeemed by Jesus's death and resurrection, belongs to Jesus as his servants (Colossians 1:13–20). Here are three implications for the 'already and not yet'.

First, Leviticus 25:1–34 reminds us that the land we live and work on does not belong to us. We are stewards of the earth, and God as the sovereign Creator is the landowner.[8] As the landowner, he has instructed the Israelites to give the land rest every seventh year, just as he has instructed the Israelites that they must rest every seventh day. While the Sabbath rest is designed to help us depend on God's sovereign provision and to remind us that he is God and we are not, Sabbath rest also protects from overwork. In the western world, we are guilty of overtaxing the earth for its resources. My suspicion is that our overworking of the land affects the Global South too, when companies from the western world make agreements with Global South governments. While we may not be CEOs or board members of those companies, we can model the wisdom of 25:1–34 by extending

---

7 See Imes, *Bearing God's Name*; Christopher J. H. Wright, *The Mission of God's People: A Biblical Theology of the Church's Mission* (Biblical Theology for Life; Grand Rapids: Zondervan, 2010).

8 See also Richter, *Stewards of Eden*, 15–28.

rest to the land where we live and work when it is in our gift to do so. This could include awareness of how we steward the earth's resources in our daily decisions, such as how we use electricity, gas, oil and water. We might also choose to eat fruit and vegetables that are seasonal and produced locally (if not in our back yard) rather than fruit and vegetables that have been greenhoused, genetically modified or imported from overseas.[9]

Second, the instructions about the Jubilee year are vital to ensure just living for everyone in the new covenant community. It is true that the new covenant community does not live in tribal land allotments. We live scattered under human governments with legal frameworks that govern how land is to be owned and sold. Moreover, the purpose of 25:35–55 is to protect the status of the Israelites as servants of the Lord. They are not to be enslaved again to human masters (i.e., reversing the Exodus event). This is true for us too. Jesus redeemed us from the power of sin and death to belong to him as his servants. We were not saved to be free. We were redeemed to belong solely to Jesus. As a new covenant community, we can embody the principle of 25:35–55 in four ways. First, as we make decisions about our own finances and property (irrespective of whether we have little or much), we need to ask whether those decisions will see us enslaved to human masters, which could detract from being wholehearted servants of Jesus. In the western world, our decisions about mortgages and credit cards often see us enslaved to our debt and repayments. This affects how we live for Jesus. We would be wise to think twice about how our spending and our quest to own property affects how we belong to Jesus as his servants in the world. Second, there are those in the new covenant community who experience financial difficulty and are in danger of losing homes due to circumstances such as loss of livelihood or the impact of marital breakdown. Embodying the instructions of 25:1–26:2 might look

9 For further reflection on this issue, see Richter, *Stewards of Eden*.

like helping our brothers and sisters in Christ financially and/or providing accommodation for them, even if temporarily. It is vital that we do this from cross-shaped generosity and not with strings attached. Third, we have brothers and sisters around the world who are in conditions of slavery, such as part of the sex trade or in sweat shops. Rather than ignore this issue, we could learn about how we can be part of freeing them from slavery so that they can live and work with dignity as they seek to follow Jesus. Fourth, God has given us these instructions for the good of his covenant community and to ensure that he is sanctified by our decisions and actions. If this is for our good, then surely extending the generosity described above to our neighbours who do not believe in Jesus would be for their good too.

The third implication for the 'already and not yet' is that 26:1–2 describes Israel's faithful response to the instructions in Leviticus 25. As we learn from Leviticus 25 that the world belongs to Jesus and that we belong to him as his servants, the prohibitions and commands from 26:1–2 apply to us too as a new covenant community. As a people who belong solely to Jesus, we too need to resist idolatry and be real with ourselves and before God as to the idols in our lives (e.g., greed, consumerism, home ownership, wanting for ourselves what others have, the ideal of the 'perfect' family).[10] A key to resisting idolatry is cultivating the spiritual discipline of taking a Sabbath rest once a week and at significant points in our calendar when we remember Jesus's work on our behalf (e.g., Good Friday). However, while Jesus does not call us to hold a building in reverence as the place where he dwells, we can honour the command to reverence the LORD's sanctuary by holding Jesus in awe (John 2:19–22) and by respecting the body of Christ as the temple of the Holy Spirit (1 Corinthians 3:16).

10 See Timothy Keller, *Counterfeit Gods: The Empty Promises of Money, Sex, and Power, and the Only Hope that Matters* (London: Hodder & Stoughton, 2009).

## *4. The consequences of obedience: blessing • Leviticus 26:3–13*

After 26:1–2 models the desired response from the Israelites, 26:3–13 describes the LORD's reciprocal response to their faithful obedience. Verse 3 introduces his reciprocal response by setting the context and then 26:4–13 accentuates how the LORD will act for Israel in light of their faithfulness.

**3** ' "If you follow my decrees and are
careful to obey my commands, **4** I
will send you rain in its season, and
the ground will yield its crops and
the trees their fruit. **5** Your threshing
will continue until grape harvest and
the grape harvest will continue until
planting, and you will eat all the food
you want and live in safety in your
land.

**6** ' "I will grant peace in the land,
and you will lie down and no one will
make you afraid. I will remove wild
beasts from the land, and the sword
will not pass through your country.
**7** You will pursue your enemies, and
they will fall by the sword before you.
**8** Five of you will chase a hundred,
and a hundred of you will chase ten
thousand, and your enemies will fall
by the sword before you.

**9** ' "I will look on you with favour
and make you fruitful and increase
your numbers, and I will keep my
covenant with you. **10** You will still
be eating last year's harvest when
you will have to move it out to make
room for the new. **11** I will put my
dwelling-place[a] among you, and
I will not abhor you. **12** I will walk
among you and be your God, and
you will be my people. **13** I am the
LORD your God, who brought you
out of Egypt so that you would no
longer be slaves to the Egyptians;
I broke the bars of your yoke and
enabled you to walk with heads held
high.

---

a 11 Or *my tabernacle*

The LORD's first action in 26:4 is that he will send rain in its season and the consequence is fruitfulness. What happens when rain occurs out of season? Often crops are destroyed because there is too much rain at the wrong time. In my Australian context, we are experiencing how rain out of season can affect our vineyards. Outside Sydney is a wine region called the Hunter Valley and our weather patterns over the past eighteen months have been chaotic, leading to the vines and ground being sodden. Too much rain at the wrong time of year affects the type of mould (botrytis) that grows on the grapes and vines. This affects the quality of the grapes. Many vineyards have thrown out entire harvests because the grapes are not of the quality needed to produce the standard of wine for which the Hunter region is renowned.

By the LORD promising to send rain in the right season, he is saying that their vines and crops will have the rain needed at exactly the right time to produce grapes and crops abundantly. There will be fruitfulness and plenty. The harvest will be so abundant that the threshing of the grain will continue until the vines are ready for the grape harvest. Moreover, the grape harvest will continue to the time that the crops need planting in the fields again. The picture is of plenty and productivity the whole year round.

The LORD's second act in 26:6–8, as he blesses his people in the land, is to grant them peace and security. For a nation to produce harvests without interruption, a vital ingredient is peace in the land and at the nation's borders. War interrupts harvests because a significant number of the field hands are Israel's warriors. Therefore, the assurance of peace in 26:6–8 is critical for a flourishing nation. However, in the event they go to war, 26:7–8 depicts the Israelites victorious over their enemies, even when their enemies' numbers outmatch their own.

Verse 9 is a sequence of first-person verbs that depict how the LORD will continue to act for his people: 'I will turn towards you, and I will make you fruitful, and I will make you increase, and I will establish my covenant with you' (my translation). The LORD's act of turning towards is a purposeful posture of favour and honour towards his people. This results in the flourishing of the nation's population and the LORD's reciprocal covenant faithfulness towards them. While 26:9 describes the fruitfulness of the people, 26:10 refocuses on the fruitfulness of the land. In 26:4–5, the picture of blessing was year-round productivity. In 26:10 the picture is of an abundance of food where the people have not finished eating one harvest when it is time for the new harvest to be stored.

The blessings culminate in 26:11–12 with an extraordinary vision. As Israel flourishes in the land, the LORD promises in 26:11 to put his dwelling place in their midst and not to abhor them. That is, the LORD will be among them and there will be no consequence. When God's people ensure that they separate impurity from the LORD's holiness, and that they embody being in a pure condition as a people set apart for the LORD in all their relationships, the LORD can dwell among his people and the Israelites will live. The outcome is that the LORD will delight in his people as he dwells among them. Verse 12 completes this vision of what the LORD–Israel relationship will be if they are faithful to the LORD's instructions: he will not only dwell among them and there be life for God's people, but he will also walk among his covenant people and he will be their God.

While 26:11 articulates the outcome that has been at the crux of Leviticus's instructions from the beginning, 26:12 extends the vision of the LORD's blessing into a future that echoes Eden where the LORD once walked in the garden (Genesis 3:8).[11] The man and the woman's desire to choose what is good and evil for themselves led to the relational breakdown that caused a permanent separation between the LORD and his people (Genesis 3:9–24). From Genesis 12:1–3, the LORD has actioned his plan to recreate a people for himself so that blessing can extend to all

11 For an Edenic allusion in 26:11–12, see Harper, *'I Will Walk Among You'*, 187–221; Milgrom, *Leviticus 23–27*, 2301; Sklar, *Leviticus*, 316; Wenham, *Leviticus*, 330.

nations. By recreating a people through Abraham's family line, he sought to restore relational order between himself and his people with the intent in Leviticus 26:12 to restore the intimate relationship of Eden where he is not only present among his people but is once more walking among them.

The LORD's reciprocal response to Israel's faithful obedience in 26:3–12 culminates in 26:13 with a declaration of the LORD's identity. Who is the LORD that he intends to restore his intimate relationship with his people and be their God? He is their covenant God who brought them out of Egypt. It was the LORD alone who broke their yokes of slavery. A yoke was a wooden bar placed over the heads of slaves and rested on their shoulders. It was a way to control a group of slaves, and the heavy wood would often cause the heads and shoulders of slaves to bow over. By rescuing the Israelites out of Egypt, the LORD broke their yokes of slavery to Pharaoh so that they could stand up properly and lift up their heads. While the Israelites were not redeemed to be free, they are redeemed to the LORD's service where they are not yoked to one another, suffering through cruel and harsh labour. Instead, they serve the LORD by ensuring that he is glorified and sanctified in their midst. In response, the LORD will cause them to flourish and grant them security in the land he has given to them.

## Moving forward into the New Testament

Israel experienced the tangible aspects of food aplenty and peace in the land when they sought their covenant God faithfully (e.g., 1 Kings 4). However, Israel's propensity towards rebellion and idolatry meant that God's covenant people experienced defeat and exile rather than peace and security. The vision of God's presence being permanently restored among his people where he will walk among them once more became a future hope beyond exile. Verses 11–12 point us forward to Revelation 21–22, where God envisions the permanent restoration of his presence among his covenant people with the crucified and risen Lamb present. Moreover, this vision in Revelation 21–22 is not a reciprocal response to our faithfulness, as we would never experience this blessing of being in God's presence if it were conditional on our faithfulness. Rather, our future hope of Leviticus 26:11–12 being fulfilled in Revelation 21–22 is entirely dependent on the faithfulness of Jesus who secured this blessing for us by his death and resurrection. However, we do not wait until Jesus's coming again to experience this blessing. God has blessed us now immensely by choosing, redeeming and sealing us with his Holy Spirit as a guarantee of our eternal inheritance, and by making known to us his purposes in Christ (Ephesians 1:3–14). Again, this is not a reciprocal blessing. This blessing for those in Christ is entirely by the riches of God's grace that he has lavished on us abundantly (Ephesians 1:7–14).

## *5. The consequences of rebellion: curse • Leviticus 26:14–46*

If the LORD will bless the Israelites with his active favour in response to their faithfulness (26:3–13), then a question emerges as to how the LORD will respond if Israel chooses to reject his ways as set out in his instructions. At the conclusion of his blessings, we saw the LORD's declaration of his identity in 26:13 as the one who redeemed the Israelites from slavery. As a people belonging to him, it is right for the LORD to expect faithful obedience from the Israelites. Similarly, it is right that he expects that they will adopt his ways and reject the ways of the Egyptians and of the Canaanites. But what will happen if Israel rejects the LORD's ways? In contrast to 26:3–13, 26:14–39 describes what happens if Israel fails to be faithful to the LORD as his covenant people and as a people belonging to him. As he warned in Exodus 34:6–7, he cannot let rebellion go unpunished.

*Punishment for disobedience*

14 ' "But if you will not listen to me
and carry out all these commands,
15 and if you reject my decrees and
abhor my laws and fail to carry out
all my commands and so violate
my covenant, 16 then I will do this
to you: I will bring on you sudden
terror, wasting diseases and fever
that will destroy your sight and sap
your strength. You will plant seed in
vain, because your enemies will eat
it. 17 I will set my face against you
so that you will be defeated by your
enemies; those who hate you will
rule over you, and you will flee even
when no one is pursuing you.

18 ' "If after all this you will not
listen to me, I will punish you for
your sins seven times over. 19 I will
break down your stubborn pride and
make the sky above you like iron and
the ground beneath you like bronze.
20 Your strength will be spent in vain,
because your soil will not yield its
crops, nor will the trees of your land
yield their fruit.

21 ' "If you remain hostile towards
me and refuse to listen to me, I will
multiply your afflictions seven times
over, as your sins deserve. 22 I will
send wild animals against you, and
they will rob you of your children,
destroy your cattle and make you so
few in number that your roads will
be deserted.

23 ' "If in spite of these things you
do not accept my correction but
continue to be hostile towards me,
24 I myself will be hostile towards
you and will afflict you for your sins
seven times over. 25 And I will bring
the sword on you to avenge the
breaking of the covenant. When you
withdraw into your cities, I will send
a plague among you, and you will
be given into enemy hands. 26 When
I cut off your supply of bread, ten
women will be able to bake your
bread in one oven, and they will dole
out the bread by weight. You will eat,
but you will not be satisfied.

27 ' "If in spite of this you still do
not listen to me but continue to be
hostile towards me, 28 then in my
anger I will be hostile towards you,
and I myself will punish you for your
sins seven times over. 29 You will eat
the flesh of your sons and the flesh of
your daughters. 30 I will destroy your
high places, cut down your incense
altars and pile your dead bodies[b] on
the lifeless forms of your idols, and
I will abhor you. 31 I will turn your
cities into ruins and lay waste your
sanctuaries, and I will take no delight
in the pleasing aroma of your offer-
ings. 32 I myself will lay waste the

land, so that your enemies who live
there will be appalled. **33** I will scat-
ter you among the nations and will
draw out my sword and pursue you.
Your land will be laid waste, and your
cities will lie in ruins. **34** Then the
land will enjoy its sabbath years all
the time that it lies desolate and you
are in the country of your enemies;
then the land will rest and enjoy its
sabbaths. **35** All the time that it lies
desolate, the land will have the rest
it did not have during the sabbaths
you lived in it.

**36** ' "As for those of you who are
left, I will make their hearts so fear-
ful in the lands of their enemies that
the sound of a wind-blown leaf will
put them to flight. They will run as
though fleeing from the sword, and
they will fall, even though no one is
pursuing them. **37** They will stumble
over one another as though fleeing
from the sword, even though no
one is pursuing them. So you will
not be able to stand before your ene-
mies. **38** You will perish among the
nations; the land of your enemies
will devour you. **39** Those of you who
are left will waste away in the lands of
their enemies because of their sins;
also because of their ancestors' sins
they will waste away.

**40** ' "But if they will confess their
sins and the sins of their ances-
tors – their unfaithfulness and
their hostility towards me, **41** which
made me hostile towards them so
that I sent them into the land of
their enemies – then when their
uncircumcised hearts are humbled
and they pay for their sin, **42** I will
remember my covenant with Jacob
and my covenant with Isaac and
my covenant with Abraham, and I
will remember the land. **43** For the
land will be deserted by them and
will enjoy its sabbaths while it lies
desolate without them. They will pay
for their sins because they rejected
my laws and abhorred my decrees.
**44** Yet in spite of this, when they are
in the land of their enemies, I will not
reject them or abhor them so as to
destroy them completely, breaking
my covenant with them. I am the
LORD their God. **45** But for their sake
I will remember the covenant with
their ancestors whom I brought out
of Egypt in the sight of the nations to
be their God. I am the LORD." '

**46** These are the decrees, the laws
and the regulations that the LORD
established at Mount Sinai between
himself and the Israelites through
Moses.

---

b 30 Or *your funeral offerings*

Verses 14–39 depict Israel's persistent unfaithfulness and the LORD's response in five cumulative situations (26:14–17, 18–20, 21–22, 23–26, 27–39). Each of these situations begins with a series of conditional clauses that begin with 'if'.[12] Conditional sentences describe what happens *if* something were to be true. For instance, the first situation begins in 26:14–15 by describing the circumstances that need to be true for the consequences described in 26:16–17 to occur. These circumstances in 26:14–15 are introduced by the word 'if': '*If* you will not listen to me and carry out all these commands, and *if* you reject my decrees and abhor my laws and fail to carry out all my commands and so violate my covenant . . .' (italics added). The LORD's response to how the Israelites despise his commands in 26:16–17 is dependent on these circumstances being true. Similarly, following this pattern from 26:14–17, the other four situations begin by describing the circumstances of Israel's unfaithfulness followed by the LORD's promise of discipline:

| | |
|---|---|
| 26:18 | If after all this you will not listen to me, I will punish you for your sins seven times over. |
| 26:21 | If you remain hostile towards me and refuse to listen to me, I will multiply your afflictions seven times over, as your sins deserve. |
| 26:23–24 | If in spite of these things you do not accept my correction but continue to be hostile to me, I myself will be hostile towards you and will afflict you for your sins seven times over. |
| 26:27–28 | If in spite of this you still do not listen to me but continue to be hostile towards me, then in my anger I will be hostile towards you, and I myself will punish you for your sins seven times over. |

There are four points to observe from the above. First, the LORD enacts his discipline against the Israelites *if* they violate the covenant relationship to which they consented at Sinai by

12 Also, Ko, *Leviticus*, 240–1.

saying, 'Everything the LORD has said we will do' (Exodus 24:3). The LORD's actions are not malicious or vindictive but rather are a just response to the Israelites' actions that are opposed to their status of being a people holy to the LORD. The LORD can avenge the wrong done without being coercive. That is, the LORD is enacting the following penalties with cause. Second, how 26:21, 23 and 27 begin reveals that the LORD does not enact punishment for punishment's sake, but rather he desires that the Israelites learn from his discipline and listen to him. Third, the descriptions are cumulative, that is, apart from the first situation in 26:14–17, every other situation is a response to the Israelites not heeding the discipline they suffered in the previous scenario. Fourth, there is an intensification in the LORD's discipline from bringing distress (26:14–17), to being placed under siege (26:23–26) and then to the eventual exile of the Israelites from the land (26:27–39).[13] As the LORD's punishment intensifies, so too does the graphic language used to depict the devastation.

However, there is a turning-point in 26:40–42. Beyond exile, when they are living in the land of their enemies, there is an opportunity for reversal. This begins in 26:40 with the Israelites reversing their attitudes towards the LORD. If the Israelites confess their rebellion, unfaithfulness and contempt, and that of previous generations, then the LORD promises in 26:42 to remember his covenant with the patriarchs.

There are two points to highlight about 26:40–42. First, the LORD's act of remembering in 26:42 is dependent on 26:41, where the Israelites' hearts need to be humbled and after they have paid the penalty for their rebellion. The LORD will not relent from his discipline until they have paid the full penalty for their violation of his covenant (see Isaiah 40:1–2). Second, the act of remembering implies action. The Hebrew language ties

13 Also, Chingota, 'Leviticus', 166; Gunjević, 'Leviticus', 137; Ko, *Leviticus*, 241–2.

together the internal disposition of remembrance and acting on that remembering so that there is integrity between the internal and the external. Thus, when the LORD promises in 26:42 to remember, it is implied that the LORD will act to reverse their circumstances as he acts in faithfulness to the Abrahamic covenant.

Verses 43–45 culminate the focus on the LORD's discipline of Israel's covenant violations by repeating the reversal depicted previously in 26:34–42. This repetition accentuates that the LORD's discipline will not be enduring. He will not continue to reject for ever. This repetition begins in 26:43 by reiterating the condition of the land from 26:34. The land does not lie desolate solely because of the land's emptiness but due to the lack of population to work the ground so that there is no harvest sown and so no harvest to grow. Verse 43c–d describes the reason for the land's forsakenness, which is that the Israelites need to pay off their debt caused by their rebellion. However, the LORD's promise in 26:44 is spoken in stark contrast to 26:43. Although the Israelites need to bear their own penalty for their rebellion in exile, the LORD declares that he will restrain his anger so that he does not destroy them completely. As Chingota highlights, 'It is important to remember that God was aiming at the reformation of the Israelites and not at their annihilation.'[14] In Exodus 32:7–33:23, the LORD gave his word to Moses that he would not destroy the people because of their rebellion and would continue to be present among his people, which formed the basis of the covenant renewal (Exodus 34). Rather than breaking faith with Israel, the LORD declares in Leviticus 26:45 that he will, for Israel's sake, remember the Mosaic covenant where, after he brought the Israelites out of Egypt in the sight of a watching world, he promised to be their God. While the Israelites may have spurned him in the sight of a watching world as his

14 Chingota, 'Leviticus', 166.

covenant people, he will not reciprocate. He will not reject for ever, but instead he will act to restore his people in covenant relationship with himself (26:42–45).

Verse 46 swiftly changes topic to announce, 'These are the decrees, the laws and the regulations that the LORD established at Mount Sinai between himself and the Israelites through Moses.' This declaration reminds the Israelites that these instructions were given by the LORD through his mediator Moses at Sinai. Moreover, they are not solely *given* but they are established between the LORD and the Israelites. As God's covenant people, they are agreeing to be bound by these instructions, including the promises of covenant blessings and curses. As the whole book concludes, this declaration in 26:46 is a reminder to the Israelites of the weight of these instructions that they have heard and which they have received.

## Moving forward into the New Testament

As the Old Testament narrative unfolds, Israel's propensity towards unfaithfulness meant that the LORD acted against Israel in accordance with the covenant curses, which culminated in the exile of the northern kingdom (2 Kings 17) and then the southern kingdom (2 Kings 24–25). While Jerusalem was restored from exile (see Isaiah 40–55; Ezra–Nehemiah), Judah remained under foreign rule and the Jewish diaspora continued. If blessing were to go to the nations by Israel fulfilling her created purpose, then the covenant curses of the law, which outline consequence for unfaithfulness, needed to be dealt with, not just the power of sin and death. For this reason, the apostle Paul wrote to the Galatian church:

> Christ redeemed us from the curse of the law by becoming a curse for us, for it is written: 'Cursed is everyone who is hung on a pole.' He redeemed us in order that the blessing given to Abraham might come to the Gentiles through Christ Jesus, so that by faith we might receive the promise of the Spirit (Galatians 3:13–14).

We are so used to talking about Jesus redeeming us from the power of sin and death, yet we forget this vital truth, which is that he bore the curse of the law for us, that is, he bore the consequence of our unfaithfulness. Douglas Moo explains:

> The curse in Scripture refers to God's judgment, a judgment that takes the form of exclusion from God's land and God's people . . . The body that was hung on a pole was under a curse because of the manner in which the person had died: executed for a heinous sin against the law of God. Paul likewise implies that Christ has suffered the curse in connection with being hung on a tree because of sin – but because of the sins of others, not his own . . . Christ suffered exclusion from the people of God and, more terribly, separation from God the Father himself, so that those people who had been excluded because of their sin could be brought back in again.[15]

As a new covenant community, we are no longer under threat of the covenant curses or of being permanently excluded from God's presence, because Jesus has become that curse for us. We now belong to Jesus and are heirs of promise and blessing that is in Christ. This truth leads us to a deeper joy in knowing Christ and releases us from the fear of being excluded from God's presence. We can have confidence in the complete and effective work of Jesus on our behalf (Galatians 3:26–29).

15 Douglas J. Moo, *Galatians* (Grand Rapids: Baker, 2013), 210, 214.

12

# Give to the Lord What Belongs to Him

## LEVITICUS 27

Leviticus 27 concludes the book by reinforcing how Israel can sanctify the Lord their covenant God who is present in their midst. How can they glorify the Lord? By giving to the Lord all that belongs to him. Leviticus 27 unpacks this emphasis in six situations. The first three situations focus on fulfilling a gift to the Lord willingly (27:2–8, 9–13, 14–25). The final three situations emphasise giving to the Lord what already belongs to him (27:26–27, 28–29, 30–33).

### *1. Honouring gifts of people to the Lord • Leviticus 27:1–8*

The first situation begins in 27:2 with the scenario where an Israelite makes an extraordinary promise to the Lord to dedicate a person to him. However, instead of the person being transferred to the Lord's service, the person who makes the vow can fulfil his promise by a financial payment where the payment equals the financial value of the person being dedicated to the Lord.[1]

1 Ko, *Leviticus*, 244, points out that the provision of this first situation is to mitigate the potential for the vow being fulfilled by human sacrifice, such as in Judges 11:34–39.

### *Redeeming what is the* LORD*'s*

**27** The LORD said to Moses,
**2** 'Speak to the Israelites
and say to them: "If anyone makes
a special vow to dedicate a person
to the LORD by giving the equiva-
lent value, **3** set the value of a male
between the ages of twenty and sixty
at fifty shekels[a] of silver, according
to the sanctuary shekel;[b] **4** for a
female, set her value at thirty shek-
els;[c] **5** for a person between the ages
of five and twenty, set the value of
a male at twenty shekels[d] and of a
female at ten shekels;[e] **6** for a person
between one month and five years,
set the value of a male at five shek-
els[f] of silver and that of a female at
three shekels[g] of silver; **7** for a person
sixty years old or more, set the value
of a male at fifteen shekels[h] and of
a female at ten shekels. **8** If anyone
making the vow is too poor to pay
the specified amount, the person
being dedicated is to be presented
to the priest, who will set the value
according to what the one making
the vow can afford.

a 3 That is, about 575 grams; also in verse 16
b 3 That is, about 12 grams; also in verse 25
c 4 That is, about 345 grams
d 5 That is, about 230 grams
e 5 That is, about 115 grams; also in verse 7
f 6 That is, about 58 grams
g 6 That is, about 35 grams
h 7 That is, about 175 grams

Verses 3–7 set the valuation depending on the sex and age of the person. Moreover, each valuation is given in the sanctuary shekel, which is the equivalent of approximately 12 grams. The assumption in 27:3–4 is that a man or woman between twenty and sixty years can bring immediate economic value to the household. Verse 5 addresses the situation where the person is between five and twenty years of age. The reason the valuation for a child is lower is that they have less economic value than a mature adult, and the same logic applies to 27:7 with the valuation of persons over sixty years.[2] Verse 8 makes provision for the poor person who cannot afford these set valuations and yet

2 Ko, *Leviticus*, 245, rightly explains that the valuation is based on economic value rather than of one's life and dignity. See also Chingota, 'Leviticus', 167.

is to make good on their promise to the LORD. In this instance, the priesthood cannot demand that the person pays more than they can afford.

Two issues may emerge for the contemporary reader of 27:2–8, irrespective of our cultural background. First, we might be a bit affronted by talking about the dedication of persons by another. How can an Israelite decide to dedicate another person? This surely diminishes the agency of the person being dedicated! But the LORD's provision in 27:3–8 is extraordinary. He does not demand that those persons promised in a vow be given to the priesthood. Instead, he gives the opportunity for the vow to be fulfilled financially without the person being given over to the LORD's Tabernacle. Rather than being irked by this situation, we could choose to see the LORD's provision as a gracious alternative that ensures that the persons being dedicated remain in their context.

Second, it is obvious that female persons have a lesser valuation relative to that of males and so suggests the devaluation of women. When we understand the valuations as reflecting economic value, we can understand why women are valued financially less than men. It is not that the text is misogynistic or devaluing the worth of women. Instead, men between twenty and sixty years of age would be seen as being in their prime in terms of strength and productivity. The household to whom they belong would gain greater profit from their work than from women of the same age. Women slaves would have been involved in the economic work of the household, but also involved in raising the household's children, serving in the household itself and most likely having children themselves. The direct economic return for their work would be less than that of a man. The same is true for children and for men and women older than sixty. Setting an economic value is not the same as devaluing the worth of women, and it would be good when reading Leviticus 27 not to confuse the two issues.

## 2. *Honouring gifts of animals to the Lord • Leviticus 27:9–13*

Verses 9–13 address a second situation where an Israelite has promised an animal to the LORD. While the first situation in 27:2–8 provides an opportunity for the Israelite to fulfil their promise to the LORD financially rather than handing over people, 27:9–13 instructs the Israelite to make good on their word with the animal that has been promised, that is, there is no ability to fulfil the vow by a financial payment.

**9** ' "If what they vowed is an animal
that is acceptable as an offering to
the LORD, such an animal given to
the LORD becomes holy. **10** They
must not exchange it or substitute
a good one for a bad one, or a bad
one for a good one; if they should
substitute one animal for another,
both it and the substitute become
holy. **11** If what they vowed is a
ceremonially unclean animal – one
that is not acceptable as an offering
to the LORD – the animal must be
presented to the priest, **12** who will
judge its quality as good or bad.
Whatever value the priest then sets,
that is what it will be. **13** If the owner
wishes to redeem the animal, a fifth
must be added to its value.

Verse 9 describes the second situation and declares that the promised animal is holy. That is, the animal is set apart to belong to the LORD because it has been promised to him. By implication, the Israelite needs to follow through with their vow since the animal's status is holy. A second implication of the animal's holy status in 27:10 is that the Israelite is prohibited from substituting the acceptable animal (i.e., 'good') for one that is unacceptable (i.e., 'bad'). If the Israelite attempts an exchange, then both the original animal and its substitute are considered holy and must be given to the LORD. Once the animal is surrendered to the LORD as an offering, 27:13 gives the opportunity for the Israelite to redeem the animal, that is, to transfer the animal by payment to belong once more to the Israelite.

What happens, though, if the promised animal is impure and so would be considered unacceptable as an offering to the LORD? Verses 10–12 instruct the Israelites to pay a valuation for the animal instead of surrendering the animal to the LORD.

## *3. Honouring gifts of property to the LORD • Leviticus 27:14–25*

After 27:2–8 and 27:9–13 focus on situations of persons and animals, the third situation in 27:14–25 instructs the Israelites about what is to happen when they set apart a house (27:14–15) and property (27:16–25) to the LORD.

**14** ‘ “If anyone dedicates their house
as something holy to the LORD, the
priest will judge its quality as good or
bad. Whatever value the priest then
sets, so it will remain. **15** If the one
who dedicates their house wishes to
redeem it, they must add a fifth to
its value, and the house will again
become theirs.

**16** ‘ “If anyone dedicates to the LORD
part of their family land, its value is
to be set according to the amount of
seed required for it – fifty shekels of
silver to a homer[i] of barley seed. **17** If
they dedicate a field during the Year
of Jubilee, the value that has been
set remains. **18** But if they dedicate
a field after the Jubilee, the priest
will determine the value according
to the number of years that remain
until the next Year of Jubilee, and its
set value will be reduced. **19** If the
one who dedicates the field wishes
to redeem it, they must add a fifth
to its value, and the field will again
become theirs. **20** If, however, they
do not redeem the field, or if they
have sold it to someone else, it can
never be redeemed. **21** When the
field is released in the Jubilee, it will
become holy, like a field devoted to
the LORD; it will become priestly
property.

**22** ‘ “If anyone dedicates to the LORD
a field they have bought, which is not
part of their family land, **23** the priest

will determine its value up to the Year of Jubilee, and the owner must pay its value on that day as something holy to the LORD. **24** In the Year of Jubilee the field will revert to the person from whom it was bought, the one whose land it was. **25** Every value is to be set according to the sanctuary shekel, twenty gerahs to the shekel.

i 16 That is, probably about 135 kilograms

A priest sets a valuation price for a property when an Israelite sets their house apart to the LORD. In 27:15, this valuation is used again if the Israelite wishes to redeem the house and so transfer it back to his or her possession. Similar logic is applied to the situation in 27:16–25 where an Israelite wishes to redeem a field that they have given to the LORD. What happens, though, if a poor Israelite must sell his land to a neighbour to pay a debt and his neighbour then sets the field apart to the LORD? In this situation, would the poor Israelite lose the right to redemption and, moreover, lose the property permanently to the priesthood if his neighbour does not redeem it? This does not seem fair to the poor Israelite. This is the reason we have the extra situation in 27:22–24, which ensures the choice of the neighbour does not permanently affect the landholding of the poor Israelite's family.

## *4. The firstborn belongs to the LORD • Leviticus 27:26–27*

So far, Leviticus 27 has addressed three situations where an Israelite chooses willingly to set apart persons, animals or property to the LORD. In these three situations, the Israelite is instructed to make good on his word and then the LORD gives appropriate provision for the Israelite to redeem what can be redeemed. The rest of Leviticus 27 addresses three situations where either animals, people or property already belong to the LORD and the Israelites are being instructed to honour what already belongs to him. The first of these three situations, in 27:26–27, pertains to the firstborn.

**26** '"No one, however, may dedicate the firstborn of an animal, since the firstborn already belongs to the LORD; whether an ox[j] or a sheep, it is the LORD's. **27** If it is one of the unclean animals, it may be bought back at its set value, adding a fifth of the value to it. If it is not redeemed, it is to be sold at its set value.

j 26 The Hebrew word can include both male and female.

Verse 26 begins with a strong prohibition, which is that no one may set apart a firstborn animal to the LORD. The reason for this prohibition is that the firstborn, irrespective of whether the animal is male or female, already belongs to the LORD. An Israelite cannot set apart to the LORD what already belongs to him. This is true of an impure animal too. Verse 27 clarifies that an Israelite is still required to bring an impure animal to a priest for a valuation, then the Israelite is to redeem the impure animal and, if not redeemed, then it is to be sold by the priesthood at its valuation price.

## *5. The redemption of those devoted to the LORD • Leviticus 27:28–29*

There is, however, a particular status of belonging that cannot be redeemed or sold. This status is of being 'devoted' to the LORD. Being devoted to the LORD is the equivalent of saying that it is 'most holy to the LORD' and therefore there is no price that is acceptable for redemption.

**28** '"But nothing that a person owns and devotes[k] to the LORD – whether a human being or an animal or family land – may be sold or redeemed; everything so devoted is most holy to the LORD.

29 ' "No one devoted to destruction[l] may be ransomed; they are to be put to death.

k 28 The Hebrew term refers to the irrevocable giving over of things or persons to the LORD.

l 29 The Hebrew term refers to the irrevocable giving over of things or persons to the LORD, often by totally destroying them.

Verse 28 is clear that any human, animal or property devoted to the LORD cannot be transferred to the ownership of another. In 27:29, this includes anyone that has been devoted to death by the LORD. The idea that persons and animals can be devoted to destruction can be uncomfortable for most readers. This is, however, limited to a particular context that we can read about in Deuteronomy 7 and 12. An Israelite does not have the freedom to devote a person to destruction; only the LORD can choose who can be devoted to destruction, and even then he limits this choice to the context of conquest where he is bringing his justice against people groups in the land of promise.[3] In this situation, where animals and people are devoted to death by the LORD, the Israelites must not keep the people or animals for themselves, but rather ensure that all that the LORD devotes to destruction is given to the LORD through death.

## *6. Every tithe belongs to the* LORD • *Leviticus 27:30–33*

The final situation in 27:30–33 addresses the topic of tithing to the LORD. Verse 30 declares that the tithe, which is one-tenth of everything produced from the land, belongs to the LORD and so is holy. This tithe is from the firstfruits of each harvest and,

3 For readers who wish to think through the issue of 'being devoted to destruction', see Charlie Trimm, *The Destruction of the Canaanites: God, Genocide, and Biblical Interpretation* (Grand Rapids: Eerdmans, 2022).

in an agrarian context, the giving of the firstfruits teaches the Israelites that the harvest belongs ultimately to the LORD. For this reason, the Israelites must take care to give to the LORD what belongs to him.

**30** '"A tithe of everything from the
land, whether grain from the soil
or fruit from the trees, belongs to
the LORD; it is holy to the LORD.
**31** Whoever would redeem any of
their tithe must add a fifth of the
value to it. **32** Every tithe of the herd
and flock – every tenth animal that
passes under the shepherd's rod –
will be holy to the LORD. **33** No one
may pick out the good from the bad
or make any substitution. If anyone
does make a substitution, both the
animal and its substitute become
holy and cannot be redeemed."'

There are two implications from 27:30–33 for the Israelite. First, although the tithe belongs to the LORD and so must be given to him, the LORD also gives provision in 27:31 for the Israelite to redeem their portion of the tithe by paying the value of the tithe plus an extra one-fifth. For the Israelite to access this right to redemption, the tithe of the harvest or livestock must first be given to the LORD so that it can be transferred back to the ownership of the Israelite with payment exchanged for the tithe. Second, 27:33 is clear that there can be no substitute or exchange. It is not too hard to imagine that Israelites may try to rebel against the command in 27:30 by trying to pass off animals with blemishes as part of the tithe and to keep those without blemish, for instance, for themselves. The LORD's instruction in 27:33 anticipates the Israelites' rebellious nature and conveys the consequence if an Israelite tries to swap the livestock. The penalty is that both the tithe of the livestock and the substitutes would belong to the LORD.

## *7. Summary • Leviticus 27:34*

The book of Leviticus concludes in 27:34 with a declaration that 'these are the commands', which refers to the instructions in the whole book, not solely those in Leviticus 27. This concluding statement reminds the Israelites that the origin of these instructions is in the LORD.

**34** These are the commands the LORD gave Moses at Mount Sinai for the Israelites.

The conclusion in 27:34 resembles a similar announcement to 26:46. Why do we have a summary of the same declaration in 27:34 that we have already heard in 26:46? Before answering this question, a second question begs to be asked: 'Why include Leviticus 27?' The answer is to emphasise honouring what belongs to the LORD as a way that Israel can ensure that the LORD is glorified in their midst.

To return to our first question, the reason Leviticus 27:34 repeats the declaration is to remind the Israelites of a critical point at the conclusion of the book. These commands are given by the LORD, that is, they have the divine authority of their covenant God. The implication is that the nation is to shape its life as a community according to these commands.

Just as this is true for Israel as the old covenant community, so too this is true for the new covenant community in 'the already and the not yet'. God has provided his Scriptures for us to make us wise for salvation in the LORD Jesus Christ and to shape us into a new covenant community among whom his name is glorified and sanctified. Our responsibility is to listen to his Scriptures, to be willing to be shaped by them and to be doers of his word and purposes in the world for his glory.

## Moving forward into the New Testament

The principle of Leviticus 27 remains unchanged as we look forward into the New Testament. As a new covenant community, we sanctify the name of the Lord Jesus by giving to him all that belongs to him. This could be voluntary gifts that are tangible and physical where, for instance, we have pledged an extra financial gift over and above our normal giving, and it could even be property that has been pledged to support the gospel ministry of a church. It is worth reiterating that these are voluntary gifts and cannot be demanded by the church, and neither must there be strings attached by the gift-giver. The motivation is a willing gift to God for the building up of his church (e.g., 2 Corinthians 9:6–11).

However, while the principle remains that we are to honour our gifts to God, we no longer have instructions about redeeming the gifts given. What we learn from the redemption instructions in Leviticus 27 is that God provides a way for gifts to be restored to the gift-giver. I would suggest that this is still true. If, for instance, the financial situation of the gift-giver changes, then it is good and appropriate for the gift-giver, with gentleness and humility, to request the restoration of the gift back to him or her. It is good and appropriate for the church to honour this request. Granted, there are complexities around this, especially if the church can no longer afford to restore the gift to the gift-giver. However, this should not hinder cross-shaped discussion about a way forward for both parties that models grace and generosity. This is also a means by which Jesus's name is sanctified by the new covenant community.

However, the gifts could also be from what already belongs to the Lord, and our regular financial giving falls into this category as a tithe. The idea of giving from our income, whether it be from little or much (see Mark 12:41–44), is acknowledging that what we have is given to us by God and ultimately all belongs to him. While we are no longer obligated to tithe particular amounts, or even to tithe at all, it is a helpful spiritual discipline to cultivate so that we are reminded with each gift that what we have is from God and not solely the work of our own hands. Tithing is an antidote to self-sufficiency and helps us to grow in generosity.

It is worth reiterating that regular financial giving could be used for spiritual abuse by the church and at no point can a church demand, shame or guilt the community into giving. Instead, the onus is on the individual believer to decide prayerfully what generous and cheerful giving looks like for their household as a means of giving to the LORD what belongs to him and so seek to sanctify the name of Jesus by their decisions.

The principle of giving to the LORD Jesus what belongs to him extends beyond the physical to the spiritual. Ultimately, what belongs to him as the crucified, risen and victorious Lamb is the praise and glory due to his name. We are to acknowledge his authority in our lives, in our church communities and in the world. As we seek to live for Jesus as a new covenant community in 'the already and the not yet', we sanctify the name of Jesus by echoing the song from Revelation 5:9–10, 12, 13:

> You are worthy to take the scroll
>   and to open its seals,
> because you were slain,
>   and with your blood you purchased for God
>   persons from every tribe and language and people
>     and nation.
> You have made them to be a kingdom and priests
>   to serve our God,
>   and they will reign on the earth . . .

Worthy is the Lamb, who was slain,
to receive power and wealth and wisdom and strength
and honour and glory and praise! . . .

To him who sits on the throne and to the Lamb
be praise and honour and glory and power,
for ever and ever!

RAISING READERS
Books Build Bright Futures

Dear Reader,

We'd love your attention for one more page to tell you about the crisis in children's reading, and what we can all do.

Studies have shown that reading for fun is the **single biggest predictor of a child's future life chances** – more than family circumstance, parents' educational background or income. It improves academic results, mental health, wealth, communication skills, ambition and happiness.[1]

The number of children reading for fun is in rapid decline. Young people have a lot of competition for their time. In 2024, 1 in 10 children and young people in the UK aged 5 to 18 did not own a single book at home.[2]

Hachette works extensively with schools, libraries and literacy charities, but here are some ways we can all raise more readers:

- Reading to children for just 10 minutes a day makes a difference
  - Don't give up if children aren't regular readers – there will be books for them!
  - Visit bookshops and libraries to get recommendations
  - Encourage them to listen to audiobooks
  - Support school libraries
  - Give books as gifts

There's a lot more information about how to encourage children to read on our website: **www.RaisingReaders.co.uk**

Thank you for reading.

hachette UK

1 National Literacy Trust, Book Ownership in 2024, November 2024 https://nlt.cdn.ngo/media/documents/Book_ownership_in_2024

2 OECD. 2021. 21st-century readers: developing literacy skills in a digital world. Paris, France: OECD Publishing. https://www.oecd.org/en/publications/21st-century-readers_a83d84cb-en.html